Eco–Logic

Logic Programming

Ehud Shapiro, editor
Koichi Furukawa, Jean-Louis Lassez, Fernando Pereira, and David H. D. Warren, associate editors

The Art of Prolog: Advanced Programming Techniques, Leon Sterling and Ehud Shapiro, 1986

Logic Programming: Proceedings of the Fourth International Conference (volumes 1 and 2), edited by Jean-Louis Lassez, 1987

Concurrent Prolog: Collected Papers (volumes 1 and 2), edited by Ehud Shapiro, 1987

Logic Programming: Proceedings of the Fifth International Conference and Symposium (volumes 1 and 2), edited by Robert A. Kowalski and Kenneth A. Bowen, 1988

Constraint Satisfaction in Logic Programming, Pascal Van Hentenryck, 1989

Logic-Based Knowledge Representation, edited by Peter Jackson, Han Reichgelt, and Frank van Harmelen, 1989

Logic Programming: Proceedings of the Sixth International Conference, edited by Giorgio Levi and Maurizio Martelli, 1989

Meta-Programming in Logic Programming, edited by Harvey Abramson and M. H. Rogers, 1989

Logic Programming: Proceedings of the North American Conference 1989 (volumes 1 and 2), edited by Ewing L. Lusk and Ross A. Overbeek, 1989

PROLOG and Its Applications, edited by Alan Bond and Basuki Soetarman, 1990

Logic Programming: Proceedings of the 1990 North American Conference, edited by Saumya Debray and Manuel Hermenegildo, 1990

Concurrent Constraint Programming Languages, Vijay A. Saraswat, 1990

Logic Programming: Proceedings of the Seventh International Conference, edited by David H. D. Warren and Peter Szeredi, 1990

Prolog VLSI Implementations, Pierluigi Civera, Gianluca Piccinini, and Maurizio Zamboni, 1990

The Craft of Prolog, Richard A. O'Keefe, 1990

Eco-Logic: Logic-Based Approaches to Ecological Modelling, David Robertson, Alan Bundy, Robert Muetzelfeldt, Mandy Haggith, and Michael Uschold, 1991

Eco–Logic
Logic–Based Approaches to Ecological Modelling

David Robertson
Dept. of Artificial Intelligence, University of Edinburgh,
Alan Bundy
Dept. of Artificial Intelligence, University of Edinburgh,
Robert Muetzelfeldt
Dept. of Forestry and Natural Resources, University of Edinburgh,
Mandy Haggith
Dept. of Computer and System Sciences, Griffith University,
Michael Uschold
Dept. of Artificial Intelligence, University of Edinburgh

The MIT Press
Cambridge, Massachusetts
London, England

This book was printed and bound in the United States of America.

Library of Congress Cataloging-in-Publication Data

Eco-logic : logic-based approaches to ecological modelling / David Robertson . . . [et al.].
    p.   cm. — (Logic Programming)
    Includes bibliographical references (p.   ) and index.
    ISBN 0-262-18143-6
    1. Ecology—Simulation methods.   I. Robertson, David.   II. Series.
    QH541.15.S5E26   1991
    574.5'01'13—dc20   90-21149
                                                                              CIP

Contents

QH
541.15
.S5E26
1991

Contents

Contents

List of Figures

Series Foreword

The logic programming approach to computing investigates the use of logic as a programming language and explores computational models based on controlled deduction.

The field of logic programming has seen a tremendous growth in the last several years, both in depth and in scope. This growth is reflected in the number of articles, journals, theses, books, workshops, and conferences devoted to the subject. The MIT Press series in logic programming was created to accommodate this development and to nurture it. It is dedicated to the publication of high-quality textbooks, monographs, collections, and proceedings in logic programming.

Ehud Shapiro
The Weizmann Institute of Science
Rehovot, Israel

Preface

This book contains a description of research carried out by the authors at the Department of Artificial Intelligence, University of Edinburgh between 1984 and 1989 as a part of the Eco–Logic project. Our concern was to make simulation modelling accessible to people with no previous knowledge of programming. As our target domain we chose ecology because this is a subject where simulation is frequently used but where only a small proportion of its practitioners really understand how simulation models work. Furthermore, many ecologists who might benefit from the use of simulation are discouraged from utilising these techniques because of their complexity. When we started work in 1984 we experimented with the use of a standard model representation language as a basis for our systems, in the hope that this would provide us with adequate expressive power. We were soon to find out that the problem was much deeper than we had expected. Users require more than simply being provided with tools for manipulating simulation models. They need more fundamental advice on how to relate the phenomena which they observe in the real world to the idealised representation necessary for simulation. Being faced with this larger problem, we began to ask ourselves whether it would be possible to make explicit the assumptions and forms of argument which provide the basis for designing simulation models. By bringing these into the open we hoped to gain insights into the process of idealisation. Logic provides a model of propriety for this task because it provides a clear separation between the axioms defining the assumptions of an argument and the inference methods used to conduct the argument. It therefore seemed interesting to find out what would happen if we applied techniques from logic to the problem of representing and reasoning about simulation models.

We decided to publish our results as a book for two reasons. First, it became apparent that in order to tackle the problem we had to consider a number of separate but interacting sub–problems. These ranged from the representational issue of finding description languages to suit our purposes, through the computational problems of automating inference in our chosen languages, to the task of designing interfaces which would make the systems usable. Since all these sub–problems influence each other it would be difficult to describe each one independently. We felt that a text which demonstrated the combination of techniques would be worth more than the sum of the descriptions of each individual part . Our second reason for writing this book is based on the observation that our research overlaps with many larger areas of research. We have drawn, for example, on information from Logic, Logic Programming, Artificial Intelligence, Simulation and Ecology. It is difficult to communicate our ideas separately to each of these groups because they tend to attend different conferences and read different sets of journals. By collating our results into a single document we hope to reach a wide variety of readers without duplication of effort.

The price which we have to pay for addressing a wide readership is that we must provide sufficient contextual information for each of the intended audiences. For example, we have tried to soften the shock of logic programming for ecologists/modellers and have included a chapter on ecological modelling for the logic programmers. There is obviously a tension between the desire to make the book self–contained and the need to reach the heart of the problem in a short space of time. We hope that we have reached a compromise which neither bores nor baffles the reader.

How to Read this Book

This book draws on experience from several different fields of research and should be of interest to the following groups of people:

Simulation modellers should be interested because we describe an alternative to the conventional method of constructing simulation models. The view which we promote, of simulation models as logical statements, will be new to most of the simulation community and is at an early stage of development. We hope that by describing our experiences using these techniques we will encourage simulation modellers to apply them more widely.

Logic programmers should be keen to discover how their techniques can be applied in the area of simulation modelling. In particular, it has been necessary to develop enhanced languages and interpreters for dealing with the implementational problems which we encountered in applying logic programming techniques to this new domain.

Artificial Intelligence researchers have provided many of the tools which we have used in our experiments. From this point of view, our work could be seen as an application of ideas from A.I. to the domain of simulation modelling. Indeed, the initial remit of our project was to construct an Intelligent Front End to a simulation package. This notion of providing a computer assistant which buffers the user from the complexities of some "back end" program ([Bundy 84]) has been a focus of our research and is of interest to the A.I. community.

Software engineers have for years been active in constructing automatic program synthesis systems. However, as Barstow pointed out ([Barstow 88]), these have mostly been able to deal only with small programs and have made very little use of information about the domain for which the program is being written. Our work, by contrast, places considerable emphasis on the use of domain knowledge to help automate the construction of larger programs. The need to integrate knowledge of the problem area with the specification of a program, both for requirements capture and subsequent maintenance, is an almost untapped vein of research.

Ecological modellers are forced, by the nature of the tools which they have available, to construct programs which are difficult for non–modelling ecologists to understand. By providing a standard notation in which to represent these sorts of models, plus techniques with which they may be more easily constructed and analysed, we hope to make simulation more widely accessible to ecologists with little computing experience, thus reducing the culture gap between modellers and non–modellers.

The wide range of people to which this book is addressed makes it difficult to produce a form of explanation which will suit all readers. We want to encourage others to join in this line of research so we must include considerable technical detail. On the other hand, we don't want to scare off those who are interested in the general principles but not in their implementation. The compromise which we have reached is to include, at the start of each chapter, a short summary of the major topics covered in that part of the book. The detailed discussion in the main body of each chapter expands on these topics and introduces other subsidiary issues. Where it is necessary to include particular algorithms or other implementational information these are given in separate figures or placed under numbered "Definition" or "Algorithm" headings for convenient reference. This allows the book to be read at three levels of detail:

- Those who want only a summary of our research should read this introductory chapter; the introduction to each subsequent chapter; and the conclusion. These readers should end up with an understanding of the general arguments but possess little substantiating detail.

- To come to grips with the evidence which substantiates our arguments (and to encounter some of the peripheral issues) it is necessary to work through the body of each chapter. Those who want the extra detail without the toil of implementation should skim over the definitions of specific algorithms.

- At the most detailed level it should be possible for a competent Prolog programmer to reconstruct the programs discussed throughout this book by following carefully the algorithms which appear throughout the text. We hope that a few people will get this far and produce their own improved versions of our experimental programs.

As an aid to readers unfamiliar with some of the terminology used in this book, we have included a short glossary in Appendix A. If you come across a term which seems unfamiliar and isn't explained in the text then it is worth scanning this appendix to see if it appears there. We have also included, in Appendix B, a list of the models used throughout the book and have summarised their relationships to eachother. The reader may find this a handy reference while working through the main text.

The Structure of this Book

Our primary aim is to demonstrate how simulation models can be made more accessible through the application of techniques from A.I. and Logic Programming. This is the core material of Chapters 7 and 8. Chapters 3 to 6 provide a foundation for Chapters 7 and 8 by supplying appropriate notation and demonstrating its utility, while Chapter 2 provides the reader with a sketch of our domain of application. The main dependencies between chapters are shown as arcs in the diagram below:

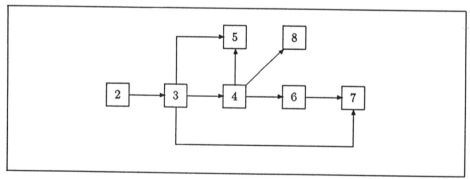

We shall use the Prolog programming language throughout this text as a reference point for the more complex notation which is required in later chapters. Chapter 3 provides an introduction to the use of Prolog for representing simulation models.

Unfortunately, it turns out that Prolog, in its "raw" form, isn't ideally suited to the sort of statements we want to make about ecological simulation models.

Therefore, in Chapter 4 we define a logic which seems better suited to our purposes – an order–sorted logic. We show how this provides a notational enhancement of basic Prolog and describe how models are represented and run in the new language. We then go on to demonstrate (in Chapter 6) how use of the sorted logic can be extended to include some of the aspects of the ecological problem associated with a simulation model.

Chapter 5 addresses a potentially crippling problem associated with the execution of these logic programs - namely that the general purpose interpreters used to run them tend to be extremely slow because they search for a solution to a given input goal in an unconstrained manner. We provide augmentations to both Prolog and sorted logic interpreters which remedy this problem (at a price). We also consider the more radical approach of translating from the sorted logic into a more conventional program in an imperative style, which can then be run in the normal way.

In Chapters 7 and 8 we describe two alternative approaches to automating the construction of simulation programs by exploiting the formal notations and inference mechanisms supplied in earlier chapters. The first of these constructs programs in Prolog using code templates (schemata) and employing simple descriptions of ecological problems to guide the model construction process. This is quite an efficient method of program construction but, because the simulation program and the problem description are represented in different languages, some of the techniques used cannot be *guaranteed* always to produce a working simulation model. In our second program construction system (Chapter 8) we show how programs which are guaranteed to run can be produced by augmenting the sorted logic interpreter from Chapter 4.

We conclude, in Chapter 9, with an assessment of the success of our experiments and the likely contribution of logic programming to simulation modelling.

Acknowledgements

The work described in this book was funded by the UK Science and Engineering Research Council and the Alvey Directorate (grants GR/C/06226, GR/D/44294 and GR/E/00730). Many people made contributions to this research. In particular, we would like to thank Dave Plummer, Jane Hesketh, Susan Niven, Paul Brna, Steve Owen, Lincoln Wallen, Elisabet Engdahl, Peter Ross, Colin Williams, Christine Pierret–Golbreich, Nigel Harding, Liam Lynch and members of the Maths Reasoning Group in the Department of Artificial Intelligence at Edinburgh.

1 Introduction

This book is concerned primarily with the problem of comprehending the structure of simulation models. By model comprehension we mean understanding the relationship between a simulation model and the real world system which it is intended to represent. Current software tools do not provide adequate support for documenting important modelling decisions and this makes it difficult for them to be understood by others. This means that key information about the assumptions which lead a modeller to choose a particular simulation model from the vast space of potential model structures is often unavailable to those who must use the model or assess its worth.

Problems of model comprehension are particularly important in the domain of ecology. Consider, for example, the question of the environmental impact of acid rain. Government must decide what action to take to reduce the acidification of water sources based not only on information about the current scope of the problem but also on predictions of future trends. Will acidification get worse and, if so, by how much ? One way of making this prediction is to build a simulation model which contains all the important components of the water cycle. When parameterised correctly and run, we would expect this model to give an accurate estimate of the future behaviour of the system – in much the same way that a carefully constructed model of, say, a chemical plant will mimic the behaviour of the real system on which it was based. The simulation modellers would then report the details of this predicted behaviour to the appropriate government authority who would use it as part of their evidence for making a policy decision. To operate correctly, this procedure must rely on several fundamental assumptions:

1. The simulation model contains all the appropriate components.

2. The parameters of the model can be measured accurately.

3. The decision makers are aware of any doubts about assumptions 1 and 2 (above) and understand the possible discrepancies which these irregularities could cause.

All of these assumptions are likely to be false. Assumption 1 will be false because, unlike engineered systems (such as chemical plants), there is no general agreement about which model components are fundamental to the modelling of acid rain and its effects. Decisions about what to include in such models are based largely on informed judgement. Assumption 2 will be false because many of the parameters of natural systems (*e.g.* rainfall) are impossible to measure precisely. We can also argue about the level of detail which is appropriate to a given problem (*e.g.* Should we measure average annual rainfall or monthly averages ? Should we represent

the spatial distribution of rainfall ?). Assumption 3 will be false because most
reports of the results of simulation modelling (even those in the specialist literature)
concentrate on the behaviour produced by the model rather than on a precise
description of the assumptions on which it is based and their ramifications through
the structure of the model. This obfuscation is not a consequence of a deliberate
attempt to deceive but often is a consequence of the complex nature of the programs
which simulation modellers write.

The nub of the problem is that techniques which work well for clearly defined
problems are not well suited to the poorly structured domains of, for example, the
environment or macro–economic analysis. In these domains the modellers may not
know if their model is correct or reliable and, worse, the decision makers may not
know that the modellers don't know. Thus, we have crucial decisions (such as environmental policy or military strategy) which are taken on the basis of predictions
which may be flawed and cannot be analysed in depth by those who must act on
their recommendations. To its users, the model is like a black box which exhibits
certain external behaviours but cannot be opened to reveal the mechanisms inside.

This is not such a problem in domains such as engineering where the key relationships are well defined (although there are other problems of software reliability). In
such domains models act as precision tools, parameterised with reliable measurements and producing output by means of the application of well defined theories.
Model comprehension presents a serious problem when there is no agreed definition
of how some system works. In these domains the construction of a model may be
thought of as the formulation of an *argument* by the modeller about how he/she
thinks the system works.

At first sight, it might seem that this view of models as arguments (although
superficially attractive) is not tenable because a conventional simulation program
is simply a sequence of instructions. It may be based on some argument about
how a modeller thinks the system operates but does not, in itself, constitute that
argument. One of the purposes of this book is to show that the distinction between
the simulation model and the arguments which it represents is an artificial one,
which has been imposed by the imperative nature of conventional programming
languages. However, it is worth making clear, with the aid of a simple example,
what we mean when we say that we may represent simulation models as arguments.

Figure 1.1 shows a simple simulation model, represented in an imperative programming language[1], which simulates the growth in height of some object over

---

[1]The notation for this program is close to that of BASIC but the precise choice of imperative
language is unimportant to our argument.

```
stoptime = 20
height = 25
for I = 1 to stoptime
        read temperature(I)
next I
for T = 1 to stoptime
        if temperature(T) > 20 then growth = height × 0.2
        else growth = height × 0.1
height = height + growth
next T
```

Figure 1.1
A basic imperative simulation program.

time. In the first 5 lines of the program the values for key variables (such as the initial height and the temperature at each time point) are obtained. The rest of the program consists of a standard "do loop" in which the time counter is incremented in steps of 1 and the height updated by a factor which varies according to the temperature at that time.

As it stands, this program bears little resemblance to anything we would grace with the name of "reasoned argument". However, it does embody an argument which we state informally below:

- The height at any time T has value N if:

    - T is not equal to 0 (the initial time point) and
    - $T1$ is equal to $T - 1$ and
    - the height at time $T1$ has value $N1$ and
    - the temperature at time $T1$ has value X and
        * $X > 20$ and growth, G, equals $N1 \times 0.2$ or
        * $X \leq 20$ and growth, G, equals $N1 \times 0.1$
    - $N = N1 + G$.

- The height at time 0 (the initial time) is 25.

This representation of our simulation model presents a clearly stated argument which defines the assumptions upon which our calculation of height will depend. It also provides a precise algorithm for computing height at any point in time. Thus, we may view it as a logical argument and, at the same time, as a simulation model.

If we accept that this is true then we must also accept that such models should meet the standards which we expect from other forms of argument, namely:

1. The notation in which we express the foundations of our argument should be:

   (a) Unambiguous (*i.e.* each symbol should have one, and only one, meaning).

   (b) Modular (*i.e.* each part of our argument should make sense when considered separately from the others).

   (c) Parsimonious (*i.e.* there should only be as much information as is necessary to fully understand the problem).

   (d) Explicit (*i.e.* the details of all assumptions should be easily accessible).

2. It should be possible to state our assumptions without committing ourselves to a particular method for deriving conclusions.

3. The development of our argument should be:

   (a) Based on sound forms of inference which we can justify to others.

   (b) Open to retrospective analysis and comparison with other arguments.

None of these qualities can be said, unreservedly, to be possessed by conventional simulation models. It is worthwhile working through the list given above to explain why this is so.

1. Conventional notation is:

   (a) Ambiguous. Often it is difficult to know, in a logical sense, what a particular structure in a program is meant to represent. Worse, the meaning of structures may change during a simulation. For example, if we allow destructive assignment to variables then some variable might have the value 25 at one point in the simulation and be re–assigned the value 999 at some subsequent point.

   (b) Non–modular. If global variables are used, these may be re–assigned values by more than one part of the program, thus violating its modularity. The imperative programming style tends to encourage this practice.

(c) Over–elaborate. The code used to represent a simulation model normally contains many keywords and symbols which have no direct bearing on the description of the system (*e.g.* "goto" statements). Such symbols exist purely to instruct the computer about how it should execute the program.

(d) Implicit. The assumptions on which the model is based tend to be buried within the procedures of the code. Because of the problems of ambiguity and non–modularity, which we mentioned earlier, it may be difficult to extract the assumptions from this tangle of procedures. Furthermore, it may be hard to distinguish *bona fide* assumptions from information derived from those assumptions during the execution of the program.

2. The procedures necessary to run the model are analogous to the strategies used to develop an argument. In the same way that arguments lead from initial assumptions to conclusions, simulation programs derive from initial data some conclusion about the behaviour of the system. Where this analogy breaks down is in the representation of assumptions and subsequent argument. Conventional simulation models merge the two together by including instructions for the running of the program among the assumptions on which it is based. It is therefore difficult to separate the information which is used to describe the problem from the information about how the argument is to be conducted.

3. Problems with the way in which an argument is developed are:

(a) We would expect each step in the development of an argument to be justifiable as correct in some abstract sense. An example of a correct form of argument is the rule of *modus ponens* which, given the assumption that some statement, A, is true and also that A implies B, allows us to conclude that B must also be true. We can justify this form of inference without worrying about the nature of the statements A and B. This allows us to maintain a clear separation between the particular problem which we want to solve and general forms of argument which we use to solve it. We can state precisely what we mean by, say, *modus ponens* in an abstract sense and apply it, without alteration, to any problem for which it is appropriate. In conventional simulation models the most general forms of argument are structures such as "do loops" and "goto" statements. On the face of it, these may seem as valid in an abstract sense as *modus ponens* and similar rules. Unfortunately, this isn't true because, while we can precisely determine what it means to apply *modus ponens*, we can only determine the precise effect of a "do loop" or "goto" statement by considering its interaction with other model structures. There is no obvious way of interpreting such statements as steps in a logical argument.

(b) All of the problems listed above make it difficult to present a coherent analysis of how a model was built; why it has a particular structure; or how it produces its conclusions. This makes comparison of different models extremely difficult, except at the superficial level of the correlation between inputs and outputs.

The desirability of standardising the notation used to describe simulation models has been acknowledged by those who construct graphical display languages in which models may be specified, examined and modified. The problem with these is that they tend to be limited to a particular style of model. For example, the STELLA system ([Lewis 86]) provides a graphical interface for models in System Dynamics notation but this interface doesn't extend to other varieties of model. In [Robertson *et al* 88] we demonstrate the representative inadequacies of such systems and describe some of the difficulties of extending their representational capacity. But even if we were fortunate enough to invent a standard notation with all the representational power which we require this would not, in itself, solve the problem of unintelligibility of model structure. Users often require explanations of models not only in terms of the structure of the model itself but with reference to those aspects of the real–world problem which led to a particular choice of model. Information about the real world is often vague and ill–defined and is therefore of a different nature to the precise, idealised structure of a simulation model.

The idea of using programs to represent and reason with imperfect and (sometimes) partial information is familiar to researchers in the field of Artificial Intelligence (A.I.). Perhaps the best known example of this is the construction of an "expert system"[2], which often involves the representation of some portion of the knowledge possessed by a human expert and the use of a inference mechanisms which can utilise that knowledge in order to solve problems with a degree of skill comparable to that of the human expert. In this enterprise it is clear from the start that the expert's knowledge is unlikely to be perfect, nor is his/her problem solving strategy likely to correspond precisely to that of other experts. It is therefore considered essential that an expert system should be able to provide an explanation of how it solves a problem. This explanation allows users to check

---

[2]A good general introduction to this area of research can be found in [Jackson 86].

for themselves that the program's reasoning makes sense and provides a safeguard against programming errors.

We have identified a deficiency in simulation models which are used to tackle problems in poorly structured domains. We have also noted that techniques for overcoming this deficiency are being developed under the general heading of Artificial Intelligence. The obvious progression is to attempt to find a representation for simulation models which allows us to apply these A.I. techniques. Our first problem is therefore to choose a notation which is conducive to the representation of reasoned argument. This notation must be sufficiently expressive to be able to represent the enormous range of model structures currently in use, while still being comparatively easy to understand. It should also be removed, as far as possible, from any confusing details of implementation which are specific to particular programming languages or hardware. Logic programming is claimed to provide precisely these characteristics. This viewpoint is expressed clearly in [Sterling & Shapiro 85]:

> Rather than being derived, by a series of abstractions and reorganisations, from the von Neumann machine model and instruction set, it is derived from an abstract model, which has no direct relationship or dependency on one machine model or another. It is based on the belief that instead of the human learning to think in terms of the operations of a computer, which some scientists and engineers at some point in history happened to find easy and cost-effective to build, the computer should perform instructions that are easy for humans to provide. In its ultimate and purest form, logic programming suggests that even explicit instructions for operation not be given but, rather, the knowledge about the problem and assumptions that are sufficient to solve it be stated explicitly, as logical axioms. Such a set of axioms constitutes an alternative to the conventional program. The program can be executed by providing it with a problem, formalised as a logical statement to be proved, called a goal statement. The execution is an attempt to solve the problem, that is, to prove the goal statement, given the assumptions in the logic program.

This approach is quite different from the conventional view of simulation modelling but offers the benefits which we desire. Some specification languages already exist for expressing the structure of models declaratively but these are either extremely complex to use or are of very limited expressive power. If we can find a logic which is sufficiently expressive to represent a wide range of simulation models and which is also easy to understand then we can view a simulation program as a set of logical axioms stating what is known about a given simulation problem. Running the program is then an attempt to find the solution to some goal statement by applying general purpose inference mechanisms.

So far, we have mentioned only the final product of the intellectual activity of simulation – the simulation model itself. However, in an ideal world we would like to build into the formal specification of each simulation model a record of the important characteristics of the real–world system which it was designed to simulate – thus making it easier for other people to reconstruct the chain of reasoning involved in that model's development. This extension of the modelling framework is not a new idea. It has been raised by several simulation researchers, including [Zeigler 84], who discuss the many levels at which a simulation model may be described. What has proved hard is to integrate in a uniform manner knowledge about the real–world problem with the description of the simulation model. Logic has its origins in the desire formally to represent and reason about phenomena observed in the real world so it is a good candidate for providing this extra facility while preserving uniformity of notation. We have chosen ecology as a domain in which to pursue our experiments because ecological modelling, being concerned with highly complex biological systems, is greatly in need of a rational framework into which can be fitted descriptions of simulation models and of the biological systems they represent. Furthermore, many ecologists do not engage in simulation modelling (because of the computational complexity of the techniques involved) but are quite capable of providing distinguishing features of the biological systems which they are studying. Representing these distinguishing features and the simulation model in a similar notation should make it easier to partially automate the process of model construction – providing guidance in the construction of models appropriate to particular real–world problems and thereby making the technology available to a wider audience.

2 Ecology and Ecological Modelling

The purpose of this chapter is to provide readers who have no previous experience of ecological simulation with a sketch of the domain to which our experiments have been applied. We begin, in Section 2.1, with a brief introduction to ecological science and then turn our attention to the activity of simulation modelling in this domain (see Section 2.2).

We argue that the modelling of ecological systems is a classic example of the application of conventional simulation techniques to a poorly understood problem. Many models are constructed on the basis of a rather arbitrary choice of modelling paradigm; model assumptions are frequently not explicitly stated; the choices that the modeller made are often not justified; and the models constructed are frequently incapable of any degree of formal validation. These problems are compounded by the fact that models are inflexible and non–transparent: it is very difficult to vary model assumptions, to explore the sensitivity of a model to alternative but equally plausible assumptions; and it is very difficult for others critically to evaluate every detail of the model.

2.1 Ecology

Ecology literally means "the study of homes". The term was coined by Haeckel in 1869 to mean the study of organisms in their organic and inorganic environment. More recently, Krebs ([Krebs 78]) has defined ecology as "the scientific study of the interactions that determine the distribution and abundance of organisms".

Ecology is essentially a science: the typical ecologist is as interested in understanding how some part of a natural biological system function as a physicist is in determining some physical principle. In addition, it is becoming obvious that an ecological understanding is essential for effectively tackling many of the problems facing mankind: pollution; the consequences of climate change; and the over–use of natural resources.

However, there are a number of characteristics of ecology that create great difficulties in trying to adopt a scientific approach.

First, ecology spans a broad range of levels of organisation:

- At the physiological level, an ecologist might be interested in the response of individual leaves to changing levels of temperature, light, and carbon dioxide.

- At the individual level, an ecologist might be interested in the energy–optimisation strategies of an animal faced with the conflicting demands of obtaining food but avoiding predators.

- At the population level, the interest might be in determining how the value of some population characteristic (such as population numbers, age–class composition, or genetic structure) varies over time or space.

- At the community level, the focus could be on determining the species composition and diversity in a range of habitats.

- At the ecosystem level, the subject of interest might be in studying the flows of energy, nutrients, or pollutants between major functional groupings (e.g the plants, herbivores and carnivores).

- At the level of the biosphere, ecological studies address the role of marine and terrestrial ecosystems in the carbon dioxide balance of the atmosphere.

Second, ecological systems are characterised by complex webs of interactions: "everything is connected to everything else". While a physicist can successfully isolate some small part of a physical system, and study it in isolation, the ecologist is aware that the object of interest affects many other ecological components, and in turn is affected by them. This makes it hard to draw boundaries, and means that answering one question – *e.g.* the population dynamics of one species – frequently requires an understanding of how this species interacts with others, their dynamics, and so on.

Third, the units of study are much less clearly defined than in other areas. In physics, chemistry, engineering and molecular biology, the units of study are obvious and discrete. In contrast, it is much less clear how an ecologist interested in pollution should represent the constituents of the system under study: individual organisms? species groupings or functional groupings?

Fourth, ecological systems are characterised by many sources of uncontrolled variation. With physical systems, the initial conditions can be specified, and external influences largely eliminated. In ecology, it is frequently difficult to know the initial state, and the role of external factors – primarily climate – introduce considerable variation. This in turn requires replication in order to detect statistically significant effects. However, the spatial size and temporal timescales of ecological systems often make it impossible to devise and implement suitably–designed and replicated experiments.

2.2   Models in Ecology

In any science, the construction of quantitative models is an important part of the scientific process. The models reflect one's understanding, and provide a formal statement of this understanding which can be evaluated by others in the scientific community.

This is especially true in ecology. It is all to easy for ecology to be approached at a descriptive level, with detailed studies of particular ecological systems at some point in space and time. However, such studies – although very common – do little towards the development of general principles.

Much of the quantitative work in ecology is statistical, resulting in the elucidation of empirical relationships between ecological quantities. However, such studies produce results which are also restricted to the particular context of the study, and fail to capture the complexity of ecological interactions (since the logistic problems mentioned above prevent the incorporation of sufficient replication to enable one to study the interaction between many variables).

Therefore, ecologists have turned to quantitative models, as tools for generalising their understanding, and for capturing the complex interactions that they perceive as being important. These models are constructed for a number of reasons:

- Most importantly, as a scientific tool, a model serves to test one's understanding: it can be regarded as a scientific hypothesis. The ecologist is stating in the model the factors that are believed to be important in governing the functioning of the ecological system. The hypothesis is evaluated by comparing the behaviour of the model system with that of the real world. The evaluation can be qualitative or quantitative:

  – Qualitative evaluation can involve an analysis of the shape of model responses to varying inputs, and qualitative feature of model behaviour, such as stability, instability, or regular oscillations.

  – Quantitative evaluation includes, for dynamic models, the comparison of model output as a function of time with observed time series. Examples include models of the population dynamics of a particular species, or changing levels of pollution in a lake.

It can also involve an analysis of the sensitivity of model output to some change in input. For example, the effect of changing the harvesting rate of a wildlife population on the population's equilibrium population size. It must be stressed, however, that this view of "model as hypothesis" has very little in common with hypothesis testing in other areas of science. First, since many models are very complex, with many sets of interacting factors, the concept of the critical experiment, whose result will support or refute the hypothesis, is rarely appropriate: rather, we think in terms of refining the model, rather than acceptance or rejection. Second, there is frequently insufficient data to permit a rigorous evaluation of a model: a model of the population dynamics of a deer population would require many years of field work to collect data on an actual population which could be compared with model output. Another way of expressing this is that many models of the same problem, based on quite different sets of assumptions, can appear to perform equally well. These problems are compounded by the difficulties of obtaining accurate measurements of ecological quantities, and by the deplorable practice of "adjusting" (fiddling) parameter values to improve model fit.

- Models are also constructed to increase one's understanding. For example, a model of an outbreak of a previously endemic pest species can suggest which of several factors is most significant in triggering the outbreak.

- Models are developed for prediction of the future behaviour of some ecological system. Examples include the use of models for predicting changes in levels of pollution and in climate, and the consequent effects of these on ecological systems. These models can be steady–state or dynamic, and are frequently used by decision makers to explore alternative scenarios (*e.g.* the impact of alternative emission controls). However, there is a very real danger that many of these models are used with little or no regard paid to the very shaky basis on which the model is based – arbitrary assumptions and guesstimated input values.

- Models are developed as management tools. These have much in common with the flight simulators used to train pilots: the model replicates the behaviour of the real system, and the user interacts with the model to observe the effects of his/her actions. Models developed for these purposes have considerable use in the teaching and training of resource managers (for example, in forestry, fisheries and wildlife management), but are little used as a serious management tool.

2.2.1   Major Model Types

Models can be classified in many different ways, and it is frequently true that the classification applies more appropriately to parts of models rather than to the model itself, and that some models can be put into more than one class.

Statistical models. These models are simply used to summarise large amounts of data in a mathematical form. The choice of the mathematical form itself has little or no theoretical justification, and the resulting parameter values, obtained by the statistical procedure, have little biological meaning. A common example is the fitting of polynomial equations to growth data, as in agricultural crops or forest stands.

Theoretical/analytical models. These are developed from simple theoretical considerations, frequently with little or nor basis in observed sets of data. These models are used to explore abstract ecological concepts, such as the coexistence of two competing species, or the relation between complexity and stability in ecological systems. The models are frequently handled analytically, and mathematical tractability is more important than ecological sense. Such models therefore tend to make highly simplistic ecological assumptions (for example, that there is a linear relationship between the amount of food eaten by a predator and the amount of food available), and this makes many of the conclusions of very doubtful value.

Numerical simulation models. Numerical simulation models involve the iterative solution of a mathematically–specified model. In a relatively few cases, such as the statistical simulation of sampling problems, the iteration is over the set of individuals in a population. In the vast majority of cases, the primary iterative loop is forward through a set of points in time. In these cases, the model specifies the changes that take place over one time step, and the model is solved by repeatedly working out changes in the system, then updating the state of the system.

Numerical simulation models may be formulated in terms of one or other of the modelling paradigms: many do not fit into a particular paradigm, and are termed "general simulation models" in the following discussion.

2.2.2   Modelling Paradigms

A modelling paradigm is a particular mathematical framework in which the system to be modelled is expressed. The advantages of using a particular paradigm is that it facilitates model construction by channelling thought into the particular modelling structures recognised by the paradigm; computational tools are available for handling the constructed model; and communication between modellers is made easier by common understanding of the meaning of the modelling constructs allowable within the paradigm. The major disadvantage of using a particular paradigm is that – as with analytical models – ecological reality is frequently sacrificed.

Differential equations. Borrowing techniques from the physical sciences, the problem is modelled as a set of ordinary linear or non–linear differential equations. This implies that the system is changing continuously, and that all rates of change are instantaneous functions of the current state of the system. The equations can be solved using established numerical methods.

Difference equations. The model is expressed in terms of the discrete change that takes place over unit intervals of time. This is justified on the grounds that:

- Many ecological processes do in fact happen more–or–less discretely (*e.g.* in many species, reproduction and mortality happen annually over a fairly short period of time).

- Even though a process may be continuous (*e.g.* plant growth), the data is collected on a discrete basis (*e.g.* daily), and therefore it is reasonable to model the system using corresponding discrete time units.

Discrete–event simulation. Time moves forward from one event to another, with unequal intervals between events. Despite the importance of this paradigm in (for example) the industrial arena, and the corresponding large number of simulation languages and packages for handling such models, this paradigm is rarely used in ecology. Probably the most common area is in the simulation of behaviour, especially the feeding behaviour of a population of individuals.

Matrix population models. The dynamics of a population divided into age–classes is simulated by multiplying a square matrix containing population fecundity and survival parameters with a vector containing the number of individuals in each age–class. The advantage of this approach is that – in the simple case – key population parameters can be derived by analysis of the matrix. For straight–forward simulation of population dynamics, little is gained by using this approach.

Markov chain models. These are used to simulate transitions between a number of states. The major area of application is in simulating succession, where each state corresponds to a successional stage, *e.g.* bare ground, shrubs, mature forest.

System Dynamics. This is a specialised form of differential equation models. The system is conceptualised as a set of compartments, with flows between them. The dynamics of each compartment is governed by a differential equation,

which is formed from the sum of the inflows into the compartment minus the
outflows from it. Each flow is in turn governed by an equation expressing
the rate of flow in terms of the values of compartments, parameters and
other variables in the model. This paradigm has the major advantage that
it matches closely on to the way that many ecologists think about ecological
systems – diagrams showing levels and flows of energy, water, nutrients and
pollutants were common in ecology even before the advent of modelling. It
minimises the extent to which the ecologist has to think in mathematical
terms, and indeed it is possible for an ecologist to specify complex and realistic
models without entering a single equation.

Cellular automata. These models provide a simple paradigm for representing
spatially–organised systems. The best known example is the Game of Life,
in which each cell on a grid is deemed to either contain an individual or
not: simple rules, expressed in terms of the occupancy of neighbouring cells,
determine whether an individual survives, dies, or reproduces.

Object–oriented modelling. In a very few instances, the object–oriented programming paradigm has been applied to modelling populations of individual
animals. This context provides the most obvious context for the application
of this approach, allowing for the creation and destruction of individuals,
message–passing between individuals as a means for triggering appropriate
behaviours, and the inheritance of attributes in a taxonomic sense.

2.2.3 General simulation models

A large proportion of ecological simulation models do not readily fit into any particular paradigm. They tend to consist of an assortment of model–building constructs,
as deemed appropriate by the model–builder for addressing a particular problem.
These are of particular interest for several reasons.

First, removing the restriction of working within a particular paradigm means
that these models are (potentially, at least) most able to capture the features of the
real system which are most suited for accurate solution of the modelling problem.
It is therefore likely that future models developed to address critical environmental
problems will be of this type.

Second, there are many more choices facing the modeller during the model design phase. This class of model is therefore the most challenging in terms of the
development of computer–based systems that can help in the model–design process,
especially for ecologists who may have little programming or modelling experience.

Third, we can speculate on the extent to which the spectrum of model–building constructs used in general simulation models can in fact be represented in a sort of "super–paradigm". This is an important point, and we will pause to consider it in some detail.

One thing that is gained by working within a particular modelling paradigm is a sort of shorthand for describing a model. This shorthand gives a declarative description of model structure: the procedural aspects needed to solve the model are implicit in the choice of modelling paradigm. General simulation models do not (conventionally) have such a shorthand description, and therefore can only unambiguously be described in procedural terms, in the form of the computer program used to implement a solution of the model. This is not an intrinsic feature of such models: it merely reflects the fact that a more general model–description language (the "super–paradigm") has not been developed.

If such a super–paradigm could be developed, which encompassed a large proportion of the modelling constructs used in existing paradigms, then these other paradigms could be viewed as sub–sets, or special cases, of the super–paradigm. By analogy with Knuth's concept of meta–fonts, from which any particular font can be implemented by a process of specialisation, we could think of the super–paradigm as being a meta–model, from which (in a similar way) any particular model could be built.

In order to put some flesh on the preceding, rather abstract, discussion, we will "walk through" the development of a particular general simulation model, considering the various choices facing the modeller, and the basis for choosing one option or the other.

2.3   Development of a General Simulation Model

An ecologist has collected data on the size of a rabbit population over a ten year period. He/she wishes to test her understanding of the factors driving the population dynamics of this species by constructing a simulation model whose output shows the same pattern over time as the real population.

The ecologist chooses the System Dynamics paradigm as a suitable one to begin with. The single compartment represents the size of the population. It can increase through a flow into the compartment representing the reproductive input into the population. It can decrease through a flow out of the compartment representing mortality.

Remember that System Dynamics is nothing more than a cosmetic interface to models based on differential equations. Therefore, what the ecologist is really saying is that the dynamics of the population can be captured with a single differential equation, with the instantaneous rate of change of the population being given by a single differential equation, equal to the reproductive rate minus the mortality rate. This assumes that the population is changing continuously: this is obviously not true in the extreme, but is taken to be a reasonable approximation.

The model is not yet complete: he/she has not specified the formulae giving the values for the rates of reproduction and mortality. These could be entered as constants, taking an average over the period of study – but this ignores the biologically obvious fact that the more rabbits there are, the greater the reproductive input into the population, and the greater the total number dying during a period of time. Therefore, the ecologist makes the assumption that both these rates depend on the size of the rabbit population. The easiest way to capture this dependency is to assume that each rate is proportional to the size of the population. This implies that each member of the population produces the same number of offspring, and has the same chance of dying, during some interval of time. These two population parameters, termed the specific reproductive rate and the specific mortality rate, are commonly–quoted parameters for many different species, so this assumption seems reasonable.

The model now has the form:

$$dN/dt = R - M$$
$$R = r \times N$$
$$M = m \times N$$

where: N = population size
R = rate of reproduction
M = rate of mortality
r = specific rate of reproduction
m = specific rate of mortality

Given an initial value for N at time zero, and values for the two parameters r and m, estimated from the population study or the literature, the model can be solved. On doing this, the ecologist observes that the model output follows an exponentially–increasing curve, whereas the real population shows considerable year–to–year fluctuations.

He/she therefore has to decide whether it is worth refining the model, and if so, how. In the following discussion, we will consider just some of the refinements that could be made, to illustrate the choices and the basis for these choices that characterise ecological modelling.

He/she might decide to refine the functional relationships in the model. This model contains two – for working out the rates of reproduction and mortality. Each of these could be made more complex by:

- making them more complex functions of rabbit population size. For example, a non–linear reproduction function could capture the notion that overcrowding at higher population sizes inhibits reproduction.

- making them functions of season, or external factors, such as climate.

- making them functions of other factors that could be incorporated in the model, such as the abundance of food and the number of predators.

In this particular instance, it is likely that the refinements would be approached by considering the specific rates, replacing the constant–valued parameter with a variable calculated from these other factors. This is a common strategy in model refinement, though in other cases we might simply replace one function with another, more complex, one.

Ideally, this process of refining relationships follows three steps:

- hypothesising that a particular factor is important;

- collecting data to characterise the relationship; and

- describing the relationship mathematically.

In practice, due to the difficulty of collecting sufficient data, many such relationships are incorporated by guessing the mathematical form of the relationship and the values of its parameters.

The model could also be refined by disaggregating the rabbit population: breaking it into smaller homogenous units. In the extreme, this could mean representing each individual in the population, which could mean adopting a completely different modelling paradigm, and introducing programming difficulties which the ecologist is unwilling to face. More typically, the population is disaggregated into smaller classes of individuals which behave similarly from the population dynamics point–of–view. An obvious basis for disaggregation in the present example is into sex classes: females reproduce and males do not, whereas we have assumed an average rate of reproduction over each individual. Additionally, it is common to split populations into age classes, to capture the difference in specific rates of reproduction and mortality between between different age groups. The implementation of the model then requires a mechanism to shift cohorts from one age–class to the next as time progresses.

A major form of disaggregation is spatial: dividing the total population into sub–populations occupying different areas of ground. The reason for doing this could be that the population is not evenly spread over the area, and that therefore population dynamics calculated from average population densities are incorrect. Or there might be spatial variation in food or predator populations. The spatial disaggregation might be in terms of some regular tesselation – grid squares or hexagons – or as some set of arbitrary polygons, perhaps reflecting natural boundaries or changes in habitat. The incorporation of spatial disaggregation requires the incorporation of migration between spatial sub–units in the model.

It was implied above, when considering functional relationships, that the model can be refined by incorporating additional components, and external factors such as climate. The external factors – those which influence the model but are not themselves influenced by it – are of considerable importance in many ecological models for capturing variation in model behaviour that cannot be explained in terms of the internal factors operating inside the model: climate frequently "drives" ecological systems to quite a large extent. The additional components could be populations of food, competitors (other herbivores) and predators.

This process of model refinement is potentially unending. For example, each of the additional components introduced to provide a better view of the rabbit population dynamics could themselves be disaggregated, and additional components introduced to provide a better account of *their* behaviour. This process is terminated by data availability, but more importantly by the insight of the modeller in balancing the cost of including additional refinements against the benefits that might accrue in terms of the accuracy of model output.

2.4   Conclusion

This chapter was intended to provide the reader with an introduction to the domain in which our experiments have been conducted. Ecology is interesting as a domain for modelling because ecological systems are highly complex and therefore it is difficult to decide how to represent them in simplified form as simulation models. A large number of modelling paradigms have been used as an aid to tackling this problem but no single paradigm has emerged as a clear favourite. We have introduced the idea of providing a general purpose specification language which would subsume a number of the conventional modelling paradigms, thus providing uniformity of notation (at a high level) for a wide range of models. This raises further questions concerning the notation to be used for such a language and the use to which it could be put in improving model comprehension. In the next chapter, we shall introduce Prolog as our first contender for the role of general purpose model specification language. Subsequent chapters will then address problems in using Prolog for this purpose and provide examples of the way in which a logic–based approach may be used to support the construction and re–use of ecological simulation models.

3 Representing Simulation Models in Prolog

Given that we wish to pursue the idea of using logic as a notation in which to represent simulation programs, the obvious starting point is with a logic programming language. Prolog is the most widely accepted of such languages. We describe the basic notation used in Prolog and show how it may be used to represent simulation models. The use of logic to represent a simulation model provides the programmer with a radically different approach to the task of simulation. Instead of providing a sequence of instructions which tell the computer how to run the model, the programmer provides a set of Prolog clauses which describe the structure of the model. These are then processed, using a standard interpreter, to provide answers to users' questions about the structure of the model at any point in the simulation.

It is important to note at this point that, although we are advocating Prolog as a useful notation in which to represent simulation models of certain kinds, we are *not* claiming that it is the pre–eminent general purpose language in which to represent simulation models. Many researchers have proposed varieties of logic which are specially tailored to the demands of particular types of simulation. For example, [Futo & Gergely 86] describes T-Prolog which extends standard Prolog to include notions of global time; [Radiya & Sargent 87] provides details of LOPPS, an adaptation of Prolog for discrete event simulation; [Cleary 89] gives examples of the use of a Horn–clause temporal logic (Starlog) for running colliding puck simulations. Other researchers have shown how common simulation methodologies can be expressed in standard Prolog ([Zajicek 86] does this for discrete–event specifications). We shall avoid becoming enmeshed in a discussion of the advantages and disadvantages of these specialist languages because this would divert attention from the topic of model comprehension. Instead, we shall try to stay as close as possible to standard logic programming methodology and notation, using Prolog as an anchor point for our study.

We demonstrate the representational benefits of specifying simulation models in logic rather than using conventional, imperative techniques. These benefits are: more explicit structure, modularity and flexibility of use. However, Prolog also has weaknesses. It is often necessary to include control information within definitions of model structures and this tends to obscure the declarative meaning of the program. Also, the models which we construct are slow to run because Prolog relies on a general purpose search procedure to solve for a particular goal, rather than relying on a sequence of finely tuned instructions (as are found in an imperative language). Partial solutions to these problems appear in subsequent chapters.

3.1   Some Prolog Examples

This book is not an introductory text on Prolog programming. A variety of such text books are available – ranging from introductory guides, of which the best known is probably [Clocksin & Mellish 84], to more extensive reference works, such as [Sterling & Shapiro 85]. In this section we shall provide the minimum amount of information necessary to understand the more complex definitions of later chapters. Readers with an interest in pursuing this topic in greater depth should consult a suitable text book or, for an introduction to Prolog for ecological modellers, study [Muetzelfeldt *et al* 88]. The primary aim of this section is to provide the reader with a first impression of what it is like to write simulation programs in Prolog. To this end we have included, in Sections 3.1.1 to 3.1.3, three simple simulation programs – each implemented in Prolog and each based on a different approach to simulation modelling. We hope that these will give the reader a feeling for the range of simulation models which can be represented in Prolog. Note, however, that we do *not* intend to provide a definitive text on how to implement simulation models in Prolog. This would be a distraction from our main goal of examining how simulation models, once described in a logic, can become easier to construct and analyse.

In Section 3.2 we concentrate more closely on this theme by comparing two representations of the same simulation model: one in a conventional imperative programming language and the other in Prolog. This allows us to illustrate some key advantages of the use of Prolog for simulation but also reveals some important disadvantages.

3.1.1   A Simple System Dynamics Example

Suppose that we have a simple model represented in System Dynamics notation ([Forrester 61]). How would we represent this in Prolog ? Figure 3.1 shows a simple System Dynamics model in which there are two state variables, *grass* and *rabbit*. The changes to these state variables over time are effected by the flows of *photosynthesis, respiration, grazing* and *defecation*[1]. The *photosynthesis* flow is from the environmental "source/sink" into *grass*. The *grazing* flow transfers material from *grass* to *rabbit*. Flows of *respiration* empty out of *grass* and *rabbit*. An additional flow of *defecation* also exists from *rabbit*. The rates of transfer for each of these flows is controlled by an equation which takes as inputs a parameter and the values of the state variables involved in that flow. We now describe how

---

[1]The material transferred by flows is often assumed to be biomass

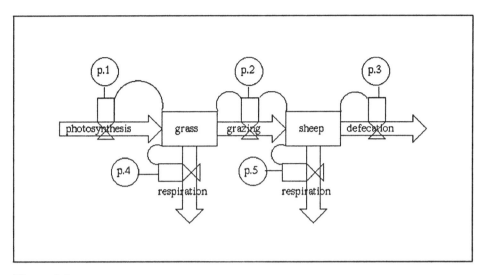

Figure 3.1
A simple System Dynamics model

this model may be represented in Prolog.

Let us begin with the state variables. Each is calculated in a similar way so we can write a general definition which covers both. We shall write *state_variable(S, T, N)* to mean that the value of the state variable S at time T is N. To define a state variable formally we must consider two cases:

- At the initial time point in the simulation, a state variable will have whatever value was set as its initial value. We write *initial_time(T)* to denote that T is an initial time and interpret *initial_value(S, N)* as meaning that the initial value of state variable S is N.[2]

$$state\_variable(S, T, N) :-$$
$$initial\_time(T),$$
$$initial\_value(S, N).$$

We can interpret the above clause declaratively to mean *"state_variable(S, T, N)* is true when *initial_time(T)* is true and *initial_value(S, N)* is true".

---

[2]Note that in these and subsequent definitions we adopt the standard Prolog convention that the names of constants in the Prolog clauses always begin with a lower case letter, while variables always start with an upper case letter.

- At times which are not initial times, a state variable will have the value, N, if: its value, Np, at the previous time point, Tp, is known; the sum, Fi, of all input flows at the previous time are known; the sum, Fo, of all output flows at the previous time are known; and N equals $Np + Fi - Fo$. To implement this definition in Prolog we need to introduce the built–in predicate, **not** P, which succeeds if the Prolog predicate, P, cannot be proved from the current set of clauses in the database. We also require the built–in predicate, N *is* E, which succeeds by evaluating an arithmetic expression, E, to obtain a number, N. Finally, we write $previous\_time(T, Tp)$ to denote that the time point before time T is Tp (see Section 3.2 for a formal definition of this predicate). Our formal definition of a state variable is then:

$state\_variable(S, T, N) :-$
        not $initial\_time(T)$,
        $previous\_time(T, Tp)$,
        $state\_variable(S, Tp, Np)$,
        $input\_and\_output\_flows(S, Tp, Fi, Fo)$,
        N *is* $Np + Fi - Fo$.

Note that this definition of a state variable is recursive: *i.e.* obtaining a value for the state variable at some time, T, depends on obtaining its value at some previous time, Tp. To complete the Prolog program for calculating any state variable we need to fill in the details of how input and output flows are obtained. The way this is done is to find the list, Li, of values for all input flows; the list, Lo, of values for all output flows; and sum the elements of Li and Lo to obtain the aggregate input values, Fi and Fo, respectively. To perform this task we make use of two Prolog utilities: $findall(X, G, L)$, which denotes that the list of all values obtained for X by solving goal G is L; and $sum\_elements(L, N)$, which denotes that the sum of all the numbers in list L is N. Finally, we write $inflow(S, T, Ni)$ when there is an inflow of value Ni into state variable S. Similarly $outflow(S, T, No)$ is true when there is an outflow of value No from state variable S. This allows us to write the Prolog clause:

$input\_and\_output\_flows(S, T, Fi, Fo) :-$
        $findall(Ni, inflow(S, T, Ni), Li)$, $sum\_elements(Li, Fi)$,
        $findall(No, outflow(S, T, No), Lo)$, $sum\_elements(Lo, Fo)$.

Our next step is to provide general definitions for inflows and outflows in terms of a common definition of flow. We introduce the predicate $flow(F, X, Y, T, N)$ to denote that the value for the flow named F from object X to object Y at time T is N.

- There is an inflow to some object if there is a flow from another object to that object. Formally:

$$inflow(S, T, N) :- flow(F, X, S, T, N).$$

- There is an outflow from some object if there is a flow from that object to another object. Formally:

$$outflow(S, T, N) :- flow(F, S, X, T, N).$$

This completes our definition of state variables in terms of flows. We now require specific equations for calculating the *photosynthesis*, *grazing*, *respiration* and *defecation* flows. These can be defined as follows.

- The value, N, of the flow, from *photosynthesis* at any time, T, can be obtained if: the value, P, of the parameter regulating photosynthesis for *grass* is known; the value, M, for the *grass* state variable at time T is known; and N equals $P * M$ (where the symbol '$*$' represents multiplication). We write $parameter(F, S, P)$ to denote that the value for the parameter regulating a flow F attached to object, S, is P. Note that the flow of photosynthesis comes from sources external to the system so we need a special object to denote this external source. This is normally referred to as the *source_sink* compartment. Thus photosynthesis is visualised as a flow from the environmental *source_sink* into *grass*. Our formal definition is:

$$
\begin{aligned}
flow(&photosynthesis, source\_sink, grass, T, N) :- \\
&parameter(photosynthesis, grass, P), \\
&state\_variable(grass, T, M), \\
&N \ is \ P * M.
\end{aligned}
$$

- The value, N, of the *grazing* flow is calculated from the value, Mg, of *grass* multiplied by the value, Mr, of *rabbit* multiplied by the value, P, of the the *grazing* parameter.

$$flow(grazing, grass, rabbit, T, N) :-$$
$$parameter(grazing, rabbit, P),$$
$$state\_variable(grass, T, Mg),$$
$$state\_variable(rabbit, T, Mr),$$
$$N\ is\ P * Mr * Mg.$$

- Both respiration flows and the defecation flow are of the same general form, each flow being determined by a parameter specific to that flow, which is applied to the state variable from which the flow leaves. The direction of flow is from the object, S, to the *source_sink* compartment: *i.e.* the flow discharges into the external environment. Using a semicolon to represent a disjunction of goals (see Glossary), we can restrict the instantiation of the variable, F, to either *respiration* or *defecation*. Our Prolog definition is therefore as follows:

$$flow(F, S, source\_sink, T, N) :-$$
$$(F = respiration\ ;\ F = defecation),$$
$$parameter(F, S, P),$$
$$state\_variable(S, T, M),$$
$$N\ is\ P * M.$$

To complete our model, all we need are definitions for the initial time in the simulation; the initial values for state variables and the values for the parameters. These can all be supplied as simple facts, such as these:

- The initial time point is 1.

$$initial\_time(1).$$

- The initial values for *grass* and *rabbit* are 1000 and 10, respectively:

$initial\_value(grass, 1000).$
$initial\_value(rabbit, 10).$

- The values for parameters are shown below:

$parameter(photosynthesis, grass, 0.4).$
$parameter(grazing, rabbit, 0.001).$
$parameter(respiration, grass, 0.1).$
$parameter(respiration, rabbit, 0.1).$
$parameter(defecation, rabbit, 0.1).$

We can now ask for various useful pieces of information about this model. For example, we could ask "What is the value for the *rabbit* state variable[3] at time 2?" by giving the Prolog goal:

| ?— $state\_variable(rabbit, 2, N).$

The Prolog interpreter would then use the definitions of model structure to solve this goal, instantiating N to 18. Figure 3.2 shows the sequence of Prolog subgoals which must succeed in order to satisfy this top-level goal. These are arranged so that the explanation of the subgoals necessary to solve for a particular goal appear beneath that goal, with indentation indicating the "depth" of the subgoal in the chain of rule applications. The reader may wish to compare in detail this explanation with the Prolog clauses supplied earlier. The main point of note is that the simulation in this case proceeds by setting up subgoals which take the simulation back through time, from requirements to establish values for state variables at times in the future to the initial values which provide the basis for their calculation. Thus, for example, it becomes necessary to establish the value of the *rabbit* state variable at time 1 in order to know the value of the *rabbit* state variable at time 2. Note that this search strategy can sometimes be inefficient. We consider this problem in Chapter 5. In the next section we shall consider a simulation model in which the execution of the program goes forwards into the future instead of backwards into the past.

---

[3]It is often implicitly assumed that state variables refer to biomass but this isn't always the case.

$state\_variable(rabbit, 2, 55.75)$ because:

    not $initial\_time(2)$

    and $previous\_time(2, 1)$

    and $state\_variable(rabbit, 1, 10)$ because:

        $initial\_time(1)$

        and $initial\_value(rabbit, 10)$

    and $findall(IS, inflow(rabbit, 1, IS), [10])$ because:

        $inflow(rabbit, 1, 10)$ because:

            $flow(grazing, grass, rabbit, 1, 10)$ because:

                $parameter(grazing, rabbit, 0.001)$

                and $state\_variable(grass, 1, 1000)$ because:

                    $initial\_time(1)$

                    and $initial\_value(grass, 1000)$

                and $state\_variable(rabbit, 1, 10)$

                and $10\ is\ 0.001 * 10 * 1000$

    and $findall(OS, outflow(rabbit, 1, OS), [1, 1])$ because:

        $outflow(rabbit, 1, 1)$ because:

            $flow(respiration, rabbit, source\_sink, 1, 1)$ because:

                $parameter(respiration, rabbit, 0.1)$

                and $state\_variable(rabbit, 1, 10)$

                and $1\ is\ 0.1 * 10$

        and $outflow(rabbit, 1, 1)$ because:

            $flow(defecation, rabbit, source\_sink, 1, 1)$ because:

                $parameter(defecation, rabbit, 0.1)$

                and $state\_variable(rabbit, 1, 10)$

                and $1\ is\ 0.1 * 10$

    and $sum\_elements([10], 10)$

    and $sum\_elements([1, 1], 2)$

    and $18\ is\ 10 + 10 - 2$

Figure 3.2
Explanation of the derivation of the value for the *rabbit* state variable at time 2

3.1.2   A Structural Growth Example

The model in Section 3.1.1 is composed entirely of ecological variables which possess numerical values. In this section we consider a model where the purpose of simulation is not simply to derive numerical values but also to "grow" a data structure. Suppose that we wish to produce a model which represents the growth of a tree, starting with the initial shoot and ending with the branch structure (without leaves) obtained after some number of years. In our idealised view of the system we shall assume that the number of new branches generated each year is determined as a function of the temperature that year and the length to which each branch grows during the following year is also a function of temperature. Further, we shall assume that each branch grows only in the year after it is created and no branches are lost with age.

Our first task is to decide how to represent the branching structure of the tree. This could be done using numerical indices to record the identity of particular branches and their lengths but this is inelegant, since it requires the addition of a considerable amount of code simply to keep track of the appropriate pointers to the branches of the growing tree. A more succinct representation is to represent the tree as a nested Prolog term of the form:

$[b(L_I, B_I), \cdots, b(L_J, B_J)]$
Where: $b(L_N, B_N)$ represents a subtree of the main tree with:
$\qquad L_N$ being the length of the main stem.
$\qquad B_N$ being a list of subtrees, composed in the same way.

The purpose of the simulation program is then to construct a nested term of the form described above, based on the temperature values each year. A Prolog program to perform this task is shown in Figure 3.3. Only 4 predicates need to be written for this model:

- $temperature(Y, V)$ provides the value, V, for temperature each year, Y.

- $stop\_time(S)$ records the time, S, at which the simulation is to end.

- $tree(Y, Branches)$ defines the nested structure, $Branches$, of the subtree grown from year Y. The two clauses for $tree/2$ determine the ways in which $Branches$ can be "grown". If Y is the final year in the simulation then there is no subtree so $Branches = []$ (see clause 1). Alternatively, if Y is earlier than the final year of the simulation then $Branches$ can be obtained if the

number of new branches, $BranchNumber$ can be obtained as a function of
the temperature, $Temp$, for that year and each of these new branches can be
developed using the predicate $branches/3$ (see below).

- $branches(N, Y, B)$ defines the list, B, of subtrees for each new branch, given
  the number of branches, N, and the year, Y. If there are no new branches (*i.e.*
  $N = 0$) then $B = []$ (see clause 1). Otherwise, if the number of new branches
  is greater than 0, a subtree is grown for the first of these new branches (using
  a recursive call to $tree/2$) and the subtrees for each of the remaining new
  branches are found by calling $branches/3$ recursively.

To run the simulation model we provide the Prolog query:

| ?— $tree(1, X)$.

This query succeeds, instantiating X to the nested term shown in Figure 3.4. To
make this term easier to interpret we have included, to its right in Figure 3.4, a
diagrammatical representation of it. The final tree structure has 4 levels of branches
– one for each year in the simulation.

Note that this example differs from the System Dynamics model of Section 3.1.1
not only because it constructs a nested data structure but also in the way in which
time passes during the simulation. In the System Dynamics model solutions were
obtained by passing *backwards* through time in order to obtain the value for a
particular ecological variable. By contrast, the tree growth example goes *forward*
through time, with each new branch forming the basis for additional subtrees at
subsequent time points. Our final example, in Section 3.1.3, adopts yet another
approach to representing the passage of time during a simulation.

3.1.3   A State Transition Example

Many ecological simulation models represent the passage of time as a sequence of
distinct time points. The state of the model during a simulation is updated at each
time point, regardless of whether any change has occurred from the previous time
point. An alternative view of a simulation is that the passage of time is represented
by transitions between states. In this view, we know that time has passed because
we observe a change in the system but it is sometimes unnecessary to know exactly
how much time has passed – we are interested in the sequence of states, not the
absolute distance in time between them. The sort of questions which we are likely
to ask of these models are of a more general nature than those for models based on

$tree(Y, []) :-$
  $stop\_time(Y).$
$tree(Y, Branches) :-$
  $stop\_time(StopTime),$
  $Y < StopTime,$
  $temperature(Y, Temp),$
  $BranchNumber\ is\ fix(0.1 * Temp),$
  $NextY\ is\ Y + 1,$
  $branches(BranchNumber, NextY, Branches).$

$branches(0, \_, []).$
$branches(N, Y, [b(Length, Branches)|Rest]) :-$
  $N > 0,$
  $temperature(Y, Temp),$
  $Length\ is\ 0.2 * Temp,$
  $tree(Y, Branches),$
  $N1\ is\ N - 1,$
  $branches(N1, Y, Rest).$

$stop\_time(4).$

$temperature(1, 10).$
$temperature(2, 18).$
$temperature(3, 20).$
$temperature(4, 14).$
$temperature(5, 8).$

Figure 3.3
A simple model of structural growth

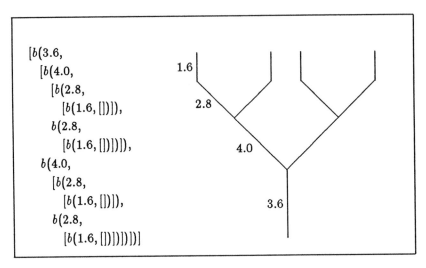

$[b(3.6,$
  $[b(4.0,$
    $[b(2.8,$
      $[b(1.6, [])]),$
    $b(2.8,$
      $[b(1.6, [])])]),$
  $b(4.0,$
    $[b(2.8,$
      $[b(1.6, [])]),$
    $b(2.8,$
      $[b(1.6, [])])])])]$

Figure 3.4
A simple tree structure

differential or difference equations. For example, we might be interested in whether
a given state could ever be obtained by any sequence of transitions between states.

We shall demonstrate this approach with the aid of a simple example. Suppose
that we have 3 different animals (call them a, b and c) and that a will prey on
b; b will prey on c; and c will prey on a. The area in which these animals live is
represented by a grid with 3 squares along each side (thus 9 grid squares in all).
Animals move by shifting from the square in which they are currently situated to
an adjoining square. Each animal moves in the direction of potential prey (*i.e.* they
actively hunt rather than browsing at random) but will not visit a square which it
has occupied previously. If an animal is ever in the same square as its prey, the
prey is eaten and thus removed from the simulation. Given these constraints on
the behaviour of the system we would like to know what sequences of states could
lead to certain animals being eaten or not eaten.

First we must decide how to represent states. Agree to name the initial state
of the system $s0$. Now new states of the system will be obtained whenever some
aspect of the system changes so we require some way of linking the changes imposed
on the system to the events which impose those changes. An elegant way of doing
this is to use a nested term of the form:

do(Action, State)
Where: *Action* is a term representing some action which has been performed.
State is either the initial state *s*0 or another term of the form:
do(Previous Action, Previous State).

The only action which it is necessary to represent in this model is the movement
of an animal from one grid square to another. We represent this action using the
term *move(A, G1, G2)* where *A* is the name of some animal; *G*1 is the location of
the grid square at which the animal was located in the previous state and *G*2 is its
new location. Agree to represent each grid square as a pair, (X, Y), where X is the
number of the column and Y the number of the row in which the square occurs.
We might draw the grid as shown below:

The diagram above shows the initial locations which we have chosen for *a*, *b* and
c, which are (respectively) squares $(1, 1)$, $(2, 2)$ and $(3, 3)$. We are now in a position
to represent any sequence of states created by moving one or more of the animals
between squares. For example, if animal, *a*, moved from square $(1, 1)$ and then
animal, *b*, moved from $(2, 2)$ to $(3, 2)$ this would produce the state:

do(move(b, (2, 2), (3, 2)), do(move(a, (1, 1), (2, 1)), s0))

which corresponds to the sequence of moves:

Figure 3.5 shows a Prolog program which can generate any valid state of the
system, based on the constraints stipulated in the initial problem description. Let
us examine each of the predicates in this program:

- *possible_state(State)* will succeed when *State* is a valid state of the system
  (*i.e.* either *s*0 or some state obtained by applying an action to a previous
  state). It is defined simply by stating that *possible_state(s0, State)* must be
  true in order to obtain a valid state (see next item). This has the effect of
  producing a valid *State*, starting with *s*0 as in initial state.

- *possible_state(State, FinalState)* succeeds if *FinalState* is a valid state of the system which can be reached from *State*. In the simplest case, this is true if *FinalState = State* (clause 1). Otherwise, it will be true if there is a possible action, *A*, which can be applied to *State* and the new state described by *do(A, State)* leads to *FinalState*.

- *possible_action(A, State)* denotes that *A* is an action which can be performed on a given *State*. Our system contains only one form of action: *move(A, G1, G3)*. This moves an animal, *A*, from grid square *G1* to square *G3*, provided that *A* is a predator on some animal, *B* and *G3* is a square on a path towards square *G2*.

- *holds(C, S)* is true when condition, *C*, holds in state, *S*. We are interested in three conditions of the system: the location of an animal; whether it has been eaten; and which squares it has visited. Let us consider each of these in turn:

    - *holds(location(A, G), S)* is true if the location of animal, *A*, is square, *G*, in state, *S*. Clauses 1 to 3 define the locations of the animals in the initial state, *s0*. Clause 4 defines the location of any animal in states other than *s0*. In such states an animal has a location determined by its most recent position in the sequence of actions, provided that it hasn't been eaten in the meantime.

    - *holds(eaten(A), S)* is true if the animal, *A*, is eaten in state, *S*. This is the case if either it has just moved into a square containing one of its predators (clause 5) or one of its predators has moved into its square (clause 6).

    - *holds(visited(A, G), S)* is true if the animal, *A*, has visited square, *G*, in state, *S*. All animals are considered to have visited their initial locations (clause 7). Otherwise, an animal which has been moved to a new location has visited that square (clause 8).

    - All conditions other than *location*, if true in some state, *S*, will remain true in any state derived from *S* by the application of a *move* action (clause 9).

- *move_in_direction(A, G1, G2, S, G3)* succeeds if animal, *A*, can move from square, *G1*, to square *G3* in the direction of square *G2*. The identity of square *G3* is determined by employing one of 4 groups of calculations and is constrained to be a square which *A* has not visited.

- *last_location*(A, S, G) is true if the last location for animal, A, in state, S, is square, G. If the most recent action in S was to move A then G is the square to which it was moved (clause 1). Otherwise, if some other animal was moved then the last location of A must be in some previous state (clause 2). Finally, if we have found no location for A by the time we reach $s0$ then its last location is simply its initial location (clause 3).

- *animal*(A) denotes that A is an animal.

- *predator*(A, B) denotes that A is a predator of B.

- *adjoining_square*$(G1, G2)$ instantiates $G2$ to a square which is next to $G1$ – either directly above, below, left or right. The value of $G2$ is also constrained by the maximum and minimum values for the rows (*max_y_square*/1 and *min_y_square*/1) and columns (*max_x_square*/1 and *min_x_square*/1).

$possible\_state(State) :- possible\_state(s0, State).$

$possible\_state(State, State).$
$possible\_state(State, FinalState) :-$
$\quad\quad possible\_action(do(A, State)),$
$\quad\quad possible\_state(do(A, State), FinalState).$

$possible\_action(do(move(A, G1, G3), State)) :-$
$\quad\quad predator(A, B),$
$\quad\quad holds(location(A, G1), State),\ holds(location(B, G2), State),$
$\quad\quad move\_in\_direction(A, G1, G2, State, G3).$

$holds(location(a, (1, 1)), s0).$
$holds(location(b, (2, 2)), s0).$
$holds(location(c, (3, 3)), s0).$
$holds(location(A, G), State) :-$
$\quad\quad \textbf{not } State = s0,\ animal(A),\ \textbf{not } holds(eaten(A), State),$
$\quad\quad last\_location(A, State, G).$
$holds(eaten(A), do(move(A, \_, G), State)) :-$
$\quad\quad predator(P, A),\ holds(location(P, G), State).$
$holds(eaten(A), do(move(P, \_, G), State)) :-$
$\quad\quad predator(P, A),\ holds(location(A, G), State).$
$holds(visited(A, G), s0) :-$
$\quad\quad holds(location(A, G), s0).$
$holds(visited(A, G), do(move(A, \_, G), \_)).$
$holds(Condition, do(move(\_, \_, \_), State)) :-$
$\quad\quad \textbf{not } Condition = location(\_, \_),\ holds(Condition, State).$

$move\_in\_direction(A, (X1, Y1), (X2, Y2), State, (X3, Y3)) :-$
$\quad\quad ((X1 < X2, X3 \text{ is } X1 + 1, Y3 = Y1);\ (X1 > X2, X3 \text{ is } X1 - 1, Y3 = Y1);$
$\quad\quad\quad (Y1 < Y2, Y3 \text{ is } Y1 + 1, X3 = X1);\ (Y1 > Y2, Y3 \text{ is } Y1 - 1, X3 = X1)),$
$\quad\quad \textbf{not } holds(visited(A, (X3, Y3)), State).$

$last\_location(A, do(move(A, \_, G), \_), G).$
$last\_location(A, do(move(A1, \_, \_), State), G) :-$
$\quad\quad \textbf{not } A = A1,\ last\_location(A, State, G).$
$last\_location(A, s0, G) :-$
$\quad\quad holds(location(A, G), s0).$

$animal(a).\ animal(b).\ animal(c).$

$predator(a, b).\ predator(b, c).\ predator(c, a).$

$adjoining\_square((X1, Y1), (X2, Y2)) :-$
$\quad\quad max\_x\_square(MaxX),\ max\_y\_square(MaxY),$
$\quad\quad min\_x\_square(MinX),\ min\_y\_square(MinY),$
$\quad\quad ((X2 \text{ is } X1 + 1, X2 \le MaxX, Y2 = Y1);\ (X2 \text{ is } X1 - 1, X2 \ge MinX, Y2 = Y1);$
$\quad\quad\quad (X2 = X1, Y2 \text{ is } Y1 + 1, Y2 \le MaxY);\ (X2 = X1, Y2 \text{ is } Y1 - 1, Y2 \ge MinY)).$

$max\_x\_square(3).\ max\_y\_square(3).\ min\_x\_square(1).\ min\_y\_square(1).$

Figure 3.5
A state transition model

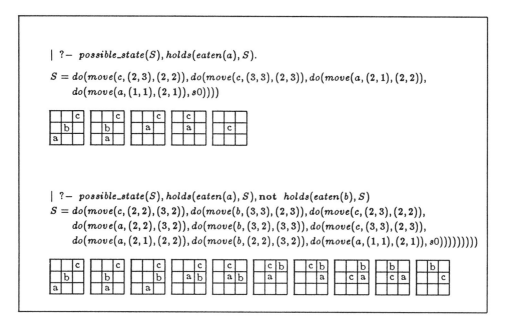

$| \ ?- \ possible\_state(S), holds(eaten(a), S).$

$S = do(move(c, (2,3), (2,2)), do(move(c, (3,3), (2,3)), do(move(a, (2,1), (2,2)),$
$\quad do(move(a, (1,1), (2,1)), s0))))$

$| \ ?- \ possible\_state(S), holds(eaten(a), S), not \ holds(eaten(b), S)$

$S = do(move(c, (2,2), (3,2)), do(move(b, (3,3), (2,3)), do(move(c, (2,3), (2,2)),$
$\quad do(move(a, (2,2), (3,2)), do(move(b, (3,2), (3,3)), do(move(c, (3,3), (2,3)),$
$\quad do(move(a, (2,1), (2,2)), do(move(b, (2,2), (3,2)), do(move(a, (1,1), (2,1)), s0)))))))))$

Figure 3.6
Example queries for state–space model

We are now in a position to use the the program from Figure 3.5 to answer
questions about possible states of the system. One possible question might be
"Is there a state of the system in which animal, a, gets eaten ?". This question,
expressed as a Prolog query, is shown in the top line of Figure 3.6. The idea is
that the first part of the query finds some possible state, S, and then S is tested to
ensure that the condition $eaten(a)$ holds in it. The first value of S for this query is
shown below the original query and we have also included a diagram showing the
sequence of states from the initial state (on the left) through to the final state (on
the right) in which the animal, a, has been eaten. Note that in the third state the
animal, b, is eaten by a and it is this move by a toward b which leaves it open to
attack from c (which, with b removed, has no predators). It would be interesting to
know if there is a valid state of the system in which animal, a, is eaten but animal,
b, hasn't been eaten. This query can be made by adding to our original query the
extra condition that $eaten(b)$ must not hold in the final state, S. A solution for
this query appears in the lower half of Figure 3.5.

The state–transition model which we have constructed is quite powerful because it is capable of exploring all states of the system. This means that if we were to add some animal which predators couldn't catch (*e.g.* if we added an animal which neither *a*, *b* or *c* prey upon) then we could use the model to confirm that there was no possible state in which it was eaten. We know that the space of possible states is finite because of the constraint that no animal can move to a grid square which it has previously visited. Thus, there is maximum of 8 potential moves for each animal. The number of animals is also limited to 3 and this number cannot increase between states (animals only get eaten and new animals aren't born). If either of these restrictions was to be lifted – for example if animals were allowed to move to any adjoining square in any state – then the space of possible states would become infinite. In these conditions we could not guarantee to find all possible states of the system, although the model might still be able to provide useful information within some explored portion of the space of possible states. We shall not dwell on these search problems because they are not our primary concern. Instead, we shall return to our main theme of simulation models as logical arguments and look more closely at the utility of Prolog for this purpose, as compared to conventional imperative techniques.

3.2   Converting Imperative Simulation Models into Prolog

The code shown in Figure 3.7 defines a simple simulation model using a stereotypic notation for a conventional, imperative programming language. For our current purposes we don't need to use a *particular* programming language because we are considering features common to many such languages (*e.g.* FORTRAN or BASIC). The program is designed to calculate the mass of a deer population (represented by the variable *mass_deer_pop*) over a time sequence from 0 to 15. This variable is calculated by summing the masses of two sub–populations of old and young deer (*mass_old_deer* and *mass_young_deer*). The mass of each of these sub–populations is calculated in the same way – by summing their growth and mortality rates – while each growth and mortality rate is calculated according to a simple coefficient of the mass of the appropriate sub–population.

Viewed as a formal description of a simulation model, the program in Figure 3.7 is lacking on several counts:

- The individual model variable names do not, of themselves, give much information about the sorts of variables that they are. For example, the variable

$mass\_old\_deer = 20$
$mass\_young\_deer = 10$
$for\ I = 0\ to\ 15$
    $mortality\_rate\_old\_deer = -0.2 * mass\_old\_deer$
    $growth\_rate\_old\_deer = 0.3 * mass\_old\_deer$
    $mass\_old\_deer = mass\_old\_deer$
                $+growth\_rate\_old\_deer$
                $+mortality\_rate\_old\_deer$
    $mortality\_rate\_young\_deer = -0.2 * mass\_young\_deer$
    $growth\_rate\_young\_deer = 0.3 * mass\_young\_deer$
    $mass\_young\_deer = mass\_young\_deer$
                $+growth\_rate\_young\_deer$
                $+mortality\_rate\_young\_deer$
    $mass\_deer\_pop = mass\_young\_deer + mass\_old\_deer$
$write\ mass\_deer\_pop$
$next\ I$

Figure 3.7
A simple imperative simulation program

mass_deer_pop, if considered in isolation from the rest of the program, could mean anything. By looking at the individual constituents of the name (realising that an underscore has been used to separate words) we could guess that it represented the attribute of *mass* of an object named *deer_pop* and we might further speculate that it might be a state variable (*i.e.* representing part of the state of the system which varies over time). These guesses could be supported by further examination of the rest of the program to find that the calculation of *mass_deer_pop* is done by reference to rate variables. However, this process is rather *ad hoc* and relies on a great deal of specialist knowledge. We would like to make the structure of the variables in the model more explicit so that others could identify more easily the sorts of variables which we have used. This is a problem of **lack of explicit structure.**

- The position of each line in the program is crucially important. For instance, if the equation for *mass_young_deer* were shifted to appear before the equation for *growth_rate_young_deer* then the program wouldn't run because the value of *growth_rate_young_deer* would not have been calculated when it cam time to find a value for *mass_young_deer*. The problem here is **a lack of modularity** in the description. That is, we cannot fully describe how a particular component of the model functions without considering the sequence in which the entire program is executed.

- The model gives, as output, the values of *mass_deer_pop* for each time point. If we wanted to also find the value of another variable (*e.g. mass_young_deer*) then we would have to insert another *write* statement into the program to print this result, even though the model hasn't changed in any important respect. We shall call this problem **lack of flexibility** because, having described the structure of the simulation model it should be possible to find the value of any variable in it without altering the original program.

With these problems in mind, we shall describe how the procedural program of Figure 3.7 can be converted into the Prolog representation shown in Figure 3.8.

First, we add more structure to the attribute and rate variable names by representing them as Prolog terms with functors *attribute* and *rate_of_change*, respectively. Both of these terms have some name (denoting the sort of variable being used); refer to some object (in this case these are populations); vary over time; and are associated with a particular value. These 4 defining characteristics are used as the arguments to these predicates, making the declaration of initial values for mass of young and old deer straightforward, using the clauses which appear in the first 2 lines of the Prolog program in Figure 3.8. Note that these clauses are cut (using the ! symbol) because we don't want any other solutions to be attempted. The effect of the cut is to inform the Prolog interpreter that if (during its attempt to solve for some subgoal) it reaches a cut within a clause then that clause will be the only one used to solve for the particular subgoal. Furthermore, the subgoals appearing in the body of the clause before the cut will be "frozen" so that they do not resucceed on backtracking. Readers who are uncertain about the use of cuts in Prolog shouldn't be too concerned because they do not loom large in this book. The key point is that cuts are a procedural notion because they provide information to the Prolog interpreter about how it should search the database of clauses. We shall return to this topic later.

Having defined the initial values, we now consider a procedure for providing the desired output of the model – the mass of the deer population. Recall that this requires us to sum the masses of old and young deer so we could try using a simple equation definition:

$$attribute(mass, deer\_pop, T, N) :-!,$$
$$attribute(mass, young\_deer, T, N1),$$
$$attribute(mass, old\_deer, T, N2),$$
$$N \text{ is } N1 + N2.$$

However, a more general description would be that we want to find all the masses of the sub–populations of *deer_pop* at the appropriate time and then sum them together, so we *actually* use a more complex procedure:

$$attribute(mass, deer\_pop, T, N) :-!,$$
$$bagof(N1,$$
$$(member(X, [young\_deer, old\_deer]),$$
$$attribute(mass, X, T, N1)), L),$$
$$sum\_list(L, N), !.$$

which could easily be adapted to handle new sub–populations by adding extra elements to the list [*young_deer, old_deer*]. In Chapter 4 we shall describe more elegant ways of handling this sort of substructure.

All the other mass calculations in the model are handled in exactly the same way so we can use a single clause to capture this information. This procedure (the 4th clause in Figure 3.8) finds the mass of any object at any time by finding the mass of that object at the previous time and adding the sum of any rates of change. The rates of change (*growth_rate* and *mortality_rate*) are also each calculated in the same way for all objects so we add a general clause for each of these (5th and 6th clauses of Figure 3.8). The only remaining definition is a means of calculating previous time points. This is done by simply subtracting 1 from the current time (clause 7 of Figure 3.8).

We now return to the deficiencies noted above for the procedural program and examine to what extent the Prolog program remedies these problems:

Explicit structure : It is easy to distinguish between attributes and rate variables and to tell which part of the expression refers to, for instance, the object to which the variable applies. It is also easy to distinguish general sorts of predicate by examining its arguments – for example constants don't vary over time and so wouldn't need a time argument. Most importantly, it is possible to leave one or more of the arguments as variables so that, for instance, we can talk about the mass of *any* object, not just some particular object.

Modularity : By making the calculations for each variable self–contained (except for the cut symbols) we are moving toward a representation where the ordering of definitions is of no consequence. For example, it doesn't matter where the *rate_of_change* clauses are placed in Figure 3.8. This means that we can, to a greater extent, concentrate on defining the components of our program without having to worry about how they will mesh together when run.

Flexibility : There are no *write* statements in our Prolog definition. Values for particular model variables would be obtained by giving an appropriate Prolog goal. Thus, the output which we required from our procedural program in Figure 3.7 would be obtained from our Prolog version by giving the goal:

| ?− *attribute*(*mass*, *deer_pop*, *T*, *N*).

for a sequence of values of T from 0 to 15. However we could also satisfy many other Prolog goals using the same Prolog program. For example:

| ?− *rate_of_change*(*growth_rate*, *old_deer*, 10, *N*).

would find the growth rate of the old deer at time 10.

$attribute(mass, young\_deer, 0, 10) :- !.$

$attribute(mass, old\_deer, 0, 20) :- !.$

$attribute(mass, deer\_pop, T, N) :- !,$
       $bagof(N1,$
               $(member(X, [young\_deer, old\_deer]),$
               $attribute(mass, X, T, N1)), L),$
       $sum\_list(L, N), !.$

$attribute(mass, X, T, N) :-$
       $previous\_time(T, Tp),$
       $attribute(mass, X, Tp, N1),$
       $bagof(N2,$
               $(member(R, [growth\_rate, mortality\_rate]),$
               $previous\_time(T, Tp1),$
               $rate\_of\_change(R, X, Tp1, N2)), L),$
       $sum\_list(L, Sum),$
       $N \ is \ N1 + Sum, !.$

$rate\_of\_change(growth\_rate, X, T, N) :-$
       $attribute(mass, X, T, N1),$
       $N \ is \ 0.3 * N1, !.$

$rate\_of\_change(mortality\_rate, X, T, N) :-$
       $attribute(mass, X, T, N1),$
       $N \ is \ -0.2 * N1, !.$

$previous\_time(T, Tp) :-$
       $Tp \ is \ T - 1, !.$

Figure 3.8
A simple Prolog simulation model

Unfortunately, our translation to Prolog hasn't been an unqualified success. Several important problems remain:

- The definitions aren't entirely independent of the execution of the program because we have included a cut in every definition. For the most part, these cuts are to ensure that each calculation is succeeds only once, which makes sense because they are really single valued functions (*e.g.* an object cannot have more than one value for its mass at any given time). Because Prolog is a relational, rather than a functional, language we have to add the extra control information necessary to prevent wasteful search for extra solutions. The most convenient way to do this in Prolog is by adding cut symbols. In Chapter 4 we provide a representation language in which we can distinguish between functions and relations, thus avoiding the corrupting influence of cuts on the modularity of our code.

- The modularity which we achieved in representation of the simulation model was achieved at the cost of devolving the task of running the model (solving some initial goal) to the Prolog interpreter. Since this is a comparatively simple, general purpose mechanism it tends to do considerably more work in running a model than would be required for a conventional, procedural program where the computer is told precisely when it should perform particular operations. In chapter 5 we consider methods for avoiding this computational overhead.

3.3   Conclusion

At the end of this chapter, the reader should have a basic understanding of how one may construct a variety of simulation models as standard Prolog programs. Our examples of Section 3.1 are not extensive but should be enough to demonstrate that Prolog can be adapted to a variety of modelling paradigms. We have also highlighted a number of advantages of Prolog as a model specification language – namely: explicit structure, modularity and flexibility. We argue that these properties are a necessary foundation for improving model comprehension because they help prevent the structure of the model being obscured by extraneous computational detail. Unfortunately there are computational problems in using the Prolog approach because some Prolog models can be unacceptably slow to run and it is often convenient to include procedural information within the Prolog program, thus re–introducing the extraneous computational detail which we sought to avoid. In the next chapter, we shall describe a special purpose model representation language which alleviates these problems and, in Chapter 5, we show how the computational inefficiency of Prolog can be tackled. A further problem is that Prolog programs are difficult for those with no training in logic programming to understand. For the purposes of model comprehension, this is of great concern because very few of the potential users of an ecological models will have any knowledge of Prolog programming. Therefore it is necessary to provide software tools which will protect users from the details of the formal notation, while allowing them to understand the structure of the program in the context of the problems which they want to solve. In Chapters 7 and 8 we give examples of these sorts of tools and show how logic can help provide a foundation for constructing them.

4 Using an Order Sorted Logic for Simulation

In Section 3.2, we introduced the use of Prolog for representing simulation models and noted that it gave several advantages over conventional procedural programs – namely, more explicit structure, modularity and flexibility. However, we were not entirely satisfied with the representational capabilities which Prolog provided. In particular, it was convenient to include in our Prolog programs a number of cuts which destroy the declarative interpretation we desire for our program specifications. These cuts are used for two reasons:

1. The model structures which we are dealing with are often functions, returning a single value. Once a value has been found for a given function there is no need to look for further values, since to do so would involve futile extra search. Unfortunately, Prolog is a relational language and so has to be "told" when to stop searching for new solutions. This is done by placing a cut symbol as the final subgoal of every clause in Figure 3.8.

2. To make our Prolog programs more compact, we often omit conditions in the body of clauses which we know are unnecessary because of cuts which commit to clauses earlier in the program. This is done for reasons of efficiency (or expediency) but its effect can be to alter the meaning of the program. For example, the 1st clause of the program in Figure 3.8 is:

$attribute(mass, young\_deer, 0, 10) :-!.$

so we know that if ever the time is 0 then the mass of young deer will have the value 10 and *no further clauses will be tried for that goal*. This allows us to write, as the 4th clause in Figure 3.8, the following algorithm for calculating masses at other times:

$attribute(mass, X, T, N) :-$
$\quad previous\_time(T, Tp),$
$\quad attribute(mass, X, Tp, N1),$
$\quad bagof(N2,$
$\quad\quad\quad (member(R, [growth\_rate, mortality\_rate]),$
$\quad\quad\quad previous\_time(T, Tp1),$
$\quad\quad\quad rate\_of\_change(R, X, Tp1, N2)), L),$
$\quad sum\_list(L, Sum),$
$\quad N \; is \; N1 + Sum, !.$

Now if this clause were ever to be applied with T instantiated to 0 then
the consequences would be disastrous: Tp would be bound to -1 and the
program, with no base case applying to negative values of time, would spin
into an infinite recursion. However, we know that, for young deer, the 1st
clause will succeed whenever the time reaches 0. Therefore, unless a time
less than 0 is specified in the top–level goal, we know that the 4th clause will
never be called in this incorrect manner. The cut in the 1st clause is used to
ensure that the 4th clause is not reached on backtracking[1].

These problems suggest that we need a more sophisticated representation language
with the following principal features:

1. It should distinguish functions from relations and the interpreter for the language should be able to use this information to control the execution of the
   program, rather than relying on control information pasted into the program.

2. It should provide an easy way of restricting the objects to which any variable
   in a clause can be instantiated, thus preventing clauses from being applied to
   objects for which they were not designed.

In the rest of this chapter we shall describe an implementation of a language
which provides these two key features. This is not intended to be a general purpose
programming language, like Prolog, although it is capable of representing a wide
range of models. Its purpose is to "clean up" the notation used to represent our
simulation models, while retaining the ability to run these models with efficiency
comparable to that of Prolog. Given the requirement for restriction of variables over
subsets of all possible objects, it seems reasonable to experiment with a variety of
order–sorted logic. A good introduction to sorted logics may be found in [Cohn 89],
from which we include the following short definition of the term:

> In ordinary (unsorted) first-order predicate calculus, the universe of dis-
> course (*i.e.* the set of individuals over which the quantifiers range) is a
> single homogeneous set. A many–sorted logic differs from this situation
> by including a set of sorts in the language and by dividing the universe
> of discourse into many subsets and assigning a sort to every subset.
> Ordinary first-order logic can be viewed as a one–sorted logic. Now,
> whereas in ordinary logic function symbols are always interpreted as

---

[1] Of course, we *could* have avoided this problem by adding extra subgoals to the fourth clause
in order to prevent it being used in the wrong circumstances. One of the purposes of this chapter
is to provide a standard method for adding this extra information.

total functions on the universe of discourse, in a many–sorted logic one can effectively have partial functions by specifying that particular function symbols are only applicable to certain sorts....Moreover the range (or co–domain) of a function symbol can be specified; given some way of assigning sorts to variables, this then naturally enables one to speak of the sort of a term in the language. Similarly, predicate symbols can be defined as only making sense on certain sorts of argument terms....Many sorted languages in which an ordering of the sorts is specified are sometimes called order–sorted languages.

In implementing our brand of order–sorted logic we have tried to keep as close as possible to the standard Prolog interpreter, in order to avoid replicating facilities which are already provided. We have retained the standard Prolog depth–first search strategy and query mechanism but have augmented this to incorporate sort restrictions on variables and a simple form of function evaluation. Our description begins, in Section 4.1, with a description of the sort hierarchy and over which we restrict the variables in our sorted logic expressions. We then describe, in Section 4.2, how the general forms of functions and predicates can be defined with respect to this sort hierarchy. In Section 4.3 we provide a notation for sorted logic axioms (analogous to the clauses of Prolog programs) and provide an algorithm for executing programs in this language in Section 4.4. In Section 4.5 we show how the sorted logic can be used to describe the simulation model introduced in Section 3.2. Finally, in Section 4.6 we provide an algorithm for translating axioms in the sorted logic into Prolog clauses, thus allowing us automatically to convert any sorted logic program into a Prolog program. This final result underlines the fact that our use of the sorted logic is not an attempt to obtain increased expressive power over Prolog but is intended to provide a language which is easier to use in specifying ecological models.

4.1   Representing Objects and Sets of Objects

In this section we provide the data structures and algorithms necessary to define a hierarchy of sets of objects appearing in ecological simulation models. We have two objectives: to provide the reader with a succinct description of the types of operation which we wish to perform on the hierarchy of sorts of objects and to demonstrate how these operations can be implemented in Prolog. Our Prolog definitions are built up incrementally as part of the discussion. Definitions 1 to 9 are a complete list of the required data structures, while Algorithms 1 to 8 together form a complete Prolog program for checking that a given object is included within a given sort, or for generating instances of objects within a given sort.

4.1.1 Simple Set Membership

The basic operation which we wish to perform is to define groups of objects in the universe of discourse and extract from them objects to instantiate variables in the axioms which define a simulation model. The simplest way to do this is to specify directly the set of objects in each group and use a set membership relation, $X \in S$, to denote that an object, X, is a member of some set, S. Since the '$\in$' operator isn't available on the Ascii keyboard we substitute the word 'in' for the symbol '$\in$' in our Prolog definitions.

Definition 1 We write Obj in $Sort$ to denote that the object, Obj, is a member of the set of objects referred to by $Sort$.

The most common usage of the expression, $X \in S$, is when S is a finite set containing some objects and X is constrained to be an element of S. For example, it would be true that the object, $wolf2$, is an element of the set, $\{wolf1, wolf2\}$ and we would write this as $wolf2 \in \{wolf1, wolf2\}$. In Prolog we can represent finite sets as lists and use the standard utility predicate, $member/2$ (see Appendix C.1.1) to obtain elements of a list. This allows us to define our first component of the $in/2$ algorithm in terms of the $member/2$ relation.

Sub–Algorithm 1
Obj in Set :–
        $member(Obj, Set)$.

Our representation of sets as lists means that we shall substitute the standard curly brackets ('{' and '}') enclosing sets for the square brackets ('[' and ']') used to represent lists in Prolog. With this adjustment in notation, Algorithm 1 allows us to check that a given object appears in a particular set or to generate instances of objects in a specific set. Thus we can have the Prolog queries:

| ?– $wolf2$ in $[wolf1, wolf2]$.
yes

| ?– X in $[wolf1, wolf2]$.
$X = wolf1$;
$X = wolf2$

4.1.2 Labelling Sets of Objects with Sort Names

The definitions of the previous section refer only to finite sets. It is inconvenient, and sometimes impossible, always to supply the full set of objects to which each variable in an axiom may be instantiated. A way around this problem is to invent names for commonly occurring groups of objects and use these names to represent the appropriate lists of objects. For instance, we might know that there were 2 animals (named $wolf1$ and $wolf2$) in our model and want to say that any animal may eat any other animal. Using the set membership notation from Section 4.1.1 we would have to write:

$$\forall X \in \{wolf1, wolf2\}, \ \forall Y \in \{wolf1, wolf2\}. \ may\_eat(X, Y)$$

This is rather long winded and we would prefer to have a name (call it '$animal$') which could represent the set $\{wolf1, wolf2\}$. This would allow us to write:

$$\forall X \in animal, \ \forall Y \in animal. \ may\_eat(X, Y)$$

To support this method of labelling sets we first require a way of associating sort labels (*e.g.* '$animal$') with the sets of objects which they represent. One way to do this is to assert the membership of each object in the set represented by the sort label. For example, to include $wolf1$ and $wolf2$ in the set represented by '$animal$' we could assert that:

$$wolf1 \in animal$$
$$wolf2 \in animal$$

Since we don't have access to the '$\in$' symbol in Prolog we use the term, $subobj(S, X)$, in an equivalent way to the $X \in S$ assertions above. Note that we could have used the symbol '**in**' (which we introduced earlier) for this purpose but it is computationally more efficient to separate the basic sort membership assertions (expressed using $subobj/2$) from the more general sort membership algorithm (expressed using **in**/2).

Definition 2 We write $\underline{subobj(Sort, Object)}$ to assert that the object referred to by $Object$ belongs to the set of objects referred to by $Sort$.

Thus, the inclusion of $wolf1$ and $wolf2$ within the sort represented by '$animal$' is written in Prolog as:

$subobj(animal, wolf1).$
$subobj(animal, wolf2).$

To be able to use the information in these new relations to obtain instances of objects referenced by sort labels we need an extra component to the Prolog definition of the **in**/2 relation. This states that an object is contained in the set referenced by a given sort label if there is a '$subobj$' relation allocating that object to the stipulated label.

Sub–Algorithm 2
Obj **in** $Sort$:—
          $subobj(Sort, Obj).$

This allows us to give the Prolog query:

| ?— X **in** $animal$.
$X = wolf1$;
$X = wolf2$

4.1.3   Arranging Sort Names into Hierarchies

Having provided the facility to represent sets of objects using convenient sort labels it is worthwhile going a step further to organise these sorts into hierarchies. For example, we might want to have a sort called '$animal$' (containing $wolf1$ and $wolf2$); a sort called '$plant$' (containing $tree1$ and $tree2$); then have a sort called '$organism$' which contains all the objects in '$animal$' and '$plant$'. We therefore need some way of saying that all the objects in one sort, $S1$, are contained within some other sort, $S2$. The membership relation from Section 4.1.2 will not do for this job because it is a relation between a single object and a sort. Instead, we use an equivalent to the standard subset relation, $S1 \subseteq S2$, to denote that $S1$ is a subsort of $S2$. For example, we could write:

$animal \subseteq organism$
$plant \subseteq organism$

to denote that objects which are in the sets of plants and animals are also in the set of organisms. Once again, we must substitute the '$\subseteq$' symbol with a name which can be composed on the Ascii keyboard, and we use the name '$subsort$' for this purpose.

Definition 3 We write $\underline{subsort(Sort, Subsort)}$ to denote that the set of objects referred to by $Subsort$ is a subset of the set of objects referred to by $Sort$.

This gives us a direct translation into Prolog of the '⊆' relations in our example:

$subsort(organism, animal)$.
$subsort(organism, plant)$.

Our Prolog definition of the in/2 relation must now be given the ability to use these $subsort$ relations to infer the membership of objects in any given sort from information about the membership of objects in subsorts of that sort. This can be achieved by stating that an object is a member of some sort if there is some subsort of that sort and the object is a member of that subsort.

Sub–Algorithm 3
Obj **in** $Sort$:−
        $subobj(Sort, Obj)$.
Obj **in** $Sort$:−
        $subsort(Sort, SubSort)$,
        Obj **in** $SubSort$.

Continuing with the example sort hierarchy from earlier in the section, this addition to the algorithm would allow us to make the following Prolog query:

| ?− X **in** $organism$.
$X = wolf1$;
$X = wolf2$;
$X = tree1$;
$X = tree2$

Notice that our algorithm will work for subsort hierarchies of any depth because of its recursive definition (*i.e.* Algorithm 3 uses the in/2 relation as part of its own definition). This is important because complex hierarchies are common in the ecological domain. A diagram of a simple ecological sort hierarchy appears in Figure 4.1. In this diagram, any sort on the left of a curly bracket contains the subsorts on the right of the bracket. Thus, '*organism*' is a subsort of '*physical_object*', which is, in turn a subsort of '*object*'. Given these subsort relations and the information that (for example) $wolf1$ was a member of '*organism*', our new definition of the in/2 relation would allow us to infer that $wolf1$ was also a member of '*object*'.

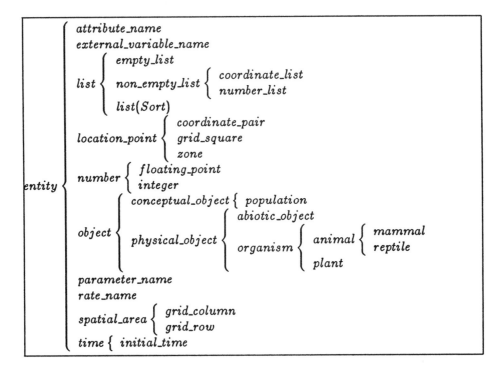

Figure 4.1
Example sort hierarchy

4.1.4   Complex Objects

In Sections 4.1.1 to 4.1.3 we have assumed that the objects referred to by sorts
would be denoted by simple, atomic names. However, it is sometimes useful to be
able to make the existence of certain objects within a given sort depend on the
existence of other objects in different sorts. For example, we might define a sort,
'*population*', which contains two objects, *population*1 and *population*2. Note that
although it is normal to think of populations as sets of objects, it is common in
models to idealise these sets as objects, in the same way that one might consider
an amorphous mass of bacteria (although composed as individuals) to behave as a
single entity. Given that we have objects representing our two populations, we might
want to define objects representing the new born of any object in '*population*'. One
way to do this would be by inventing new object names (say *new_population_1* and
new_population_2) but by doing this we lose information about the dependency of
the new–born objects on the existence of the objects in *population*. This creates
a practical problem because if we later removed the object *population_1* we would
still retain the object *new_population_1*, even though it is no longer required in the
sort hierarchy. We want to be able to say that an object of the form, $new\_born(X)$,
will exist for any object of sort, *population*. Put formally, this might be expressed
as:

$$object \supseteq \{new\_born(X) \mid X \in population\}$$

A more general form of this definition is:

$$S \supseteq \{\mathcal{T}(X_1, \cdots, X_N) \mid (X_1 \in S_1 \ \& \ \cdots \ \& \ X_N \in S_N)\}$$

That is, we want to be able to construct an object of sort, S, consisting of a term
$\mathcal{T}$ with arguments X_1 to X_N which are constrained to be of sorts S_1 to S_N. To
include this facility in our Prolog definition of the in/2 relation, we first require a
way of denoting the relationship between the arguments of a complex object and
the restrictions on those arguments. For this, we introduce the Prolog predicate,
sort_term/3:

Definition 4 We write $\underline{sort\_term(Sort, Term, Constraints)}$ when *Term* is a complex term representing an object in *Sort* and *Constraints* is the conjunction (represented as a list) of sort restrictions on *Term*.

The *new_born* in *population* example given above would be handled by adding
the *sort_term* definition:

$sort\_term(object, new\_born(X), [X$ in $population])$.

which states that the sort *object* contains all terms of the form $new\_born(X)$ such that X in *population*. We now need to provide our Prolog algorithm for **in**/2 with the ability to generate correct instances of complex objects by referring to the *sort_term* definitions. This is done by adding a clause which states that an object is contained within a given sort if there is a *sort_term* definition linking the object to the sort and all the sort constraints in the list of sort restrictions are satisfied. Since the set of sort constraints can be of any length we require an extra predicate (which we shall call *satisfiable_constraints*) to work down the list of constraints, testing that each can be satisfied using the **in**/2 relation. The necessary additions are shown below.

Sub–Algorithm 4

Obj **in** $Sort$:—
$\qquad sort\_term(Sort, Obj, Consts)$,
$\qquad satisfiable\_constraints(Consts)$.

$satisfiable\_constraints([Obj$ **in** $Sort|Rest])$:—
$\qquad Obj$ **in** $Sort$,
$\qquad satisfiable\_constraints(Rest)$.
$satisfiable\_constraints([])$

   Following the population example above, we could obtain the instances of sort, *object*, as follows:

| ?— X **in** $object$.
$X = population\_1$;
$X = population\_2$;
$X = new\_born(population\_1)$;
$X = new\_born(population\_2)$

4.1.5   Adding Relations Between Sorts

In Section 4.1.4 we considered the need to represent objects whose existence depended on the existence of other objects. A further, related, problem arises when one or more sets of objects are already defined and we want to define a sort containing those objects which satisfy some condition on the stipulated sets. This is best explained by following an example. Suppose that we have two sorts, named '*zebra*' and '*antelope*', and wish to state that all *zebra* compete with all *antelope*. This can be done by constructing a *competition* relation which is contingent on its arguments being of the appropriate sorts:

$competitor(A, B) \leftarrow A \in zebra \ \& \ B \in antelope$

To represent this relationship between predicates and sorts in Prolog, we add another new form of definition:

Definition 5 We write $sort\_relation(Relation, Constraints)$ when $Relation$ is a relation between objects and $Constraints$ is the conjunction (represented as a list) of sort restrictions on $Relation$.

This allows the competition relation described above to be expressed as:

$sort\_relation(competitor(A, B), [A$ in $zebra, B$ in $antelope])$

As before, we require an augmentation of our algorithm for the **in/2** relation which allows it to use these new definitions. We need to be able to find any object which could be instantiated to a stipulated argument of the *Relation* term and which is consistent with the set of *Constraints* applying to that relation. In order to indicate that *Relation* needs to be treated in this way, rather than as a normal sort, we enclose it within a special term: $srelation(Relation)$. Our algorithm is then:

Sub–Algorithm 5
Obj in $srelation(Relation) :-$
            $sort\_relation(Relation, Consts),$
            $satisfiable\_constraints(Consts).$

Continuing the zebra and antelope example, suppose that *zebra* contains the objects $z1$ and $z2$ while *antelope* contains the objects $a1$ and $a2$. We might want to restrict the instances of some variable, X, to those objects which compete with $z1$. Stated formally, we want the objects in the set:

$\{X \mid competitor(z1, X)\}$

To do this in Prolog, we can use the goal:

| ?– B in $srelation(competitor(z1, X))$.
$X = a1$;
$X = a2$

4.1.6   Infinite Sets

So far we have considered sorts defined over finite sets of objects but many of the
sorts which are referred to in simulation models are defined either over large sets of
objects which the user does not want to enumerate or over infinite sets of objects.
The former case will be tackled in Section 6. Our concern in this section is with
infinite sets of objects. The most obvious example of this is the use of real numbers
as the values of numerical variables in the model. It is inconceivable, in practice,
that we could enumerate all the numbers which might be used in most models
so we need an extra facility to cope with these infinite sets. The idea is that if
some predicate, P, involving object, X, is available to test that X belongs to some
standard sort, S, then we use the success of P to indicate that the object belongs
to S. Put more formally, we can write:

$$S \supseteq \{X \mid P(X)\}$$

In the case of numbers, there is normally in Prolog a built–in procedure, $number(X)$,
which can be used to test whether X is a number. In this case, our formal definition
would be:

$$number = \{X \mid number(X)\}$$

To represent this relationship in Prolog we add definitions of the form:

Definition 6 We write $sort\_test(Sort, Obj, Test)$ when Obj is a variable referring
to an object in $Sort$ and $Test$ is a procedure which determines whether Obj is in
$Sort$.

This allows us to define the sort *number* using:

$$sort\_test(number, N, number(N)).$$

The addition needed to our algorithm for computing the **in/2** relation is straightforward. An object is considered to be contained within some sort if there is a
sort_test definition providing a test to determine membership of the object in the
sort and the test succeeds.

Sub–Algorithm 6
Obj **in** $Sort$:–
        $sort\_test(Sort, Obj, Test)$,
        $Test$.

This bypasses the problem of infinite sorts but a price has to be paid for this extra flexibility : we cannot *generate* all the members of an infinite sort, we can only *test* whether a given object belongs to a given infinite sort. For example, the goal:

| ?− 0.169 in *number*.

will succeed but the goal:

| ?− *X* in *number*.

is prevented because the particular number represented by *X* is unknown. This has important implications in Sections 4.2 and 4.3 where we discuss the use of sort restrictions on the variables of formulae.

4.1.7 Intersection and Union of Sorts

Our current definition of in/2 permits tests for inclusion in a single sort or relation between sorts. However, it is common to talk about intersections of sorts. We might, for instance, talk about carnivorous animals, in which case we are referring to the intersection of the sorts, *carnivore* and *animal*. This intersection operation can be expressed as a conjunction of set operations – when we find an object which is in the intersection of *carnivore* and *animal* this must be because it is a member of *carnivore* and of *animal*. In formal notation (using the '∩' symbol to represent sort intersection) we could write:

$$X \in carnivore \cap animal \leftrightarrow X \in carnivore \ \& \ X \in animal$$

More generally, we can say that an object, X, is in the intersection of two sorts, S_1 and S_2, if and only if it is a member of S_1 and also a member of S_2:

$$X \in S_1 \cap S_2 \leftrightarrow X \in S_1 \ \& \ X \in S_2$$

A similar principle can be used to obtain the union of sorts. For example we might want to define the sort of objects which are either *zebra* or *antelope*. An object would be contained in this union if and only if it was contained in either of the sorts. Expressed formally:

$$X \in zebra \cup antelope \leftrightarrow X \in zebra \ or \ X \in antelope$$

More generally, we can say that an object, X, is in the union of two sorts, S_1 and S_2, if and only if it is a member of S_1 or is a member of S_2:

$$X \in S_1 \cup S_2 \leftrightarrow X \in S_1 \text{ or } X \in S_2$$

As usual, the limitations of the Ascii keyboard force us to invent new names to represent the set intersection and union operators. We have chosen to use the names 'and' and 'or' for this purpose because of the aforementioned equivalence between intersection and conjunction and between union and disjunction.

Definition 7 We write *Sort1 and Sort2* to denote the intersection of sort *Sort1* and sort *Sort2*.

Definition 8 We write *Sort1 or Sort2* to denote the union of sort *Sort1* and sort *Sort2*.

Prolog uses a comma to represent conjunction and a semicolon to represent disjunction. With this change in notation, it is possible to translate the formal definitions of sort intersection and union directly into our Prolog definition of the **in/2** relation:

Sub–Algorithm 7
Obj in (*Sort1 and Sort2*) :−
        Obj in *Sort1*,
        Obj in *Sort2*.
Obj in (*Sort1 or Sort2*) :−
        Obj in *Sort1*;
        Obj in *Sort2*.

This allows sort intersection goals such as:

| ?− X in *carnivore and animal*.

to succeed, binding X to any object which is in both *carnivore* and *animal*. It also allows sort union goals such as:

| ?− X in *antelope or zebra*.

which would bind X to any object which is in *antelope* or *zebra*.

4.1.8   Membership of Inverses of Sorts

The final refinement required of the in/2 relation is to cater for sorts from which an object is excluded. Put more formally, we want to be able to say that an object, X, is a member of the inverse of a sort, S if and only if it is in the universe of discourse, U, but is not a member of S.

$$X \in \overline{S} \leftrightarrow X \in U \;\&\; \neg X \in S$$

For example, we might want to talk about all animals which aren't carnivores. Put more formally, we want to find any object which is in the sort, *animal*, but is not in the sort, *carnivore*:

$$X \in animal \,\cap\, \overline{carnivore}$$

The simplest way to implement this form of sort definition in Prolog is to make use of Prolog's built–in negation operator. Different dialects of Prolog have different symbols for negation but we shall use the term, **not** P, to denote that some Prolog predicate, P, cannot be satisfied. Note that in Prolog the fact that a goal, **not** P, cannot be satisfied does not mean that P is *proved* to be false, only that it cannot be proved true. In the context of the sort hierarchy, this means that we assume that an object is not contained in some sort if we cannot prove that it is contained within that sort. The limitations of the Ascii keyboard again force us to introduce a new term to represent the inverse symbol:

Definition 9 We write $inv(Sort)$ to denote the inverse of set $Sort$.

The final addition to the in/2 algorithm to provide this feature is:

Sub–Algorithm 8
Obj **in** $inv(Sort)$:–
      not $(Obj$ **in** $Sort)$.

This allows the "animals and not carnivores" statement which we gave earlier to be expressed as the goal:

| ?– X **in** *animal and inv(carnivore)*.

This completes our definition of the in/2 relation. In the next section we shall consider how the sort restrictions may be linked to the axioms which are needed to define simulation models in the sorted logic.

4.2   Declaring Functions and Predicates

4.2.1   User Defined Functions and Predicates

Having provided (in Section 4.1) a mechanism with which we can restrict the objects permitted as constraints for a variable in the logic we now require a notation for describing the general forms of functions and predicates involving these variables. We shall consider predicates first, since the definitions of these are simpler. Predicates are often described formally in sorted logics as functions from arguments of particular sorts to some boolean result (*i.e.* they are either true or false). For example, we might have a predicate, $may\_eat(A, B)$, which is permitted to hold for objects of sort *animal*. In many text books this would be written formally as:

$$may\_eat : animal \times animal \mapsto bool$$

Of course, these symbols aren't available in Prolog and there is an additional complication because of the computational requirement to distinguish sort restrictions which must be applied when a predicate is first called from sort restrictions which are applied only after the predicate succeeds. We shall return to this problem shortly but first provide our Prolog notation for representing predicate definitions.

Definition 10 We write $def(Term, pred(InputConsts, OutputConsts))$ to denote that *Term* is a predicate with variables restricted according to the constraint sets *InputConsts* and *OutputConsts* – where the *InputConsts* constraints must hold at the time the predicate is called and the *OutputConsts* constraints must hold after the predicate has succeeded.

Returning to our previous example, we can define a general form of a predicate $may\_eat(A, B)$ which holds when an animal A may eat an animal B:

$$def(may\_eat(A, B), pred([A \text{ in } animal, B \text{ in } animal], []))$$

Notice that, although we have put the sort restrictions on A and B in the *InputConsts* set, we could have put them in the *OutputConsts* set instead. The only difference would have been that the tests for sort membership are performed earlier in the execution of the program if the restrictions appear in the *InputConsts* set.

Why do we ever need to distinguish between *InputConsts* and *OutputConsts*? The reason lies in our need to restrict objects over infinite sorts (see Section 4.1.6). If we have a predicate which has as one of its arguments a variable which is a member of an infinite sort and that variable is expected to be bound at some point after the predicate is called then we cannot test for membership of that variable in the infinite sort until after the variable has been bound to some object. Since the only point at which we are certain that the binding should have occurred is when the predicate finally succeeds we must assign this sort restriction to the *OutputConsts* set. To clarify this point, consider a predicate *maximum_y_coord*(*Coords, C*) which holds when *C* is a coordinate pair from the list *Coords* of coordinate pairs which has a value for its "y" coordinate greater than or equal to the "y" coordinate of any other coordinate in *Coords*. Both *Coords* and *C* are restricted over infinite sorts (all lists of coordinates and all coordinates, respectively) but we know that *Coords* should be bound to a list of coordinates when the predicate is called, otherwise it would be impossible to select a maximum. However, *C* is likely to be a variable when the predicate is called, since typically we will use this predicate to find a maximum from a list of coordinates. Therefore, it must appear in the *OutputConsts* set so the correct definition is:

$$def(maximum\_y\_coord(Coords, C),$$
$$pred([Coords \text{ in } coordinate\_list], [C \text{ in } coordinate\_pair]))$$

The notation for defining functions is similar to that given above for predicates. For example, we might have a function named '*attribute*' which takes as arguments objects of sort *attribute_name*, *object* and *time* and returns an object of sort *number*. In the conventional mathematical notation this would be represented as:

$$attribute : attribute\_name \times object \times time \mapsto number$$

Our Prolog representation of this form of definition is as follows:

Definition 11 We write $def(Term, fun(InputConsts, OutputConsts, ResultS))$ to denote that *Term* is a function with variables restricted according to the constraint sets *InputConsts* and *OutputConsts* (where the *InputConsts* constraints must hold at the time the function is called and the *OutputConsts* constraints must hold after the function has succeeded) and *ResultS* is the sort of the object obtained by evaluating *Term*.

Using this Prolog notation, we can define the *attribute* function, used earlier, as:

$$def(attribute(S, X, T), fun([S \text{ in } attribute\_name, X \text{ in } object, T \text{ in } time], [], number))$$

4.2.2   System Functions and Predicates

Although our primary aim is to make explicit the computational structure of simulation models, some of the functions and predicates which we shall use are more appropriately regarded as "built in" features implemented directly in Prolog. The main reasons for this are:

Clarity : If we have a function which performs a standard, mundane task – such as finding the "y" values in a list of coordinates – then there is little point in defining this explicitly in the sorted logic (although this *could* be done). It is more convenient to regard the procedure for evaluating this function as "given" and assume that it will never need to be redefined by the users of the system.

Efficiency : Some functions would take a long time to execute if defined entirely in the sorted logic. The multiplication function is a good example of this.

For those predicates which we want to implement directly in Prolog we provide mapping statements in the following way:

Definition 12 We write $sys\_pred(Term, (InputConsts, OutputConsts), Proc)$ to denote that $Term$ is a predicate implemented using the Prolog $Procedure$ which satisfies the sort restriction set $InputConsts$ before the procedure, $Proc$, is called, and satisfies the sort restriction set $OutputConsts$ if $Proc$ succeeds.

Using this notation we can define the predicate $A = B$, meaning that the object A unifies with the object B, as a direct mapping to the corresponding Prolog unification procedure (see Appendix A for a definition of the term "unification"):

$$sys\_pred(A = B, ([], [A \text{ in } universal, B \text{ in } universal]), A = B)$$

In this example A and B can be any two objects so their sorts are restricted by the maximally general $universal$ sort. Note also that both sort restrictions are placed in the $OutputConsts$ set because the unification procedure may itself bind one or other of the variables.

Our definitions of built in functions are similar to those for predicates, with the addition of an extra argument to restrict the sort of the object returned when the function is evaluated:

Definition 13 We write $sys\_fun(Term, (IConsts, OConsts), RSubst, Proc)$ to denote that $Term$ is a predicate implemented using the Prolog procedure, $Proc$, which satisfies the sort restriction set $IConsts$ before $Proc$ is called ; satisfies the sort restriction set $OConsts$ if $Proc$ succeeds ; and the result of the evaluation satisfies the sort restriction $RSubst$.

The multiplication function is defined using this notation as:

$$sys\_fun(A * B, ([A \text{ in } number, B \text{ in } number], []), C \text{ in } number, C \text{ is } A * B).$$

the idea being that if A and B are numbers the Prolog procedure C is $A * B$ is executed and the result C tested to ensure that it is a number. Note that by placing the sort restrictions on A and B in the $IConsts$ set we ensure that both variables are instantiated before the Prolog procedure is called. This is essential for the procedure to succeed.

4.2.3 Meta–Logical Functions and Predicates

The final class of functions and predicates which must be considered are meta–logical ones (see Appendix A for a definition of the term "meta–logical"). For example, we often have to find the set, S, of all objects, X, such that a particular predicate, P, is satisfied for X. In Prolog, this is done using the built in predicate $setof(X, P, S)$. The key point is that, when $setof(X, P, S)$ is used in standard Prolog, all the solutions for P are found, using the Prolog interpreter, and these form the set, S. At first sight, it might seem that in order to incorporate this predicate into the sorted logic interpreter we could simply map this predicate onto the appropriate Prolog procedure, using the sys_pred declaration from Section 4.2.2:

$$sys\_pred(setof(X, P, S), ([], [X \text{ in } universal, P \text{ in } universal, S \text{ in } list]), setof(X, P, S))$$

This is *incorrect* : first because P will be a predicate, not an object ; second (and more importantly) we don't want to call P directly as a Prolog goal from within $setof$ because the standard Prolog interpreter can't interpret the sorted logic. What we want to to say is "find the set of all objects X such that P can be solved *using the sorted logic interpreter* and store these as list S." We introduce a new definition for this purpose:

Definition 14 We write $meta\_pred(Pred, Proc)$ to denote that the sorted logic predicate, $Pred$, can be implemented using the Prolog procedure, $Proc$.

We can now give a workable declaration for the $setof$ predicate as:

$$meta\_pred(setof(X, P, S), setof(X, solve(P, X), S))$$

where $solve(P, X)$ is a top level call to the sorted logic interpreter which solves predicate P, returning the solution X.

Meta–functions can be defined in a similar way to meta–predicates. The only difference is that an extra argument must be added to record the result obtained for the evaluation of the function:

Definition 15 We write $meta\_fun(\overline{Fun, Res, Proc})$ to denote that the sorted logic predicate, $Pred$, can be implemented using the Prolog procedure, $Proc$, returning the result Res.

We can now provide a $setof$ function which returns the set of all values for a given function:

$$meta\_fun(setof(F), S, setof(R, solve(F, R), S))$$

This definition takes the sorted logic function $setof(F)$ (where F is some other sorted logic function) and implements this using the Prolog procedure $setof(R, solve(F, R), S)$ (where S is the result returned from the $setof$ function).

4.3 Defining Sorted Logic Axioms

In Section 4.1 we provided a definition of the 'in' relation for determining the membership of an object in a sort. In this section we introduce a language for describing a simulation model using axioms in the sorted logic. We introduce the sorted logic notation for axioms by using as an example a simple model which contains a single object, named $plant1$. The mass of $plant1$ has a value of 20 at an initial time point and increases by 10 at every successive time point. Formally, we can represent this using two equations. The first states that the value for the mass of $plant1$ at any initial time must be 20:

$$\forall T \in initial\_time \; attribute(mass, plant1, T) = 20$$

The second axiom states that for any time other than the initial time the mass of $plant1$ will be equal to the mass at the previous time plus 10:

$$\forall T \in time \; and \; inv(initial\_time)$$
$$attribute(mass, plant1, T) =$$
$$attribute(mass, plant1, previous\_time(T)) + 10$$

These axioms have a standard form which we must represent in Prolog. Each contains a '=' symbol which separates some function on the left from another function on the right, the value of the function on the left being obtained by evaluating the function on the right. This is analogous to the arrangement in Prolog, where the truth of the head of a clause is determined by satisfying the subgoals in its body. All the variables in the sorted logic axioms are universally quantified over the appropriate sorts of objects, using the sort notation from Section 4.1.

Conversion of these axioms into Prolog is almost direct, given some minor changes in notation. Our first step is to take advantage of the fact that all variables are universally quantified, thus allowing us to remove the '∀' symbols and regard them as implicit. Then we need to remove the '=' symbol to prevent confusion with Prolog's use of the same symbol as a unification operator. We have chosen to replace the '=' with '⟸' because this indicates the direction of evaluation of the functions during computation. We next require a Prolog operator to connect the set of sort restrictions to the functions. We have chosen the '#' symbol for this purpose. Finally, we must consider the set of sort restrictions on the axiom. Since this set may contain varying numbers of sort restrictions (depending on the number of variables in the axiom) it is convenient to represent it as a Prolog list. Furthermore, we need to distinguish those restrictions which need to be applied when the axiom is called from those which must be enforced when the axiom has been evaluated. Therefore, we split the list of sort restrictions into a pair of "input" and "output" sort restrictions, in a similar way to Section 4.2.1. To summarise, if we start with a formal statement of the form:

$$\forall X_1 \in S_1 \cdots \forall X_N \in S_N \; \mathcal{F}_1(X_1, \cdots, X_N) = \mathcal{F}_2(X_1, \cdots, X_N)$$

where $X_1 \cdots X_N$ are variables appearing in functions $\mathcal{F}_1$ and/or $\mathcal{F}_2$ and $S_1 \cdots S_N$ are the sorts over which the variables range, then the translation into Prolog produces a clause:

$$([X_1 \in S_1 \cdots X_J \in S_J], [X_K \in S_K \cdots X_N \in S_N])\#$$
$$\mathcal{F}_1(X_1, \cdots, X_N) \Leftarrow \mathcal{F}_2(X_1, \cdots, X_N)$$

If we apply this translation to the two axioms in our example model, we obtain
the Prolog clauses:

$([T \in initial\_time], []) \# attribute(mass, plant1, T) \Leftarrow 20.$

$([T \in time \ and \ inv(initial\_time)], []) \#$
$\qquad attribute(mass, plant1, T) \Leftarrow$
$\qquad\qquad attribute(mass, plant1, previous\_time(T)) + 10.$

In Section 4.4 we show how to build a Prolog interpreter for this notation. To
conclude the current section we summarise the basic symbols and their interpretation.

Definition 16 A well formed term in the logic can be any of the following:

- An <u>object</u>, belonging to a sort hierarchy defined using the notation in Section 4.1.

- A <u>function</u> (declared using the notation in Section 4.2) for which each argument is either an object, as defined above, or a well formed function.

- A <u>predicate</u> (declared using the notation in Section 4.2) for which each argument is either an object, as defined above, or a well formed function.

- A sort restricted term $(InputConsts, OutputConsts)\#Term$ where $Term$ is
  either a function or predicate (as defined above) or a variable appearing in
  $InputConsts$ or $OutputConsts$. $InputConsts$ is a set of sort constraints
  which must hold before $Term$ is called. $OutputConsts$ is a set of sort constraints which must hold after $Term$ is called.

- A derivation expression $\underline{Fun_1 \Leftarrow Fun_2}$ where Fun_1 and Fun_2 are well formed
  functions, possibly with sort restrictions. The interpretation of this expression
  is that the value of Fun_1 is that obtained by evaluating Fun_2.

- An implication expression $\underline{Pred_1 \leftarrow Pred_2}$ where $Pred_1$ and $Pred_2$ are well
  formed predicates, possibly with sort restrictions. The interpretation of this
  expression is that $Pred_1$ is true if $Pred_2$ is true.

4.4   An Interpreter for the Sorted Logic

Sections 4.1 to 4.3 provide a complete description of the sorted logic notation. We
now describe an interpreter which allows these sorted logic axioms to be executed as
a logic program. To get a feel for what is involved, consider the following example.

Suppose that we have supplied a definition of a function, *append/2*, for concatenating two lists, as shown below:

$([X$ in $list], [])\#append([], X) \Leftarrow X.$

$([H$ in $universal, T$ in $list, L$ in $list], [])\#append([H|T], L) \Leftarrow [H|append(T, L)].$

The first of these axioms states that the result of appending an empty list to a list X is just X. The second axiom states that the result of appending a list with first element H and remaining elements T to a second list L is the list containing H as its first element, followed by the result of applying the *append/2* function to the lists T and L. We shall use the predicate *solve(Term, R)* to denote that the input sorted logic expression, *Term*, has the solution, R. We would expect the following behaviour from the sorted logic interpreter:

| ?− *solve(append([1, 2], [3, 4]), R)*.
$R = [1, 2, 3, 4]$

This query succeeds, binding R to the concatenated list.

| ?− *solve(append(1, 2), R)*.
no

In this case, the query fails because neither 1 nor 2 are lists and so the arguments to *append/2* are of the wrong sorts.

| ?− *solve(append([1 + 2, 2 * 3], [9]), R)*.
$R = [3, 6, 9]$

This query succeeds, evaluating all the arithmetic expressions in the list to obtain their numeric values.

In describing the algorithm for performing this task, we provide 4 interacting sub–algorithms (Algorithms 9 to 12). The first of these (Algorithm 9) describes the main *solve/2* procedure. The role of this part of the algorithm is threefold:

- To determine the identity of a given input expression (*e.g.* whether it is a conjunction, disjunction, sort restricted term, meta–function, ordinary function, *etc*).

- If the input expression is a term restricted over some sets of input and output sorts then it must ensure that the input sort restrictions are applied before the term is passed to other parts of the algorithm and that the output sort restrictions are applied after the expression has been processed.

- If the input expression is an ordinary term (*i.e.* not one of the special functions or predicates caught earlier in the algorithm) then the term must first be standardised by evaluating all its arguments. This simplifies subsequent unification. If the expression is a function it must then be passed to the evaluation procedure. Alternatively, if it is a predicate then it must be passed to the algorithm for establishing it as a relation.

Algorithm 9 We write $\underline{solve(Term, Result)}$ to denote that the sorted logic $Term$ is solved to obtain its $Result$ when :

- $term\_class(primitive, Term)$ **THEN** $Result = Term$.
- **OTHERWISE IF** $Term = (Obj \text{ in } Sort)$ **THEN** :
    - **IF** Obj **in** $Sort$ **THEN** $Obj = Result$.
- **OTHERWISE IF** $Term = (A \text{ and } B)$ **THEN** :
    - $solve(A, RA)$ **AND**
    - $solve(B, RB)$ **AND**
    - $Result = RA \text{ and } RB$.
- **OTHERWISE IF** $Term = (A \text{ or } B)$ **THEN** :
    - $solve(A, RA)$ **AND** $Result = RA$ **OR**
    - $solve(B, RB)$ **AND** $Result = RB$
- **OTHERWISE IF** $Term = [H|T]$ **THEN** :
    - $solve(H, R)$ **AND**
    - $solve(T, Rest)$ **AND**
    - $Result = [R|Rest]$.
- **OTHERWISE IF** $Term = ((Ins, Outs)\#Tm)$ **THEN** :
    - $satisfiable\_constraints(Ins)$ (Algorithm 4) **AND**
    - $solve(Tm, Result)$ **AND**
    - $satisfiable\_constraints(Outs)$.
- **OTHERWISE IF** $meta\_fun(Term, Result, Call)$ **THEN** :

- *execute Call* **AND**

- *Term = Result.*

- **OTHERWISE IF** *meta_pred(Term, Call)* **THEN** :

  - *execute Call.*

- **OTHERWISE IF** *nonvar(Term)* **THEN** :

  - *standardise_term(Term, ETerm)* (Algorithm 10) **AND** :

    * **IF** *term_class(function, ETerm)* **THEN** *eval(ETerm, Result)* (Algorithm 11).

    * **OTHERWISE IF** *term_class(predicate, ETerm)* **THEN** *establish(ETerm, Result)* (Algorithm 12).

Given the definition of *solve*/2 which we introduced in Algorithm 9, it is easy to evaluate any sorted logic term simply by unpacking each of its arguments; solving it to obtain its result; and remaking the term with the same principal functor but substituting the results as its arguments.

Algorithm 10 We write $\overline{standardise\_term(Term, ETerm)}$ to denote that a *Term* in the sorted logic can be standardised to form the term, *Eterm*, with all its arguments fully evaluated, when:

- *Term* has functor *F* and ordered set of arguments *Args* **AND**

- For each *A* in *Args solve(A, R)* (Algorithm 9) and return the values for *R* in the ordered set *RArgs*.

- *ETerm* has functor *F* and set of arguments *RArgs*.

Evaluation of an input term to obtain some result requires two cases to be considered. If there is a system function which unifies with the term and for which all the sort restrictions before and after the calling of the appropriate procedure are consistent, then the result is obtained from that procedure. This caters for functions which we don't want to define explicitly as axioms in the logic. Any other function can only be evaluated by referring to the sorted logic axioms so an evaluation expression is selected which, when standardised, unifies with the input term [2] and for which any associated sort restrictions are consistent. The result is then the value obtained by solving the right hand side of the evaluation expression.

---

[2] In our implementation we make this more efficient by only selecting evaluation expressions which solve for a term with the same principal functor as the input term.

Algorithm 11 We write $eval(Term, Result)$ to denote that a sorted logic function, $Term$, evaluates to produce the value, $Result$, when:

- $sys\_fun(Term, (Ins, Outs), Result\ in\ Sort, Call)$ **THEN** :
  - $satisfiable\_constraints(Ins)$ (Algorithm 4) **AND**
  - $execute\ Call$ **AND**
  - $satisfiable\_constraints(Outs)$ **AND**
  - $Result\ in\ Sort$ (Section 4.1).
- **OTHERWISE IF** $term\_class(defined\_function, Term)$ **THEN** :
  - $(Ins, Outs)\#Term1 \Leftarrow Body$ **AND**
  - $standardise\_term(Term1, ETerm1)$ (Algorithm 10) **AND**
  - $Term = ETerm1$ **AND**
  - $satisfiable\_constraints(Ins)$ **AND**
  - $solve(Body, Result)$ (Algorithm 9) **AND**
  - $satisfiable\_constraints(Outs)$.

The algorithm for establishing predicates is similar to that for evaluating functions, except that we distinguish between facts and rules in addition to system predicates. This means that the interpreter will attempt to satisfy a relational query from the available facts before attempting to apply rules, which is a departure from the standard Prolog interpretation algorithm. However, since we do not allow cuts in our axioms the ordering should make no difference to the total number of results obtained – although the order in which they are found may vary.

Algorithm 12 We write $establish(Term, Result)$ to denote that a sorted logic predicate, $Term$, is satisfied from the sorted logic axioms to produce a ground instance, $Result$, when:

- $sys\_pred(Term, (Ins, Outs), Call)$ **THEN** :
  - $satisfiable\_constraints(Ins)$ (Algorithm 4) **AND**
  - $Call$ **AND**
  - $satisfiable\_constraints(Outs)$ **AND**
  - $Result = Term$.
- **OTHERWISE IF** $term\_class(defined\_predicate, Term)$ **THEN** :

- **EITHER** :

  * $(Ins, Outs)\#Term1$ **AND**
  * $standardise\_term(Term1, ETerm1)$ (Algorithm 10) **AND**
  * $Term = ETerm1$ **AND**
  * $satisfiable\_constraints(Ins)$ **AND**
  * $satisfiable\_constraints(Outs)$ **AND**
  * $Result = Term.$

- **OR** :

  * $(Ins, Outs)\#Term1 \leftarrow Body$ **AND**
  * $standardise\_term(Term1, ETerm1)$ **AND**
  * $Term = ETerm1$ **AND**
  * $satisfiable\_constraints(Ins)$ **AND**
  * $solve(Body, \_)$ (Algorithm 9) **AND**
  * $satisfiable\_constraints(Outs)$ **AND**
  * $Result = Term.$

Note that our unification algorithm contains no occurs check. In other words, we have to be careful not to unify terms such as X and $f(X)$ because this would create an infinite recursion in the unification algorithm, which would attempt to construct the infinitely nested expression: $f(f(f(\cdots)))$. This is a standard problem which stems from our reliance on Prolog to do most of the pattern matching in the algorithm[3].

4.5 An Example Model in the Sorted Logic

To demonstrate how the sorted logic which we defined in Sections 4.1 to 4.4 can actually be used to represent simulation models, we return to our running example from Section 3.2. Our first task is to define the objects in our model, using the sort hierarchy definitions from Section 4.1. We first add all the time points as objects of sort *time*, ranging from 0 to 15. These define the time frame in which we are currently interested. We also add the integer 0 as a sub–object of *initial_time*. We have three populations in our model – *deer_pop*, *young_deer* and *old_deer* – so we add these as sub–objects of *population*. We also have one attribute name

---

[3]Some dialects of Prolog are now provided with the option of an occurs check, which solves this problem.

$subobj(time, 0)$. $subobj(time, 6)$. $subobj(time, 11)$.
$subobj(time, 1)$. $subobj(time, 7)$. $subobj(time, 12)$.
$subobj(time, 2)$. $subobj(time, 8)$. $subobj(time, 13)$.
$subobj(time, 3)$. $subobj(time, 9)$. $subobj(time, 14)$.
$subobj(time, 4)$. $subobj(time, 10)$. $subobj(time, 15)$.
$subobj(time, 5)$.
$subobj(initial\_time, 0)$.
$subobj(population, deer\_pop)$.
$subobj(population, young\_deer)$.
$subobj(population, old\_deer)$.
$subobj(attribute\_name, mass)$.
$subobj(rate\_name, growth\_rate)$.
$subobj(rate\_name, mortality\_rate)$.
$sort\_relation(subpopulation(A, deer\_pop), [A$ in $[young\_deer, old\_deer]])$.

Figure 4.2
Additions to universe of discourse for simple example model

(*mass*) and two ecological variables which determine the rate of change of the attribute over time (*growth_rate* and *mortality_rate*) so we add these as sub–objects of *attribute_name* and *rate_name*, respectively. These are all the objects which need be considered but we also have to capture the information that *old_deer* and *young_deer* are sub–populations of *deer_pop*. We do this by using a *sort_relation* statement (Definition 5) as follows:

$sort\_relation(subpopulation(A, deer\_pop), [A$ in $[young\_deer, old\_deer]])$.

This states that the relationship of *subpopulation* holds between *deer_pop* and each object in the set [*young_deer, old_deer*]. It is worth noting, in passing, that it would have been possible to use a *sort_term* definition to achieve the same effect (see Section 4.1.4). The complete set of sort declarations is shown in Figure 4.2.

We can now define a simulation model in the sorted logic using the axioms shown in Figure 4.3. We have used the same number of axioms as there were clauses in the Prolog program of Figure 3.8 and the model structure represented by each axiom in the sorted logic is similar to the corresponding clause in the Prolog program. However, there are a number of important differences between these two representations of the same model.

- Because the sorted logic interpreter can distinguish functions from predicates and will attempt to find a solution to a function only once, we can dispense with the "cut" symbols placed at the end of each Prolog procedure to force determinacy.

- By being careful to restrict the sorts of objects for each axiom to only those for which that axiom is intended we have been able to dispense with the "cut" symbols placed to prevent certain clauses being called with incorrect instantiations of variables.

- All of the calculations in the sorted logic program are performed by the evaluation of nested function expressions. In the Prolog version, the same effect is produced by satisfying each part of the evaluation in sequence, as subgoals, and explicitly passing the results of each stage to the appropriate arguments of subsequent subgoals, using shared variables. This means that the Prolog version contains a large number of extra variable names, the sole purpose of which is to pass around the results of previous parts of the computation.

Having defined the model as shown in Figures 4.2 and 4.3 we can "run" it in a variety of ways. The simplest way is just to ask for the value of some model variable at a particular time – for example we can make the query "What is the mass of the deer population at time 3 ?" and obtain the value:

| ?− $solve(attribute(mass, deer\_pop, 3), N)$.
$N = 39.9299$

Alternatively, we may want to find the value of the mass of the deer population at more than one time. We can ask this question by making time a variable, T, in our query and restricting this over some subset of times (in this example the subset contains just times 2 and 3):

| ?− $solve(([T \text{ in } [2, 3]], [])\#attribute(mass, deer\_pop, T), N)$.
$T = 2, \quad N = 36.2999$;
$T = 3, \quad N = 39.9299$

$([T \text{ in } initial\_time], [])\#attribute(mass, young\_deer, T) \Leftarrow 10.$
$([T \text{ in } initial\_time], [])\#attribute(mass, old\_deer, T) \Leftarrow 20.$

$([X \text{ in } srelation(subpopulation(X, deer\_pop)),$
$\quad T \text{ in } time \text{ and } inv(initial\_time)], [])\#$
$attribute(mass, X, T) \Leftarrow$
$\qquad attribute(mass, X, previous\_time(T))$
$\qquad +sum(bagof(([R \text{ in } rate\_name], [])\#$
$\qquad\qquad\qquad rate\_of\_change(R, X, previous\_time(T)))).$

$([T \text{ in } time], [])\#attribute(mass, deer\_pop, T) \Leftarrow$
$\qquad sum(bagof(([Y \text{ in } srelation(subpopulation(Y, deer\_pop))], [])\#$
$\qquad\qquad\qquad attribute(mass, Y, T))).$

$([X \text{ in } srelation(subpopulation(X, deer\_pop)), T \text{ in } time], [])\#$
$rate\_of\_change(growth\_rate, X, T) \Leftarrow$
$\qquad 0.3 * attribute(mass, X, T).$

$([X \text{ in } srelation(subpopulation(X, deer\_pop)), T \text{ in } time], [])\#$
$rate\_of\_change(mortality\_rate, X, T) \Leftarrow$
$\qquad -0.2 * attribute(mass, X, T).$

$([T \text{ in } time], [])\#previous\_time(T) \Leftarrow T - 1.$

Figure 4.3
A simple model in the order–sorted logic

A more complicated question is "When are the values for mass of the deer population less than 40 ?" In the Prolog program this question could not be asked without adding information about the individual time points which we wanted to consider. We have already provided this information in the sorted logic as part of the sort definitions. The query is therefore straightforward:

| ?− $solve(([T \text{ in } time], [])\#attribute(mass, deer\_pop, T) < 40, R)$.
$T = 0$,
$R = 30 < 40$;

$T = 1$,
$R = 32.9999 < 40$;

$T = 2$,
$R = 36.2999 < 40$;

$T = 3$,
$R = 39.9299 < 40$;
no

Finally, we can build up yet more complex questions by combining other system functions with those from the model. For example, we provide a system function called $fplot$ which takes two arguments – a dependent model variable and an independent model variable – and returns a set of pairs of values in which each pair contains the value of an independent variable followed by the associated value of the dependent variable. In other words, it produces a plot of dependent against independent. Using this function, we can ask the question "What is the plot of mass of the deer population against time over times from 0 to 3 ?":

| ?− $solve(fplot(([T \text{ in } [0, 1, 2, 3]], [])\#attribute(mass, deer\_pop, T), T), R)$.

The resulting instantiation of R is:

$R = [(0, 30), (1, 32.9999), (2, 36.2999), (3, 39.9299)]$

4.6   Translation from the Sorted Logic to Prolog

It is clear, from cursory examination, that there is a strong similarity between the sorted logic notation and standard Prolog. To make this link more formal, we describe below an algorithm for automatically translating any sorted logic axiom into an equivalent Prolog clause. Translation from the sorted logic to Prolog is useful in a practical sense because it gives the ability to develop a model in the sorted logic (perhaps using a construction system like those described in chapters 7 and 8) and then convert the model into a Prolog program which could be ported to other systems. The algorithm given below is a simplified version of the working implementation (we have left some of the more tricky details out) but it contains sufficient detail to demonstrate the general principles involved.

Algorithm 13 We write $sl\_to\_prolog(S, P)$ to denote that the sorted logic axiom S can be translated into the Prolog clause P when:

1. **IF** S is a primitive (*i.e.* an object or variable) **THEN** $P = S$.

2. **OTHERWISE IF** S is an evaluation expression of the form $(Ins, Outs)\#A \Leftarrow B$, where Ins is the set of input constraints and $Outs$ is the set of output constraints, **THEN** :

    -   $sl\_to\_prolog(A, P1)$ where $P1$ is a sequence of Prolog terms derived from A **AND**

    -   Remove the last conjunct, C, from $P1$, leaving the residual conjuncts R **AND**

    -   $sl\_to\_prolog(B, P2)$ **AND**

    -   P is the Prolog term $C :- Body$, where $Body$ is the ordered sequence of conjunctive goals formed from the elements of $Ins \cup R \cup P2 \cup Outs$ and terminated with a cut symbol.

3. **OTHERWISE IF** S is an evaluation expression of the form $A \Leftarrow B$, with no sort restrictions, **THEN** proceed as for part 2 but leave out the conjuncts representing input and output sort restrictions.

4. **OTHERWISE IF** S is a rule of the form $(Ins, Outs)\#A \leftarrow B$, where Ins is the set of input constraints and $Outs$ is the set of output constraints, **THEN** proceed as for part 2 but leave out the terminating cut symbol at the end of the resulting Prolog clause.

5. **OTHERWISE IF** S is a rule of the form $A \leftarrow B$, with no sort restrictions, **THEN** proceed as for part 2 but leave out the conjuncts representing input and output sort restrictions and the terminating cut symbol.

6. **OTHERWISE IF** S is of the form $(A \ and \ B)$ **THEN** :

   - $sl\_to\_prolog(A, P1)$ **AND**

   - $sl\_to\_prolog(B, P2)$ **AND**

   - P is the ordered sequence of conjunctive goals formed from $P1$ followed by $P2$.

7. **OTHERWISE IF** S is of the form $(A \ or \ B)$ **THEN** :

   - $sl\_to\_prolog(A, P1)$ **AND**

   - $sl\_to\_prolog(B, P2)$ **AND**

   - P is the term $(P1; P2)$.

8. **OTHERWISE IF** S is a meta–function or meta–predicate **THEN** apply special purpose translation rules for it to return a conjunction of goals P.

9. **OTHERWISE IF** S is a system or user–defined function or predicate with functor, F, and ordered sequence of arguments A **THEN**

   - Take each element, E, of A in sequence and apply the algorithm: $sl\_to\_prolog(E, R)$.
     Store each term, R, as it is found, in the ordered set $A1$, being careful to introduce and carry forward variables for transferring the results of computations between Prolog goals **AND**

   - Reconstruct the final goal, G, in the sequence as a term with principal functor F and, if S is a function, add an extra variable to its existing arguments which should be carried forward from the previous translation of the original term **AND**

   - P is the ordered sequence of conjunctive goals formed from $A1$ terminated by G.

This algorithm, when applied to all the axioms of our example sorted logic program from Figure 4.3, yields the Prolog program shown in Figure 4.4. This translated version shows clearly the general effect of the algorithm. Consider, for example, the third clause in the program, which started out as the sorted logic axiom:

$([X$ in $srelation(subpopulation(X, deer\_pop)), T$ in $time$ and $inv(initial\_time)], [])\#$
$attribute(mass, X, T) \Leftarrow$
$\qquad attribute(mass, X, previous\_time(T))$
$\qquad + sum(bagof(([R$ in $rate\_name], [])\#$
$\qquad\qquad\qquad rate\_of\_change(R, X, previous\_time(T))))).$

and is translated into the Prolog clause:

$attribute(mass, X, T, C)$:−
$\qquad X$ in $srelation(subpopulation(A, deer\_pop)),$
$\qquad T$ in $time$ and $inv(initial\_time),$
$\qquad previous\_time(T, D),$
$\qquad attribute(mass, X, D, E),$
$\qquad bagof(F, (R$ in $rate\_name, previous\_time(T, H),$
$\qquad\qquad\qquad rate\_of\_change(R, X, H, F)), I),$
$\qquad sum\_list(I, J),$
$\qquad C$ is $E + J, !.$

By comparing the two, we can see that the nested function on the right hand side of the $\Leftarrow$ arrow has been replaced in the Prolog version with a sequence of 5 subgoals; the last of which uses the built in Prolog predicate, $is/2$, to calculate the final value, C. The variables E and J, used to calculate C, are used to pass forward the results of calculating the mass of X at previous time D and the sum of the list of values, I, respectively. The variables D and I play similar roles. The input sort restrictions applied to $attribute(mass, X, T)$ in the sorted logic appear as the first two goals in the body of the Prolog clause, thus ensuring that these sort restrictions are called before any of the other goals.

If we compare the translated Prolog program of Figure 4.4 to the hand–coded Prolog program of Figure 3.8 the two are identical, except for the extra sort checking subgoals, using the $in/2$ predicate, which are present in the translated program. These sort checks make the translated code modular, in the sense that the ordering of clauses in the program doesn't matter, which is not the case for the hand–coded program.

4.7   Conclusion

This chapter introduced the use of a sorted logic as a means of representing simulation models. This notation doesn't provide any increase in representational power

$attribute(mass, young\_deer, A, 10) :-$
    $A\ in\ initial\_time, !.$

$attribute(mass, old\_deer, A, 20) :-$
    $A\ in\ initial\_time, !.$

$attribute(mass, A, B, C) :-$
    $A\ in\ srelation(subpopulation(A, deer\_pop)),$
    $B\ in\ time\ and\ inv(initial\_time),$
    $previous\_time(B, D),$
    $attribute(mass, A, D, E),$
    $bagof(F, (G\ in\ rate\_name, previous\_time(B, H),$
            $rate\_of\_change(G, A, H, F)), I),$
    $sum\_list(I, J),$
    $C\ is\ E + J, !.$

$attribute(mass, deer\_pop, A, B) :-$
    $A\ in\ time,$
    $bagof(C, (D\ in\ srelation(subpopulation(D, deer\_pop)),$
            $attribute(mass, D, A, C)), E),$
    $sum\_list(E, B), !.$

$rate\_of\_change(growth\_rate, A, B, C) :-$
    $A\ in\ srelation(subpopulation(A, deer\_pop)),$
    $B\ in\ time,$
    $attribute(mass, A, B, D),$
    $C\ is\ 0.3 * D, !.$

$rate\_of\_change(mortality\_rate, A, B, C) :-$
    $A\ in\ srelation(subpopulation(A, deer\_pop)),$
    $B\ in\ time,$
    $attribute(mass, A, B, D),$
    $C\ is\ -0.2 * D, !.$

$previous\_time(A, B) :-$
    $A\ in\ time,$
    $B\ is\ A - 1, !.$

Figure 4.4
Prolog code obtained by translation from simple sorted logic model

compared to Prolog (we show in Section 4.6 how any program in the sorted logic can be translated into standard Prolog). Its value is in providing explicit control over the sets of objects to which variables in the program may refer. This, in combination with a more sophisticated mechanism for function evaluation, makes it easier to avoid the use of procedural information within the model. From the point of view of model comprehension, we claim that the sorted logic provides a more natural way to express information about groupings of objects and the properties of these groups. This makes it a useful notation in Chapter 6, where we consider the need for a formal representation of users' ecological problems, as well as the completed model. Before addressing this topic we shall digress slightly, in the next chapter, to consider the problem of increasing the speed of execution of models in Prolog and the sorted logic.

5 Running Logic–Based Simulations

In previous chapters, we have demonstrated that first order logic (in the form of Prolog or the order–sorted logic) is useful for representing simulation models but it suffers from one major drawback. It is often very slow to run – prohibitively so for many simulation models. A major cause of this problem is that the same goal is often called (and thus re–executed) many times during a simulation, despite the fact that it has only a single solution. These redundant computations make the search spaces for many logic simulation programs very large. Some means must be found of reducing the size of the search space and thereby reducing run time.

Other researchers have tackled this problem in various ways. Explanation based generalisation and partial evaluation techniques were incorporated into the PRO-LEARN interpreter ([Prieditis & Mostow 87]) but this system could not handle the cut symbol. In previous chapters we have argued against the use of cuts because they corrupt the declarative interpretation of the simulation model. Although we want to remove cuts from our specification of the simulation model we may require cuts in the code in order to improve efficiency at run time so it is prudent to allow for the use of cut in interpreters which are intended for general use. In this chapter we investigate the more straightforward technique of recording the results of satisfying particular goals and accessing these to satisfy those goals directly if they are called subsequently. This technique has much in common with the "caching" strategy used for Interlisp code in the Memoise system ([Mostow & Cohen 85]). Closely related work has also been done independently by Steve Owen ([Owen 87]) on Prolog interpreters for use in reasoning about protein topology. Like PROLEARN, the interpreters described in Owen's paper did not handle cuts. In Section 5.1 we show how the technique of recording successful goals can be applied in Prolog interpreters which can handle cut (but not side–effecting predicates such as $assert/1$ and $write/1$). These techniques are then applied (in Section 5.2) to the sorted logic interpreter. We provide some estimates for the savings in run time obtained using the interpreters which we have constructed. Although these savings are large, they may still not be large enough for many applications. Therefore, in Section 5.3, we consider the use of a special purpose mechanism to translate a limited range of sorted logic programs into a procedural language which can then be run in the conventional way. First, we give a summary of the problem, in the context of simulation programs. Note that the language which we use to summarise the problem is not Prolog notation but the problem applies equally to Prolog.

Many simulation programs consist of a series of dependencies between various quantities in the simulation model. These dependencies may be interwoven in complex networks. A simple example of this sort of dependency network occurs when some attribute (*e.g.* the mass of rabbit) at time step T is calculated as a function $(\mathcal{F}_1)$ of its value at the previous time step $(T-1)$ and the value of another attribute (*e.g.* the mass of grass) at the previous time. Suppose that the mass of grass is also a function $(\mathcal{F}_2)$ of the masses of rabbit and grass at the previous time step and that the initial values (at $T = 0$) for mass of rabbit and grass are 10 and 100 respectively. This gives us the expressions:

$$mass(rabbit, T) = \mathcal{F}_1(mass(rabbit, T-1), mass(grass, T-1))$$
$$mass(grass, T) = \mathcal{F}_2(mass(rabbit, T-1), mass(grass, T-1))$$
$$mass(rabbit, 0) = 10$$
$$mass(grass, 0) = 100$$

Now suppose that we want to know the value for $mass(rabbit, 3)$. This involves the nested evaluation of functions as shown in the following diagram, where sub–functions are indented and execution of the "program" is from top to bottom. The evaluation goes backwards through time to previous values of mass, rather than forwards through time. The reason for this is that the equations allow the calculation of mass at *any* time point later than the initial time. Therefore, a computation which applied these equations forward through time from the initial time would (if unconstrained) be non–terminating.

$$mass(rabbit, 3) = \mathcal{F}_1(mass(rabbit, 2), mass(grass, 2))$$
$$\quad mass(rabbit, 2) = \mathcal{F}_1(mass(rabbit, 1), mass(grass, 1))$$
$$\quad\quad mass(rabbit, 1) = \mathcal{F}_1(mass(rabbit, 0), mass(grass, 0))$$
$$\quad\quad\quad mass(rabbit, 0) = 10$$
$$\quad\quad\quad mass(grass, 0) = 100$$
$$\quad\quad mass(grass, 1) = \mathcal{F}_2(mass(rabbit, 0), mass(grass, 0))$$
$$\quad\quad\quad mass(rabbit, 0) = 10$$
$$\quad\quad\quad mass(grass, 0) = 100$$
$$\quad mass(grass, 2) = \mathcal{F}_2(mass(rabbit, 1), mass(grass, 1))$$
$$\quad\quad mass(rabbit, 1) = \mathcal{F}_1(mass(rabbit, 0), mass(grass, 0))$$
$$\quad\quad\quad mass(rabbit, 0) = 10$$
$$\quad\quad\quad mass(grass, 0) = 100$$
$$\quad\quad mass(grass, 1) = \mathcal{F}_2(mass(rabbit, 0), mass(grass, 0))$$
$$\quad\quad\quad mass(rabbit, 0) = 10$$
$$\quad\quad\quad mass(grass, 0) = 100$$

The important point made by the above diagram is that the values which have to be calculated in order to obtain $mass(grass, 2)$ are identical to those required for $mass(rabbit, 2)$ – only the functions ($\mathcal{F}_1$ and $\mathcal{F}_2$) differ. This can introduce a considerable amount of redundancy into the computation. Consider the following example, which is a simplified form of the previous *rabbit–grass* example:

Suppose that we have the expressions:

$$a(L) = \mathcal{F}_1(a(L-1), b(L-1))$$
$$b(L) = \mathcal{F}_2(a(L-1), b(L-1))$$
$$a(0) = K1$$
$$b(0) = K2$$

To obtain a value for any of the quantities $a(L)$ or $b(L)$, where L is an integer greater than 1, we must find values for each instance of $a(L-1)$ and $b(L-1)$ and apply the evaluation mechanism recursively until we reach the base cases $a(0)$ and $b(0)$. Considering this as a search problem, we can say that the branching rate during the execution of the program is determined by the number of subexpressions of the functions (in this case 2). The number of levels in the search tree between two quantities, $G(L')$ and $G(L'')$ is $L' - L''$ (*e.g.* the number of levels between the quantities $a(5)$ and $b(2)$ is 3). In these circumstances, we can calculate the number of times a particular quantity is calculated during execution of a program according to the equation:

$$N = Branch\_rate^{(L\_initial - L\_target)}$$

Where: *NCalls* is the number of times a quantity is calculated.

   Branch_rate is the branching rate of the search tree.

   L_initial is the level of the initial query.

   L_target is the level of the quantity which is calculated N times.

This is a severe problem if the branching rate is high and there are a large number of levels. For example, our initial query was $a(20)$ then $a(10)$ would be calculated 1024 times. If we increase the branching rate to 5 and the difference in levels to 20 then the target quantity is calculated approximately 9.54×10^{13} times. We should only have to calculate a given quantity *once* in any simulation because it is a physical impossibility for the same quantity to have different values at the same time.

   Of course the picture isn't quite as black as it would seem from our example, since in it we maximised the number of interdependencies between functions. Normally we would not expect so many interdependencies but there is sufficient recalculation in the execution of many logic simulation programs to make it worth considering ways in which some of this redundancy could be removed. This chapter describes some implementations of meta–interpreters for this purpose (see Appendix A for a definition of "meta–interpreter"). We first describe a meta–interpreter for Prolog programs (Section 5.1). We then (in Section 5.2) show how similar techniques can be integrated into the sorted logic interpreter from Section 4.4. Finally, (in Section 5.3) we demonstrate a more radical solution – that of translating sorted logic programs into a procedural language which can be executed more efficiently.

An analysis is provided of the benefits obtained by storing the results of function evaluation. The results of this analysis show that the exponential increase in run time with depth of recursion using the standard interpreters is reduced to a linear increase when using the meta–interpreters. This can result in a reduction in run time of several orders of magnitude for simulations in which the level of recursion is high. Note that the results presented in this chapter apply only to conventional Prolog programs and our variety of sorted logic. Other varieties of logic applied to simulation, such as the T-Prolog ([Futo & Gergely 86]) and Starlog ([Cleary 89]) systems mentioned in Chapter 3, have different representations of the passage of time, which it is not the purpose of this book to address.

5.1 Meta–Interpreters for Prolog

Our experiment consists of two phases: first the design of an interpreter which, for Prolog programs, reduces the redundancy of computation described above; then the testing of this interpreter on the hand–coded simulation program of Figure 3.8 and the automatically translated program of Figure 4.4 to provide quantitative comparisons of their performance. The success of the experiment will be judged by the reduction in execution time achieved using the meta–interpreter relative to the execution time using the standard Prolog interpreter.

5.1.1 Design of the Interpreters

Two strategic decisions must be made when designing augmented meta–interpreters: first we must decide how to replicate the standard Prolog interpreter explicitly; then we must choose augmentations to this core mechanism in order to achieve the desired efficiency saving. We begin by considering each of these decisions independently and then show how they are merged to form our experimental interpreter.

Replicating the Standard Prolog Interpreter   There are a large number of ways of implementing the Prolog interpreter in Prolog. We are not interested in a detailed analysis of such implementations. We simply want an efficient implementation which is amenable to adaptation. In [Robertson 88] we describe a similar experiment which tested two different implementations of meta–interpreter. For our current experiment we shall use the simplest and most efficient of these, based on a version written by Peter Ross at the Department of Artificial Intelligence, University of Edinburgh.

Every interpreter described in this chapter is accessed via a top–level call to the $psolve/1$ predicate. For example, a standard Prolog query:

| ?- $foo(X)$.

would be made using the meta–interpreter by making the query:

| ?- $psolve(foo(X))$.

As a gentle introduction to the cut–handling interpreter we shall first consider a simple interpreter which does not handle cuts. Figure 5.1 shows an example of this sort of simple interpreter.

Only two clauses in Figure 5.1 require further explanation. Clause 3 takes care of the case where the goal passed to $psolve/1$ is a meta–predicate (such as $setof/3$ which finds the set of all successful calls of some goal). We could simply call these goals directly, thus omitting clause 3 altogether. However this would cause parts of the program to be interpreted directly by Prolog rather than via the meta–interpreter. For example, consider the $setof/3$ predicate mentioned above. Suppose that our query is $setof(X, foo(X), Set)$. If we simply call this goal then we find all solutions to the goal $foo(X)$ but these would be obtained using the standard Prolog interpreter, not our meta–interpreter. We want the meta interpreter do perform any search necessary to obtain solutions for the goal, $foo(X)$. Therefore the appropriate call should be $setof(X, psolve(foo(X)), Set)$ [1]. The $psolve\_meta\_pred/2$ goal provides a bridge between the goal provided as standard Prolog and the goal required internally by the interpreter (see Figure 5.2). Definitions of $psolve\_meta\_pred/2$ appear in Figure 5.2. The second complication to our simple interpreter arises from the need to differentiate between goals for which Prolog can find clauses (using the built–in $clause/2$ predicate) and those for which it cannot (*i.e.* predicates which are built–in, compiled or interfaced to another programming language). If clauses cannot be found for a given goal then it can be interpreted only by being

---

[1]Note that this problem also arose in the sorted logic interpreter of Section **4.2.3**

```
psolve((A, B)) :–!,
        psolve(A),
        psolve(B).
psolve((A; B)) :–!,
        psolve(A); psolve(B).
psolve(Meta) :–
        psolve_meta_pred(Meta, Call), !,
        Call.
psolve(Goal) :–
        not direct_call(Goal), !,
        clause(Goal, SubGoals),
        psolve(SubGoals).
psolve(Goal) :–
        Goal.
```

Figure 5.1
Simple interpreter which cannot handle cut

$psolve\_meta\_pred(setof(I, P, Set), setof(I, psolve(P), Set)).$
$psolve\_meta\_pred(setof\_or\_empty(I, P, Set), setof\_or\_empty(I, psolve(P), Set)).$
$psolve\_meta\_pred(for\_each(A, L, P, B, List), for\_each(A, L, psolve(P), B, List)).$
$psolve\_meta\_pred(\text{not } Goal, \text{not } psolve(Goal)).$

Figure 5.2
Meta–predicate declarations for Prolog interpreter

called directly (*i.e.* outside the meta–interpreter). This is ensured by testing that a particular goal is not a direct call (using *direct_call*/1) before using *clause*/2.

A Meta–Interpreter which Handles the Cut Symbol The code for our cut handling interpreter is given in Figure 5.3. It provides a neat way of implementing cuts by exploiting Prolog backtracking. The *psolve*/2 predicate in this program contains, as its second argument, a variable which is instantiated to the flag 'cut' whenever a cut is backtracked over (see first two clauses of *psolve*/2). This is used to force failure of clause bodies in which the 'cut' flag gets set (see sixth clause of *psolve*/5). In other words, the interpreter communicates when it has backtracked over a cut and prunes the search tree using that information. Note the use of the equivalence operator ('==') in the third clause of *psolve*/2. This tests whether two terms are identical without forcing variables to be instantiated. Thus the goal $Cut1 == cut$ succeeds only if $Cut1$ is instantiated to 'cut' before the goal is called.

```
psolve(Goal) :−
        psolve(Goal, _).

psolve(!, _).
psolve(!, cut) :−!.
psolve((A, B), Cut2) :−!,
        psolve(A, Cut1),
        (Cut1 == cut, Cut2 = cut; psolve(B, Cut2)).
psolve((A; B), Cut) :−!,
        (psolve(A, Cut); psolve(B, Cut)).
psolve(Meta, _) :−
        psolve_meta_pred(Meta, Call), !,
        Call.
```
Augmentation for unique solutions (see Figure 5.4).
```
psolve(Goal, Cut) :−
        not direct_call(Goal), !,
        clause(Goal, SubGoals),
        psolve(SubGoals, Cut),
        ((Cut == cut, !, fail); true).
psolve(Goal, _) :−
        Goal.
```

Figure 5.3
A meta–interpreter which handles cuts

Augmenting the Standard Interpreter to Reduce Recomputation   A description of the search problem experienced using conventional Prolog–style interpreters for simulation has been given at the beginning of this chapter, where we argued that a great deal of this search could be avoided by storing the results of previous computations, rather than replicating them for each Prolog goal. We shall now describe the way in which we chose to augment the interpreter of Figure 5.3 to provide this facility. As pointed out by Steve Owen in [Owen 87], there are two main categories of goal to be considered:

Uniquely satisfiable goals. Our examples from the beginning of this chapter involved finding the value of attributes of particular objects at given times (*e.g. $mass(rabbit, 10) = N$*). These functions are uniquely satisfiable, in that they return one, and only one, result (a rabbit cannot have two different values for its mass at the same time). If we know that a particular goal is uniquely satisfiable then we can store the result of its solution when it first succeeds and refer to this if it is ever called again. We shall refer to these stored results as **lemmas**.

Re–satisfiable goals. Of course, many goals have several solutions. For example, a test for the proximity of a given object to any other might have several solutions for each instance of an object which is in proximity. In this case, we could generate all possible lemmas originating from a particular goal, rather than simply recording a lemma for the first call. This is likely to be expensive but, once done, the solutions for a re–satisfiable goal can subsequently be looked up from the lemmas rather than recalculated.

In the experiments described in [Robertson 88], recording of lemmas for re–satisfiable goals was not found to produce run times any shorter than those obtained by simply recording lemmas for uniquely satisfiable goals. Furthermore, attempting to generate lemmas for re–satisfiable goals may also lead to non-termination of the execution of some programs by forcing premature exploration of parts of the search space. For these reasons, we shall confine our attention to uniquely satisfiable goals.

Recording Uniquely Satisfiable Goals   The additional code necessary to record lemmas for uniquely satisfiable goals is quite simple. The necessary additions appear in Figure 5.4. They should be added to the code for the appropriate basic interpreter at the point shown by the box in Figure 5.3. An informal statement of the algorithm is as follows: if a goal is known to have a unique solution and a lemma for it already exists, then commit to that lemma; otherwise, if it has a unique solution, try to find a solution and add it as a lemma (the code for adding

```
psolve(Goal, _) :-
        unique_soln(Goal),
        lemma(Goal), !.
psolve(Goal, Cut) :-
        unique_soln(Goal), !,
        clause(Goal, SubGoals),
        psolve(SubGoals, Cut), !,
        ((Cut == cut, !, fail); true),
        add_lemma(Goal).
```

Figure 5.4
Additions to Prolog meta–interpreter for recording unique solutions

lemmas is described in Appendix C.1.2). The information determining whether a given goal has a unique solution is hand coded for our sample simulation programs (see Section 5.1.2), using the *unique_soln/2* predicate (see Figure 5.5).

At this point it is worth noting two important problems associated with using the unique solution definitions of Figure 5.5.

First, we have to decide under which conditions a goal has a unique solution. This decision is often difficult for Prolog programs because it is not always easy to guess when, and under what conditions, a given predicate will succeed only once during a simulation. Second, to decide whether or not a given goal is uniquely satisfiable it is often necessary to test whether its arguments are instantiated [2]. For example, *attribute/4* has a unique solution only if its first 3 arguments are instantiated (*i.e.* if we know the identity of the attribute name, object and time at which we require the value of the attribute). These tests must be done correctly, otherwise a predicate may be considered uniquely satisfiable when it is not. They are also executed each time a goal passes through the interpreter, thus lengthening run time. In Section 5.2 we show how the use of the sorted logic can help solve these problems.

---

[2]Strictly, the test should be for groundness (see Appendix A) but in this case the distinction isn't important

$$unique\_soln(attribute(Att, Obj, T, \_)) :-$$
$$nonvar(Att),$$
$$nonvar(Obj),$$
$$nonvar(T),!.$$
$$unique\_soln(rate\_of\_change(Rate, Obj, T, \_)) :-$$
$$nonvar(Rate),$$
$$nonvar(Obj),$$
$$nonvar(T),!.$$
$$unique\_soln(previous\_time(T1, \_)) :-$$
$$nonvar(T1),!.$$
$$unique\_soln(previous\_time(\_, T2)) :-$$
$$nonvar(T2),!.$$

Figure 5.5
Unique solution definitions for the test simulation programs

5.1.2 Analysis of the Efficiency of the Interpreters

In section 5.1.1 we described a basic Prolog meta–interpreter. We then extended this interpreter to record lemmas for uniquely satisfiable goals. We now analyse the efficiency of these interpreters in relation to the standard Prolog interpreter.

We have chosen 2 programs on which to test the interpreters: the simple hand-coded program from Figure 3.8 ; and the program in Figure 4.4 obtained by automatic translation of the sorted logic program from Figure 4.3. These programs produce the same external behaviour ; their main difference being that the program in Figure 3.8 places no restrictions on the sorts of object which can be used as arguments to predicates, while the program in Figure 4.4 imposes sort restrictions.

Several points are worth making about this code:

- The primary aim when originally constructing the test programs was to be able to find the value of the *mass* attribute of the population *deer_pop* at given times. This corresponds to goals of the form $attribute(mass, deer\_pop, T, N)$, where T is instantiated to some integer, greater than or equal to 0, representing a time point in the simulation.

- To solve for goals of the sort given above it is necessary to recurse back through the sequence of time points until initial values for particular attributes are found and apply equations to the results of this recursion, in a similar manner to the examples given at the beginning of this chapter. The greater the value for time in the top level goal, the greater the number of levels in the recursion during execution of the program. As we explained earlier, the amount of search done by the standard Prolog interpreter tends to increase exponentially with the number of levels in the recursion.

- The test program contains numerous examples of uniquely satisfiable goals. For example, the goal $attribute(A, X, T, N)$ is uniquely satisfiable if A, X and T are instantiated. The unique satisfiability conditions for our analysis appear in Figure 5.5.

Each of the two test simulation programs was run by giving the goal:

$$attribute(mass, deer\_pop, T, N)$$

with values of T from 0 to 15. For larger values of T, the test program takes a long time to run (over an hour of real time in some instances) so we have timed the interpreters over single runs rather than finding an average over a number of runs. It turns out that the important differences between interpreters are sufficiently large to be clear even with this rudimentary timing procedure. Each test program was run in 3 ways and the results plotted on the graphs in Figure 5.6 (for the hand coded program) and Figure 5.7 (for the automatically translated program). These graphs plot the CPU time required for a simulation to be completed against the value given for T on that run. The sequences of points appearing on each graph are:

- Runs using the standard Prolog interpreter (shown by a "•" symbol).

- Runs using the unique solution interpreter but removing any lemmas between runs (plotted using a "○" symbol).

- Runs using the unique solution interpreter and retaining lemmas generated in runs with lower T values (shown by a "⋆" symbol).

Note that CPU times have been plotted on a logarithmic scale to base 10. This allows us to compress the wide range of values onto a readable graph and is also particularly suitable for responses which are likely to be exponential. Several aspects of the graphs are of interest:

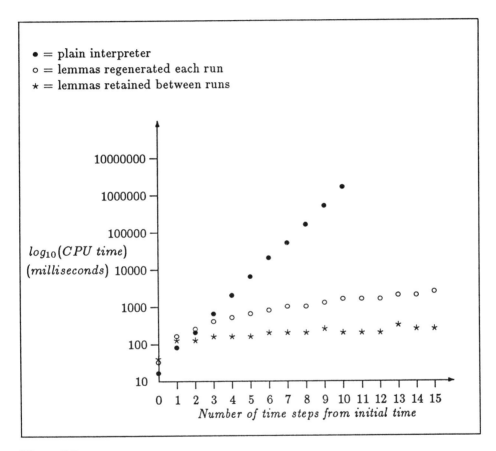

Figure 5.6
Performance of interpreters on hand–optimised program (log scale)

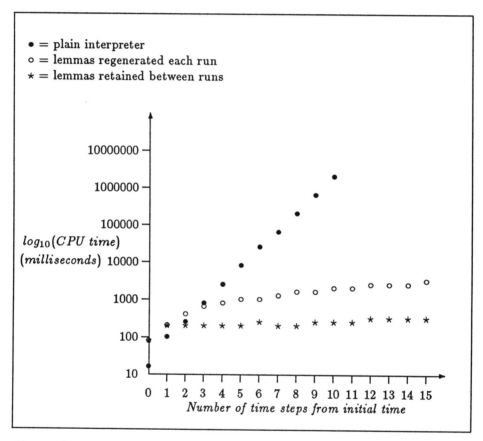

Figure 5.7
Performance of interpreters on automatically translated program (log scale)

- Run times for the automatically translated program are slightly larger than for the hand coded version but this difference is insignificant by comparison with the total run times involved.

- The timings for the standard Prolog interpreter increase exponentially for both test programs with increasing values of T, as expected.

- The response curve is similar for all the augmented interpreters. At low values of T the times for augmented interpreters are greater than those for the standard Prolog interpreter because of the extra layer of computation involved in using a meta–interpreter. However, the increase in run time with increasing T is much less steep for the augmented interpreters and at values of T greater than 4 the augmented interpreter outpaces the standard Prolog interpreter. At T = 9 the augmented interpreters solved the test goal in approximately one thousandth of the time taken by the standard interpreter.

We have described an implementation of a Prolog meta–interpreter which can handle the cut operator and shown how this can be augmented to store lemmas for uniquely satisfiable goals. The tests described in this section and in [Robertson 88] indicate that storing lemmas can give reductions in run time of several orders of magnitude for some simulations (at the cost of the extra memory required to store the lemmas). By comparing run times against an index (T) of level of recursion in the program we established that (for the test example) storage of lemmas made run time respond almost linearly to level of recursion. This compares favourably to the exponential increase in run time experienced using the standard Prolog interpreter.

We have also highlighted a fundamental problem in applying the unique solution interpreter to standard Prolog programs – namely, that it is difficult to decide when a particular Prolog goal is guaranteed to have a unique solution. In the next section we show how this problem can be avoided in the sorted logic by augmenting its interpreter to record lemmas.

5.2 Meta–Interpreters for the Sorted Logic

We have already supplied a meta–interpreter for the sorted logic in Section 4.4 and it is easy to adapt this to record lemmas for uniquely satisfiable goals. Since we know that all functions in the language are uniquely satisfiable (they return only one result) then we need change only the evaluation procedure, detailed in Algorithm 11. Only two alterations are required: the addition of an initial check for an existing lemma before attempting to evaluate a function using the standard procedure; and the assertion of the result for any user–defined function as a lemma. The adapted evaluation algorithm is shown below:

Algorithm 14 We write $eval(Term, Result)$ to denote that a sorted logic function, $Term$, is evaluated using recorded lemmas to produce its value, $Result$, when:

- $term\_class(defined\_function, Term)$ AND $lemma(Term, Result)$ THEN STOP .

- OTHERWISE IF $sys\_fun(Term, (Ins, Outs), Result\ in\ Sort, Call)$ THEN :
  - $satisfiable\_constraints(Ins)$ (Algorithm 4) AND
  - $execute\ Call$ AND
  - $satisfiable\_constraints(Outs)$ AND
  - $Result\ in\ Sort.$

- OTHERWISE IF $term\_class(defined\_function, Term)$ THEN :
  - $(Ins, Outs)\#Term1 \Leftarrow Body$ AND
  - $standardise\_term(Term1, ETerm1)$ (Algorithm 10) AND
  - $Term = ETerm1$ AND
  - $satisfiable\_constraints(BIns)$ AND
  - $solve(Body, Result)$ (Algorithm 9) AND
  - $assert(lemma(Term, Result)).$

Performing similar tests to those done using the Prolog meta–interpreters, but this time using the sorted logic interpreter and the sorted logic program from Figure 4.3, gives the performance results shown in Figure 5.8. These are similar to the results obtained for the translated Prolog program (see Figure 5.7). This suggests that the overhead of interpreting the sorted logic axioms is not greatly different from that of interpreting a conventional Prolog program and similar efficiency gains can be achieved by storing lemmas for uniquely satisfiable goals.

5.3 Translation to an Imperative Language

In the preceding sections we have demonstrated that the problem of exponential increase in run time with level of recursion can be drastically reduced for logic programs by recording the values for uniquely satisfiable functions. However, even with this improvement the logic programs will still, in some cases, take an unacceptably long time to run. One solution to this problem is to view the logic program as a

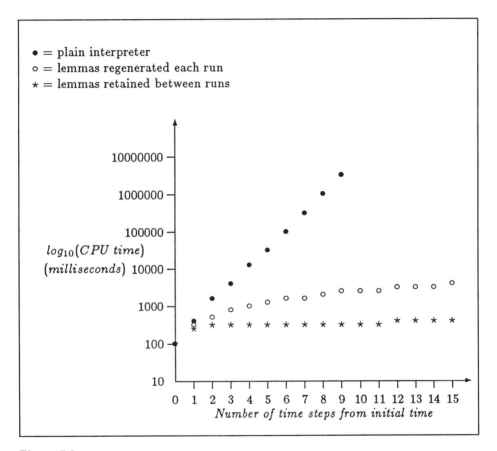

Figure 5.8
Performance of order–sorted logic interpreters (log scale)

specification for a conventional imperative program and provide a means of translating the clauses of the logic program into a sequence of instructions constituting a behaviourally equivalent imperative program. In the general case this is extremely hard, since programs including, for example, relations do not translate easily into discrete packages of instructions. Furthermore, the presence of cuts in Prolog code destroys its modularity, exacerbating the problem.

Fortunately, it is possible to isolate a class of programs in the sorted logic for which automatic translation into procedural code is comparatively straightforward. Recall that the sorted logic is cut free and distinguishes between functions returning a single value and predicates which may succeed many times. If we have a sorted logic program containing only function evaluation expressions (*i.e.* Terms of the form $A \Leftarrow B$) and at any time in the simulation there is only one possible way in which any given model variable can be calculated and we know the goal for which the program was designed to solve, then we can derive an imperative version of this program, using the special purpose translation algorithm given informally as Algorithm 15. The basic idea of this algorithm is that the appropriate set of equations for the imperative program is obtained by finding all the instances of the axioms[3] (instantiating over their input sort constraints) and converting each of these instances to a procedural equation – converting any structured terms to scalar variables in the process. The resulting set of equations is then sorted to ensure that the value of each variable is computed only when the variables used to calculate it also have values (we shall refer to this form of sorting as a "topological sort"). Initial value assignments are extracted from the sorted logic axioms by finding all instances of expressions which contain a primitive value on the right hand side of the "$\Leftarrow$" symbol. Finally, a time loops is placed around the sorted equations and a write statement added to print out the values for the goal of the simulation.

Algorithm 15 We write $procedural\_translation(Goal, Axioms, Prog)$ to denote that there is a translation from a set of sorted logic *Axioms* to a set of statements, *Prog*, comprising an imperative program which will calculate values for *Goal*, when:

- $make\_procedural\_variable\_name(Goal) = GoalName$ **AND**
- Find the *initial_time* object, I, in the sort hierarchy **AND**
- Find the maximum value, F, for *time* in the sort hierarchy **AND**
- Convert each axiom, A, in *Axioms*, into an equation in the procedural language by applying the translation $inst\_ax(A, E)$ exhaustively and store the E terms in the set $PAxioms$ **AND**

---

[3]excluding any axioms, such as $previous\_time/1$, which are only used to reference time points

- Extract from *PAxioms* all equations of the form: $X = Val$, where Val is a number. These are the initial values for the corresponding X procedural variables and are stored in the set *InitVals*. *Equations* is the set of equations remaining after *InitVals* have been removed from *PAxioms* **AND**

- *topological_sort*(*FName*, *Equations*, *SortedEqns*) **AND**

- *Prog* = *InitVals* ∪ [*'for I'* = *I to F*] ∪
  SortedEqns ∪ [*write FName*, *'Next I'*]

ensuring that the order of the sets and the ordering of elements within each set is preserved.

We write $\underline{make\_procedural\_variable\_name(Term) = Name}$ when a *Term* in the sorted logic is converted into an atomic *Name* in the procedural program by:

- Extracting from *Term* an ordered set, *Nset*, of the functors and atomic arguments encountered during a depth–first, left–right traversal of the structure of *Term*.

- Converting *Nset* into an atom containing all the atoms from *Nset*, in their original order, connected by underscores.

We write $\underline{inst\_ax(Term, Equation)}$ when *Equation* is an equation in the procedural language, derived from the sorted logic *Term* according to the algorithm:

- Find an instance, *Iterm*, of *Term* by instantiating any variables in it which are restricted over input sort sets (excluding those of sort *time*) **AND**

- For every subterm, *Stm*, of *Iterm* which does not contain one of the arithmetic operators $(=, +, -, *, /)$, **EITHER** apply a special purpose translation rule *special_inst(Stm)* = *PStm* **OR** convert *Stm* into a procedural variable name by applying the algorithm *make_procedural_variable_name(Stm)* = *PStm* **AND** replace *Stm* with *PStm* in *Iterm*. *Equation* is the result of performing all such replacements.

We write $\underline{topological\_sort(FName, Equations, SortedEqns)}$ when *SortedEqns* is a sequence of equations in the procedural program, obtained by ordering the elements of the set *Equations* in such a way as to ensure that for each procedural variable *PV* in the right–hand side of any equation in *SortedEqns* there is a preceding equation of form $PV = PT$. The last element of *SortedEqns* is of the form $FName = PT1$

```
attribute_mass_old_deer = 20
attribute_mass_young_deer = 10
for I = 0 to 15
    rate_of_change_mortality_rate_old_deer = −0.2 ∗ attribute_mass_old_deer
    rate_of_change_growth_rate_old_deer = 0.3 ∗ attribute_mass_old_deer
    attribute_mass_old_deer = attribute_mass_old_deer
                            +rate_of_change_growth_rate_old_deer
                            +rate_of_change_mortality_rate_old_deer
    rate_of_change_mortality_rate_young_deer = −0.2 ∗ attribute_mass_young_deer
    rate_of_change_growth_rate_young_deer = 0.3 ∗ attribute_mass_young_deer
    attribute_mass_young_deer = attribute_mass_young_deer
                            +rate_of_change_growth_rate_young_deer
                            +rate_of_change_mortality_rate_young_deer
    attribute_mass_deer_pop = attribute_mass_young_deer + attribute_mass_old_deer
write attribute_mass_deer_pop
next I
```

Figure 5.9
An imperative simulation program, translated from the sorted logic

Applying this translation algorithm to the sorted logic program in Figure 4.3 produces the procedural program shown in Figure 5.9[4]. This code is behaviourally identical to the imperative program which we started off with in Figure 3.7; only the names of variables are longer – reflecting the structure of the terms which we used in the sorted logic.

To give a flavour of how the translation process works, we shall describe how the *inst_ax* procedure is applied exhaustively to the fifth clause in Figure 4.3. This clause is:

$$([X \text{ in } srelation(subpopulation(X, deer\_pop)), T \text{ in } time], [])\#$$
$$rate\_of\_change(growth\_rate, X, T) \Leftarrow$$
$$0.3 ∗ attribute(mass, X, T).$$

The first step is to find all the instances of this term by finding all valid combinations of instances of objects for the sort restrictions on the formula (excluding objects of sort *time*). Since the only instances are for *young_deer* and *old_deer* (subpopulations of *deer_pop*) the instances of formulae are:

---

[4]As in our earlier examples of imperative code, this program is not in a particular programming language but the code is similar to standard imperative languages, such as BASIC.

$$rate\_of\_change(growth\_rate, old\_deer, T) \Leftarrow$$
$$\qquad 0.3 * attribute(mass, old\_deer, T).$$
$$rate\_of\_change(growth\_rate, young\_deer, T) \Leftarrow$$
$$\qquad 0.3 * attribute(mass, young\_deer, T).$$

We then use the *make_procedural_variable_name* algorithm to obtain unique, atomic names for the variables in our equations, producing the final equations:

$$rate\_of\_change\_growth\_rate\_old\_deer =$$
$$\qquad 0.3 * attribute\_mass\_old\_deer.$$
$$rate\_of\_change\_growth\_rate\_young\_deer =$$
$$\qquad 0.3 * attribute\_mass\_young\_deer.$$

It is important to note that, although the translation mechanism is useful both as a way of improving run–time efficiency and to cater for users who require procedural programs for reasons of portability, it is *not* general purpose. It relies on a large number of assumptions about the particular expressions which appear in the sorted logic. In particular, it doesn't try to translate *previous_time*/1 functions because these are only used to reference time points. In the imperative program the task of updating the time counter is performed by the "do loop" which increments the counters I and N on each cycle. This makes the use of the *previous_time* function unnecessary. A further problem is that we have placed heavy reliance on special purpose translation rules to handle functions such as *setof*/1 (where the translation mechanism finds the set of all instances and puts these in the procedural equation) and *sum*/1 (where it puts "+" symbols between all elements of the list being summed). The degree to which this sort of translation mechanism can be generalised and extended to cater for more complex simulation programs remains an open question.

5.4   Conclusion

This chapter is something of a digression from our main theme of model comprehension. However, the requirement to actually run completed simulation models is of fundamental importance and deserves detailed consideration. The problem of run–time inefficiency doesn't occur for all logic–based models but does arise in an important class of models - namely, those which make heavy use of the repeated application of recursive functions. We have described two techniques for reducing

this problem. The first involves the use of an enhanced interpreter for the logic programs, which stores the results of previous computations for functions which return
a single, unique result. Massive savings in run time can be achieved by this method
but at the expense of extra memory required to store the appropriate results of
function evaluation. Our second technique was to provide a special purpose mechanism for translating sorted logic programs into a conventional imperative language
which can then be used to run the model more efficiently. The drawback with this
method is that it only works for a restricted class of sorted logic programs and
relies on a number of domain–dependent assumptions about the interpretation of
particular axioms in the logic program. The problem of program transformation is
not a central theme of this book and our discussion in this respect serves merely to
make the point that translation from logic to imperative programs is possible. In
the next chapter, we shall return to our main theme of model comprehension and
consider the requirement for a formal description of users' ecological problems.

6 High Level Problem Descriptions

In previous chapters we have described how sorted logic can be used to provide a declarative representation of simulation models. We demonstrated how those sorted logic models could be run directly, using a Prolog–style interpreter, or, in some cases, translated automatically into procedural programs. We claim that the use of sorted logic to represent model structure provides greater clarity (because the structure of the program is made more explicit) and increased modularity (since each axiom can be defined without worrying about when it will be executed during a run of the program). In the introductory chapter we also suggested that the logic used to represent simulation models might be extended to represent the key characteristics of the real–world systems which the models were intended to represent. This would allow a record to be kept of some of the assumptions which were made during model construction and therefore make it more easy for models to be analysed and compared. It would also raise the possibility of using such knowledge to partially automate the process of model construction (we return to this topic in Chapter 7). We shall refer to a set of sorted logic axioms describing the features of an ecological system as a **problem description**.

Why is it necessary to distinguish a problem description from the simulation model which is constructed in response to that problem ? There are both theoretical and practical reasons for doing this:

- The theoretical reason is that the simulation model is only the final product of a sometimes lengthy process of description and analysis of some real–world problem. Normally, this information is discarded once the model is constructed, since it isn't necessary to the functioning of the model. However, if we view simulation models as arguments based on certain assumptions then it becomes important to retain as much as possible of the problem description because this will provide evidence of the reasons for making these assumptions about model structure.

- The practical reason is that it is useful to have a separate level of description at which users may state the major components of the problem which they wish to represent. This coarse grain description provides context for subsequent development of the simulation model and allows more guidance to be provided during model construction. It also aids automatic model explanation and provides a basis for fast prototyping of alternative models to solve a given problem.

It is important to realise that we are not advocating the representation of real–world problems in their entirety. This would appear to be an insuperable problem because we do not, ourselves, possess a complete understanding of the problems which we seek to model. Our claim is a much more modest one: that for limited categories of problem it is possible to define certain key aspects of the problem to be of central importance in determining the structure of the simulation model. It is this subset of key properties of the real world which we must be able to represent formally. We are therefore in the business of finding partial, domain–specific problem descriptions rather than complete, domain–independent ones.

We need a formal notation in which to represent problem descriptions and we must be able to link the statements in the problem description to the structure of the simulation model. It makes sense to use the same notation (in our case the sorted logic) for both simulation model and problem description, thus making it easier to link the two. Despite this similarity in notation, the way in which the problem description is used is rather different from the process of running the simulation model. It is necessary for users to be allowed to provide partial information about a problem and the computer must be able to prompt users to add detail to this incomplete description. This has important implications for the inference mechanisms which we employ:

- Much of the reasoning must be abductive (see Glossary), as compared to the running of the simulation model which is exclusively deductive. For example, we will often be in a position where the user has provided a piece of information, A, and there are, say, two rules which would allow us to conclude A: $A \leftarrow B$ and $A \leftarrow C$. Even though we do not know if B or C is true we may suggest either as a possible cause of A, thus refining our problem description.

- It is not always possible to rely on users to enumerate all the objects referred to in their problem descriptions. Users often want to make general statements about sets of objects without specifying which objects those sets contain. The inference mechanisms must be able to operate without having to refer to named objects.

6.1 Partitioning of Information

In order to represent problem descriptions we need a formal notation. All our problem description formulae are represented in the same notation but it will be helpful to divide them into several distinct groups, according to the use to which they will be put by the system. The purpose of each group is summarised below and will be fully discussed later :

Established formulae are those formulae which are true of a particular modelling problem. For example a user may want to state that all objects of sort *wolf* have an attribute of *mass*. This is represented by the formula:

$$established(([A \text{ in } wolf], [])\#has\_attribute(mass, A)).$$

Problem description rules are of two types. The most straightforward are those which are considered to always be true in any ecological system. For example, if there is a predation relationship between two organisms then there must also be an eating relationship between those organisms. In our notation this becomes:

$$pd\_rule(([A \text{ in } organism, B \text{ in } organism], [])\#$$
$$eating(A, B) \leftarrow$$
$$predation(A, B)$$

However, there is another class of problem description rules which have a more subtle interpretation. These are used to imply general properties of the ecological system from certain key conditions of the system, in relation to the model. An example of a general property of an ecological system is whether its spatial representation is important to its functioning. One condition under which this is true is when some attribute of objects in the system varies with location. In our notation this is represented by the following rule:

$$pd\_rule(([A \text{ in } object, Att \text{ exist } attribute], [])\#$$
$$spatial\_representation(A)) \leftarrow$$
$$varies\_with(Att, A, location, A)$$

We have introduced an extra piece of notation in this formula by using a term of the form, X **exist** S, in the list of sort restrictions to represent the information that the formula is valid for *some* object, X, of sort, S. We shall refer to this form of sort restriction as *existential* because it relies upon the existence of a single object of the stipulated sort. This compares to the *universal* sort restriction denoted by a term of the form, X **in** S, which stipulates that the formula applies over *any* object, X, of sort, S. Note that this rule doesn't allow us to infer that the simulation model must automatically contain a spatial representation. A user could, with justification, decide to ignore spatial considerations when constructing a model, even though they were evident in the ecological system. Nevertheless, it is possible to use this type of rule to form a bridge between the ecological component of the problem description and the model representation, as we show in Section 6.3.

Modelling rules represent implications which are always true in any simulation model. For instance, if it is true that in the model the chosen location representation for some set of objects is grid squares then it must also be true that there is some number of rows in the grid and some number of columns (we assume a rectangular grid).

$$model\_rule(([A \text{ in } object], [N \text{ in } integer])\#$$
$$number\_of\_grid\_rows(N) \leftarrow grid\_squares(A)$$

$$model\_rule(([A \text{ in } object], [N \text{ in } integer])\#$$
$$number\_of\_grid\_columns(N) \leftarrow grid\_squares(A)$$

Listings of typical problem description and modelling rules appear in appendices C.3 and C.4. These will be referred to again in Chapter 7 where we discuss their use in a system to guide users in the construction of simulation models. In the rest of the current chapter we shall discuss in more general terms the way we want to deal with problem description information, showing how this sometimes requires a departure from the Prolog–style interpreter which we described in Chapter 4.

6.2   Preserving the Validity of Rules

There are two contrasting interpretations of problem description rules. This sort of distinction is discussed at greater length in [Bundy 87] but we consider it sufficiently important to highlight it here:

- We could interpret them as *suggested* problem description formula. The idea here is that we try to guess what we would like to have suggested under given conditions and build this information into the rules. This is the approach commonly used in expert systems which apply condition–action rules to solve a given problem. The problem with this approach is that the discipline of ensuring that the consequent of every rule will *always* be true whenever its antecedent is true has been abandoned (see Appendix A for a definition of "antecedent" and "consequent"). The consequent has the status of a "suggestion", which may be true or false, regardless of the truth of its antecedent.

- An alternative, which we favour, is to insist that the rules we write are logically valid. That is, the implication of consequent from antecedent will always hold if the antecedent is true. It may be much harder to extract logically valid rules from ecologists than to obtain procedural rules for generating suggestions, since ecologists may not be conscious of using definite rules or, if they do, they may not be able to express them directly as formulae in a logic. We argue that this initial effort is justified by subsequent benefits obtained by being able to test, in a principled way, for consistency of the knowledge base – thus making it easier to extend and maintain.

It is worth emphasising the practical value of avoiding a procedural interpretation of problem description rules. To do this we use an example:

A valid suggestion might be that if an organism grows then some size attribute which it possesses will be observed to increase with its age. We could denote this with the following condition–action rule:

$$increases\_with(mass, A, age, A) \quad \text{IF} \quad grows(A)$$

We can demonstrate that this is not a logically valid implication by considering the case where A is a plant which grows (so $grows(A)$ is true) but is grazed by some herbivore at a rate exceeding its rate of growth (so $increases\_with(mass, A, age, A)$) is false). We could convert this rule into a logically valid one by simply switching the consequent and antecedent:

$$([A \text{ in } organism], [])\#grows(A) \leftarrow increases\_with(mass, A, age, A)$$

The reading of this rule is that if it is true that some size attribute of any organism is observed to increase with some age attribute of that organism, then it will be true that the animal grows. Making this alteration does not rule out the possibility that an increase in size with age could be suggested if growth were established. What it ensures is that this suggestion cannot be made deductively – it can only be made abductively. The value of this is that we can distinguish between abductively generated suggestions – which may or may not be true for a given established antecedent – and deductions – which will always be true if our rules are logically valid.

6.3   The Importance of Abduction

Our attitude to the construction of modelling rules is similar to that described for the problem description rules in Section 6.2 – namely, that they should be logically valid and not condition–action structures. Consider the following two modelling rules:

If we have a grid square representation for the object A then we have a spatial representation for the object A.

$$model\_rule(([A \text{ in } object], []) \#$$
$$spatial\_representation(A)) \leftarrow$$
$$grid\_squares(A)$$

If we have a zone representation for the object A then we have a spatial representation for the object A.

$$model\_rule([A \text{ in } object], []) \#$$
$$spatial\_representation(A)) \leftarrow$$
$$irregular\_zones(A)$$

These both contain as consequents the *spatial_representation* predicate, which can be established by deduction from the user's problem description (see above). Such predicates provide a means of bridging the gap between ecological description and simulation model, since they allow the system to isolate formulae which influence model structure on the basis of formulae established when describing ecological systems. In general, the process of *establishing* these bridging formulae is deductive, based on information supplied by the user, while the *definition* of model structure from established bridging formulae is chiefly abductive.

   To demonstrate why abduction is so important to us, consider what would happen if, in order to use deduction to derive information about model structure from *spatial_representation* statements, we reverse the implication arrows in the rules listed above. If we apply deduction exhaustively to these rules, given an established *spatial_representation* formula, we shall overgenerate model structure because the consequents must *all* be true. In fact, we want only one of them to apply, since they happen to be alternative definitions of spatial representation. By keeping the direction of implication the way it was initially and using abduction we can present these as alternatives without invalidating the logic.

This still leaves the problem of preventing the abduction mechanism from suggesting spatial representation alternatives, regardless of the fact that they cannot all apply to the same model. We prevent this happening by checking for abductively generated statements which will lead to contradictions ([Cox & Pietrzykowski 86]). This is described along with the abduction algorithm in section 6.6. Before describing our mechanisms for deduction and abduction it is necessary to tackle the problem (which we raised earlier) of unifying sorted logic formulae when the names of all objects within a sort may not be known. This is the subject of the next section.

6.4   Unifying Sorted Logic Formulae

For the sorted logic simulation models of Chapters 4 and 5, queries were always solved by finding an *instance* which satisfied the top level goal. When reasoning about problem descriptions we shall need a greater variety of inference mechanisms (both abductive and deductive). To support these new varieties of inference we require a procedure for unification of sorted logic formulae which, if successful, will return a set of substitutions which apply to the unified formulae. For example, we want to be able to unify the two formulae :

$([A \text{ in } wolf, B \text{ in } animal], [])\#predation(A, B).$
$([A \text{ in } animal, B \text{ in } rabbit], [])\#predation(A, B).$

to obtain a new formula with the scope of variables A and B restricted to a sort which is compatible with the sort restrictions on both terms. In our example, this new formula is:

$([A \text{ in } wolf, B \text{ in } rabbit], [])\#predation(A, B).$

Unification of sorted logic formulae is a well known problem which is discussed thoroughly in [Walther 85]. Fortunately, we can rely on Prolog's own unification mechanism to take care of most of the work – the additional requirement being a mechanism for determining the greatest lower bounds on the substitutions applying to the unified formulae. The standard definition for the sort, S_3, which is the greatest lower bound of two sorts, S_1 and S_2, in a sort hierarchy, S, is expressed by the formula:

$$S_3 \subseteq S_1 \ \& \ S_3 \subseteq S_2 \ \& \ \forall S_4 \in S (S_4 \subseteq S_1 \ \& \ S_4 \subseteq S_2) \to S_4 \subseteq S_3$$

which says that the greatest lower bound, S_3, must be a subsort of S_1 and of S_2 and that any other sort, S_4, which is a subsort of both S_1 and S_2 must also be a subsort of S_3. To reduce the computational overhead involved in some of the algorithms of this chapter, we constrain our sort hierarchy to be a tree (*i.e.* there is no instance of a sort with two different parent sorts). This means that we cannot say things like "cats are a subsort of animals and of carnivores" because cats are allowed only one parent sort. This restriction can be lifted, but at a price, as we demonstrate later. Note also that the "occurs check" problem which we mentioned at the end of Section 4.4 also applies here.

Algorithm 16 We write $unifies(Term1, Substs1, Term2, Substs2, Substs3)$ to denote that for a formula with a set $Substs1$ of sort substitutions applying to term $Term1$ and a formula with a set $Substs2$ of sort substitutions applying to term $Term2$ unification is successful, constructing the new substitution set $Substs3$ applying to the unified terms.

$unifies(Term1, Substs1, Term2, Substs2, Substs3)$ only if :

- $Term1$ and $Term2$ unify as Prolog terms.

- The following constraints applied to $Substs1$ and $Substs2$, yield $Substs3$.

  - For each member of $Substs1$ of the form V in $Sort1$ (where V is a Prolog variable and $Sort1$ is a defined sort) there is a corresponding member of $Substs2$ of the form V in $Sort2$, such that
  $max\_shared\_substitution(Sort1, Sort2) = Sort3$ and $Sort3 \in Substs3$.

  - For each member of $Substs1$ of the form Obj in $Sort1$ (where Obj has been instantiated to some object when unifying $Term1$ and $Term2$ and $Sort1$ is a defined sort) $Obj \in Sort1$.

The function $max\_shared\_substitution(Sort1, Sort2) = Sort3$ holds if any one of the following conditions are satisfied :

- **IF** $Sort1 \subseteq Sort2$ **THEN** $Sort3 = Sort1$.
- **IF** $Sort2 \subseteq Sort1$ **THEN** $Sort3 = Sort1$.

where $S1 \subseteq S2$ signifies that the sort referred to by $S1$ is a more specific sort than that referred to by $S2$ (*i.e.* all the objects in the set referred to by $S1$ are also in the set referred to by $S1$ (see Section 4.1).

The result of applying this unification algorithm to the example which we provided at the beginning of this section would be:

$unifies(predation(A, B), [A$ in $wolf, B$ in $animal],$
$\qquad predation(A, B), [A$ in $animal, B$ in $rabbit],$
$\qquad [A$ in $wolf, B$ in $rabbit])$

Note that the above definition of *max_shared_substitution* only works if the sort hierarchy is a tree. If we were to extend the algorithm to handle graphs, we would need to cater for the case where $Sort1$ and $Sort2$ shared a common descendant. This condition can be described as follows:

- $Sort3 \subseteq Sort1$.

- AND $Sort3 \subseteq Sort2$.

- AND there is no instance of a sort, $Sort4$, such that:

  - $Sort4 \subseteq Sort1$.
  - AND $Sort4 \subseteq Sort2$.
  - AND $Sort3 \subseteq Sort4$.

Implementing this condition would make the unification procedure considerably less efficient.

6.5 The Deduction Mechanism

Since we are are assuming that our problem description rules can never allow a false formula to be inferred from a set of established formulae[1], we can apply a basic exhaustive forward chaining mechanism whenever a new formula is added to the problem description. That is, we can take each rule, of the form $A \leftarrow B$, for which B can be established from the database and add the new information, A, if it is not already present.

---

[1]Assuming a sound inference procedure.

This strategy is appealing because it ensures that as many formulae as possible are available for use by other inference mechanisms – particularly the abduction mechanism (section 6.6). However, it could leave the system vulnerable to two notorious problems. First, in order to ensure that deduction is exhaustive the system must attempt to establish the antecedents of all rules. This is computationally expensive – especially if a number of new formulae are added to the problem description during deduction. Second, it might be possible that vast numbers of new formulae could be deduced from the problem description, making it unmanageable. Fortunately, these problems have not emerged in our current system, largely because we have a small number of non–recursive rules and input templates. Our hope is that the number of rules can be kept low, while still allowing control over the generation of a wide range of simulation programs. Our optimism is supported by observing that the current system, although possessing a tiny set of rules and input templates, can already guide the construction of complex simulation programs (see section 7.4). However, it may become necessary to subdivide our knowledge base more finely, into collections of rules for particular sub–domains of ecology (*e.g.* for forestry, hydrology or fisheries). These types of constraint on the size of the knowledge base are not specific to the ecological modelling domain. The problem (and the solution of restricting the domain of application) is common in most applications of knowledge–based systems. Our exhaustive deduction mechanism is:

Algorithm 17 We write $exhaustive\_deduction(\Theta, \Delta, \Gamma) = \Delta'$ to denote that from a universe of discourse Θ, problem description Δ and a rule base Γ we can derive the new problem description Δ' by exhaustively applying a deductive inference mechanism, according to the algorithm:

- $exhaustive\_deduction(\Theta, \Delta, \Gamma) = \Delta'''$ **IF** :
  - Find a rule in Γ of the form $Term1 \rightarrow Term2$ with substitution set $Substs1$ such that:
    * $established(Term1, Substs1, \Delta, Substs2)$ (Algorithm 18) **AND** .
    * Find the subset $Substs3$ of substitution elements in $Substs2$ which apply to variables in $Term2$ **AND** .
    * Add the term $Term2$ under substitution set $Substs3$ to Δ, forming the new problem description Δ'.
  - **AND** $exhaustive\_deduction(\Theta, \Delta', \Gamma) = \Delta''$
  - **AND** $\Delta''' = \Delta' \cup \Delta''$.
- **OTHERWISE** $exhaustive\_deduction(\Theta, \Delta, \Gamma) = \Delta$

To complete the algorithm we require a mechanism for establishing a sorted logic formula (possibly containing conjunction or disjunction) directly from the current problem description. This is defined as follows:

Algorithm 18 We write $established(Term1, Substs1, \Delta, Substs3)$ if a given term $Term1$ under substitution set $Substs1$ can be established directly from a problem description Δ, returning the restricted substitution set $Substs3$. This is true when:

- **IF** $Term1$ is of the form: $Term2\ and\ Term3$, **THEN** :
  - $established(Term2, Substs1, \Delta, Substs2)$ **AND**
  - $established(Term3, Substs2, \Delta, Substs3)$.

- **OTHERWISE** , if $Term1$ is of the form: $Term2\ or\ Term3$, **THEN** :
  - $established(Term2, Substs1, \Delta, Substs3)$ **OR**
  - $established(Term3, Substs1, \Delta, Substs3)$.

- **OTHERWISE** , find in Δ a term $Term2$ under substitution set $Substs2$, such that $unifies(Term1, Substs1, Term2, Substs2, Substs3)$ (Algorithm 16).

6.6   The Abduction Mechanism

Our abduction procedure is used to generate a set of all formulae which appear as antecedents to rules for which the consequents are established (under a possibly restricted substitution set) and which are not inconsistent with the current problem description.

Algorithm 19 We write $valid\_abduction(\mathcal{F}, \Delta, \Gamma)$ to denote that a formula $\mathcal{F}$, consisting of a term $Term1$ under substitution set $Substs1$ is a valid abduction, given problem description Δ and rule base Γ when :

- There is some rule $\mathcal{R}$ in Γ of the form $Term1 \rightarrow Term2$ under substitution set $Substs1$, such that $established(Term2, Substs1, \Delta, Substs2)$ **AND**
- $\neg\ inconsistent(Term1, Substs2, \Delta, \Gamma)$ (Algorithm 20).

6.7   Consistency Checking

In section 6.3 we introduced the idea of restricting the number of new formulae generated by the abduction mechanism by pruning out those abductions which lead to inconsistencies in the problem description.

Algorithm 20 We write $inconsistent(Term1, \theta, \Delta, \Gamma)$ to denote that a term $Term1$ under substitution set $Substs1$ is inconsistent with $\Delta \cup \Gamma$. Our algorithm for detecting inconsistency is :

- Add $Term1$ under substitutions $Substs1$ to Δ, forming Δ' **AND**

- $exhaustive\_deduction(\Delta', \Gamma) = \Delta''$ (see section 6.5) **AND**

- For some term $Term2$ under substitution set $Substs2$ in Δ'':

  - $complement((Term2, Substs2)) = (Term3, Substs3)$ **AND**

  - $established(Term3, Substs3, \Delta'', Substs4)$

Where, $complement(\mathcal{F})$ is a function which returns the negation of the formula $\mathcal{F}$.

In other words, if we make all possible deductions from the problem description with the suspect abduced formula added and then find that some contradiction between complementary formulae is obtained, then the problem description is inconsistent.

6.8   The Problem of Completeness of High Level Descriptions

A distinguishing feature of the domains in which we are interested is that they are not precisely understood in the way which one might understand the functioning of a bridge or electric circuit. In some cases there may not even be a consensus on the identity of the important features of the domain. This raises the question of how to ensure that the terms incorporated into the problem description are sufficient to meet the demands of its users. We need some way of deciding, out of the myriad details of real–world problems, which are appropriate to retain in the problem description and which should be omitted.

One way of making these decisions is to begin with a fixed range of model structures and concentrate only on those parts of the problem which are key in deciding when and how to apply those structures in the domain. In other words, we begin by considering which types of simulation model we wish users to build and work "upwards" to determine the problem descriptions necessary to support them. This was the approach which was used in constructing the EL system (see Chapter 7). Its advantage is that additions to the problem description are always relevant to the requirements of subsequent simulation modelling. Its disadvantage is that it tends to restrict the knowledge base to a narrow range of applications and there is no guarantee that a problem description which has been developed for one set of models will extend to other models in related domains.

Even if we can provide some comprehensive set of primitives which may be used to describe a given domain, there remains the problem of determining standard ways of using these primitives. Frequently, it is possible to express similar information in very different ways within the same notation. For example, we have already discussed three ways of representing sub-populations of objects: using *subsort* relations (Section 4.1.1); using *sort_term* definitions (Section 4.1.4); and using *sort_relation* definitions (Section 4.5). On one hand, it is sometimes beneficial to provide a variety of ways of expressing the same concept, thus allowing users to choose the representation that best suits them. On the other hand, too much variety can be confusing unless it is anchored within a standard framework.

In order to provide some degree of standardisation of notation across a large domain it is necessary to become involved in an investigation of a formal theory of the domain itself. It is important to realise that this doesn't require the construction of some grand unified theory of how the real–world system operates. What is required is the collection and precise definition of the key concepts in that domain. For example, in ecology B.S. Niven has provided formal definitions of basic concepts, such as "niche" and "environment" ([Niven 82]) and these have recently been represented in the Z specification language ([Abel 90]). These definitions are still a long way from providing all the detail necessary to control the generation of simulation models but they provide a starting point for the development of a problem description at the most general level. The question which remains to be answered is whether the formal theories being developed independently in the ecological domain can be extended to encompass the demands for problem descriptions to support ecological modelling.

6.9 Conclusion

The purpose of this chapter was to explain why a formal representation of a user's ecological problem is necessary in order to support the development of a model to solve that problem and to allow that model to be understood in the context of the problem. The construction of problem descriptions is the most difficult aspect of model comprehension because users aren't always able to identify the key features of their problem and/or exclude those features which are of no importance. It is necessary to make it easier for users to identify aspects of their ecological problem which are relevant to the construction of simulation models and to use the ecological information supplied by users to extract details of the appropriate simulation models. To support this activity we have adapted the unification algorithm of the sorted logic to deal with unification of sorts without requiring the objects contained within each sort to be enumerated. This is important because users often want to make general statements about the ecological system without committing themselves to particular sets of objects. We have also described a mechanism for abductive inference, which we shall use as part of the dialogue mechanism in the next chapter.

7 Model Construction Using Prolog Schemata

In Chapters 3 and 4 we have shown how a variety of simulation models may be represented in notations based on logic. In Chapter 6 we have demonstrated how a similar notation may be used to represent key features of the domain which the model is intended to represent. We require a program which is capable of bridging the gap between a user's conception of a problem in his/her domain and the formal representation of that problem required to produce a simulation model, thus aiding model construction and comprehension. This type of package is often referred to as an Intelligent Front End ([Bundy 84]) and has the general architecture shown in Figure 7.1.

The idea is that the instructions required by the application package are represented formally in the task specification. The IFE program enables users to add information to the task specification in a way which is understandable to them. It is able to do this because it is provided with sufficient information about the application to be able to shield users from a large portion of its complexity. In this chapter we shall describe a program, named EL – an IFE which utilises the sorted logic problem description language from Chapter 6 to provide an interface for constructing Prolog simulation programs. We then discuss two of its "descendants" – HIPPIE and NIPPIE.

Simulation program generators are not new. A survey of some of these systems can be found in [Ulgen & Thomasma 89] who distinguish two basic varieties: domain independent and domain dependent. Domain independent IFE's possess no explicit knowledge of the problem which is to be solved using the simulation model and therefore can supply little guidance to the user beyond that which can be derived from the syntax of the application language. The MAGEST system ([Aytac & Oren 86]) is an example of this approach. It provides a front end to the GEST simulation language by supplying users with a library of standard model structures and an interface which permits them to be connected together in ways which are syntactically correct. To use MAGEST (and other domain independent IFE's) it is necessary to possess some prior knowledge of the simulation language

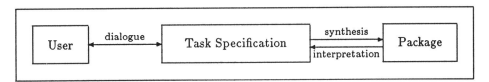

Figure 7.1
Architecture of a general IFE System

and to have experience of representing problems in the appropriate notation. This step between conceptualisation of the problem and specification of the simulation model is often the most difficult part of the exercise.

A natural reaction to this problem is to produce domain dependent IFE's which are finely tuned to the requirements of a narrow domain of application and, within this domain, provide support for the conversion from initial problem to simulation model. It is this kind of support which is necessary in order to permit users with no formal training in logic to construct logic–based simulation programs. The disadvantage of relying heavily on domain information is that the mechanisms used to process this information are often specific to the domain for which they were developed and cannot transfer to other domains. To reduce this problem in EL we have tried, where possible, to base its means of operation on domain independent inference methods and to maintain a clear separation between these and the domain knowledge required for our ecological application.

Although still a prototype, EL is interesting for several reasons :

- As well as representing conventional model structures (such as those for System Dynamics), it constructs programs which are not easily represented in standard simulation notations.

- It utilises the modularity inherent in the structure of Prolog programs to divide the task of program construction neatly into nested sets of goals and subgoals.

- It does not operate directly as a program editor. Instead it extracts from the user a description of the ecological problem which requires simulation and uses this information to guide the construction of the final program, thus linking the model to the problem description.

- It supports interaction with the user during all stages of program development. This gives it the flexibility to allow the user some free choice over the shape of the final program, rather that automatically churning out some "standard" result.

- The way in which EL constructs programs provides a foundation for a simple, but powerful, mechanism for reconstructing previous model construction sessions. This helps users to comprehend model structure by linking it to relevant components of the problem description.

7.1   Overview

The EL system consists of two distinguishable subsystems and these, combined with our Prolog interpreter from Chapter 5, form a system with three interacting components. The core of the EL system (often referred to simply as EL) has the task of helping users to construct ecological simulation programs. It is, in turn, composed of two subsystems: a problem description system which helps the user describe the problem which the simulation model must represent and a program generator which produces the completed Prolog simulation program. The completed program which can either be run as standard Prolog or loaded into the simulation interpreter from Chapter 5, which replaces the standard Prolog interpreter with a variant which often provides faster execution for simulation programs. The final component of the system allows users to load programs which have been previously built by EL and provides a simple structured explanation of the decisions made when constructing them. Figure 7.2 shows the general architecture of the system, with ovals representing repositories of data; rectangles enclosing mechanisms; and arrows showing dependencies between data/mechanisms. For convenience of reference, each box on the diagram is labelled with the section of the book in which it is described.

Our discussion will initially concentrate on the definition of building blocks (*schemata*) with which EL constructs simulation programs (these are defined in section 7.2). We could construct simulation programs directly from a database of schemata, using a simple schemata application mechanism but this would put a great burden on users to decide which schemata to apply to a given ecological problem (schemata are quite complex structures). To help reduce the range of schemata which are candidates for representing a particular part of a simulation model we add an extra component to the database – the **problem description** (described in Chapter 6). The role of the problem description is to represent important features of the problems faced by ecological users. EL extracts this information from users with the aid of a knowledge base of ecological and modelling rules (see Chapter 6). The mechanisms which constitute the core EL system are described in Section 7.3, while Section 7.4 contains a supporting example of these mechanisms in operation. Having completed our description of the core EL system, we describe, in section 7.5 the description subsystem. We conclude with a discussion of possible extensions which could be made to the existing program.

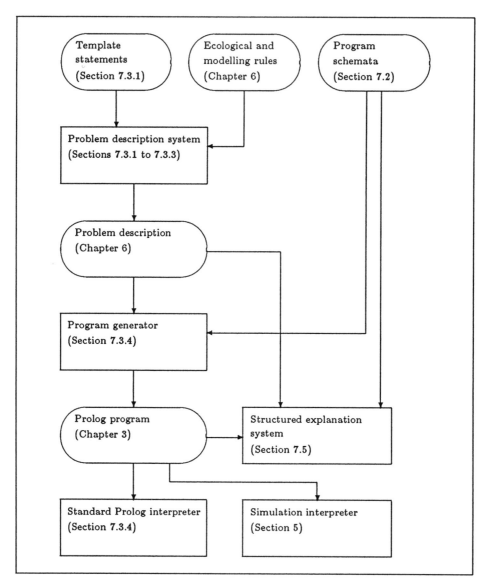

Figure 7.2
General plan of the EL system

7.2   Prolog Program Schemata

At the heart of every program construction system must lie some mechanism for
generating the completed program.   In EL the completed program is in Prolog
so we require a means of generating the Prolog code appropriate for the sorts of
problems faced by our target group of users (ecologists). To do this, we introduce
the notion of a Prolog schema. A schema can be thought of as a way of packaging the Prolog code needed to implement some part of of the simulation model.
This packaging stipulates the conditions under which a particular structure should
be used and specifies the other forms of structure necessary for it to operate in a
working model. The idea of integrating model structures with information about
the conditions under which they should be used has been pursued in many domains. The work which seems most similar to EL is that of the EDORA project
([Pave & Rechenmann 85]) which produced the SHIRKA system. This system also
employed schema–like structures which were contained within a frame–based system. In EL, a schema is defined as follows:

Definition 17 We write $schema(Name, Goal, Subgoals, Clauses, Acts, Precond)$
to define a valid program schema, where:

- *Name* is a list which provides a name for the schema.

- *Goal* is the simulation goal for which the schema solves.

- *Subgoals* is a list of new goals which the schema generates.

- *Clauses* is a list of Prolog clauses introduced into the simulation program by
  the schema.

- *Acts* is a list of procedure calls (actions) which must be satisfied before the
  schema, once selected by the user, can be applied.

- *Precond* is a procedure call (precondition) which must be satisfied before a
  schema can be used in a given context.

We describe the details of schemata application in section 7.3.4. For now, we
restrict our attention to the structure of schemata without considering the mechanisms with which they are manipulated. It is worth highlighting several aspects of
schemata, in preparation for the detailed examples which follow.

- Each schema solves for exactly one *Goal*. A schema cannot solve for a conjunction or disjunction of goals. This is a restriction on the expressiveness of
  schemata but considerably simplifies the schemata application mechanism.

- A schema is guaranteed (if correctly described) to solve its stipulated simulation goal if its *Precondition* and *Action* procedures execute successfully and all its *Subgoals* can be satisfied.

- The preconditions to schemata are used to block out those schemata which are inapplicable, given previously established problem description information, and to instantiate various elements of a schema, prior to its further manipulation by a user.

- *Action* procedures are executed when a user has chosen a particular schema for use in program construction. These procedures may involve some interaction with users.

One may think of these schemata as contributing parts of a plan for a simulation program. The *Goal* for which a schema solves may then be viewed as a task during plan formation and a schema's *Subgoals* as subtasks which must be performed to complete this task.

In order to understand in depth the examples of subsequent sections it is necessary to be familiar with the schema notation. To help the reader to get a feel for the way in which schemata are constructed we shall devote the rest of this section to some detailed examples. These schemata (in combination with more schemata from Appendix C.2) will be used in Section 7.4 when we walk through an example of EL at work. To make the arguments of each *schema* definition clearly distinguishable we list each argument separately, rather than enclosing them within a *schema* predicate.

7.2.1 Constants

We shall describe the first of our schemata examples (Schema 1) in detail. It solves for the goal $parameter(P, O, \_)$ by adding the code:

$$parameter(P, O, V) :- V = N.$$

Its action list contains a procedure which prompts for a value (N) for the parameter and is guaranteed to return some number. The precondition argument is the atom '*true*', which always succeeds. Therefore, this schema will be valid in any context. The list of actions contains a single call to *prompted_input*/4, which prompts the user for the value of the parameter of the object. The subgoal list is empty so no new subgoals will be created as a result of applying this schema. A formal definition of this schema is given below:

Schema 1 $['assign\ a\ value\ to\ parameter', P, of, O]$
Goal: $parameter(P, O, \_)$
Subgoals: $[]$
Clauses: $[(parameter(P, O, V) :- V = N)]$
Actions: $[prompted\_input(['Value\ for', P, of, O,' >>'], number(N), [], [N])],$
Precondition: $true$

7.2.2 Simple Equations

It is obviously of key importance to be able to include equations in schemata so we shall spend some time on a simple example from a previous model before considering more complex schemata. In Section 3.1.1, where we defined a basic System Dynamics model, we introduced the following Prolog clause to calculate the flow of photosynthesis from the environmental source–sink into grass. This was done simply by multiplying the *grass* state variable by a photosynthesis parameter specific to *grass*:

$$flow(photosynthesis, source\_sink, grass, T, N) :-$$
$$parameter(photosynthesis, grass, P),$$
$$state\_variable(grass, T, M),$$
$$N\ is\ P * M.$$

We could generalise this clause to form the code in a schema for calculating any flow of this type by replacing *photosynthesis, source_sink* and *grass* with variables (we shall name these variables, F, $X1$ and $X2$, respectively). The goal for which the schema solves would then be $flow(F, X1, X2, T, N)$. In order to ensure that this goal could be satisfied from the program we would need clauses for $parameter(F, X2, P)$ and $state\_variable(X2, T, M)$. These are the subgoals of the schema (*i.e.* goals which must be processed by further schema application). We shall assume that there is no need to reference the problem description or interact with the user when applying this schema, so the Actions list is empty and the Preconditions are set to '*true*'. This gives us the following schema:

Schema 2 $['calculate\ flow', F, 'from', X1, to, X2]$
Goal: $flow(F, X1, X2, T, N)$
Subgoals: $[parameter(F, X2, P),\ state\_variable(X2, T, M)]$
Clauses: $[(flow(F, X1, X2, T, N) :-$
                   $parameter(F, X2, P),$
                   $state\_variable(X2, T, M),$
                   $N\ is\ P * M)]$
Actions: $[],$
Precondition: $true$

We now consider a slightly more complex equation: a calculation of the relation $previous\_time(T, T1)$, where T is some integer time value and $T1$ is the previous time value. The extra complexity of this definition comes from the need to apply a different calculation depending on whether T or $T1$ is instantiated when the goal is called. The first clause of the schema caters for the case where $T1$ is a variable and is calculated from the value of T. The second clause applies when T is a variable and is calculated from $T1$. Apart from this, the schema definition is straightforward – the only point of interest being the introduction of the subgoal $time\_step(S)$ which must be satisfied in order for the schema to be applicable (*i.e.* the system must obtain, by the application of other schemata, extra code sufficient to satisfy this subgoal).

Schema 3 $['decide\ how\ to\ calculate\ a\ previous\ time\ in\ the\ simulation']$
Goal: $previous\_time(T, T1)$
Subgoals: $[time\_step(S)]$
Clauses: $[(previous\_time(T, T1) :-$
                   $integer(T),$
                   $var(T1),$
                   $time\_step(S),$
                   $T1\ is\ T - S),$
               $(previous\_time(T, T1) :-$
                   $integer(T1),$
                   $var(T),$
                   $time\_step(S),$
                   $T\ is\ T1 + S)]$
Actions: $[]$
Precondition: $true$

The schema for implementing a simple competition equation is considerably more complex. This schema is applicable only if the attribute A is of sort *size* or *energy*.

It fires a single action procedure which prompts the user for a name for some object which competes with the object O (if this information is not already known). This example demonstrates that the subgoals generated by the schema need not correspond to those generated by the program associated with that schema. As part of solving the goal $attribute(A, O, T, N)$ the program recurses on the same predicate with $T1$ (the time previous to T) as its new time argument. Although $attribute(A, O, T1, N2)$ is a subgoal of the program, it is *not* a subgoal of the schema because the program for solving this subgoal is the same as for $attribute(A, O, T, N)$. Note, however, that there is a schema subgoal to obtain the attribute, A, of the competing object, $O1$, because the means of calculating this attribute of $O1$ may differ from that introduced for the object, O.

Schema 4	$[A, of, O,'\, is\; determined\; by\; a\; simple\; competition\; equation']$
Goal:	$attribute(A, O, T, N)$
Subgoals:	$[initial\_time(T),$
	$\quad previous\_time(T, T1),$
	$\quad initial\_value(A, O, N),$
	$\quad attribute(A, O1, T1, \_),$
	$\quad parameter(self\_inhibition\_coefficient, O, S),$
	$\quad parameter(competition\_coefficient, O1, C)]$
Clauses:	$[(attribute(A, O, T, N1) :-$
	$\qquad not\; initial\_time(T),$
	$\qquad previous\_time(T, T1),$
	$\qquad attribute(A, O, T1, N2),$
	$\qquad attribute(A, O1, T1, N3),$
	$\qquad parameter(self\_inhibition\_coefficient, O, S),$
	$\qquad parameter(competition\_coefficient, O1, C),$
	$\qquad N1\; is\; N2 + (1 - N2 * S - N3 * C)),$
	$\quad (attribute(A, O, T, N4) :-$
	$\qquad initial\_time(T),$
	$\qquad initial\_value(A, O, N4))]$
Actions:	$[prompted\_input(['Name\; of\; object\; which\; competes\; with', O],$
	$\quad atom(O1), [], [O1])]$
Precondition:	$(valid\_object\_for\_type(size, A); valid\_object\_for\_type(energy, A))$

7.2.3 More Complex Procedures

Our first example of schemata for more complex procedures involves finding the value of an attribute by summing its sub-attributes. This example is interesting because the program it introduces is determined by information from the problem description. Note that the tail of the program list contains the variable *DescendantRels* which is instantiated to a list of relations defining the sort hierarchy between O and any objects to which it refers. The new subgoals generated by the schema (*SubGoalList*) are also dependent on the problem description, since they are the attribute goals $attribute(A, O', T, N')$ such that O' is a member of the set (*DescObjs*) of objects for sort O. Note that each member of *DescObjs* will be of the form $subt(P, S)$ where P is a parent object and S is a sub-object of P.

Schema 5 $[A, of, O,' is the sum of', A,' for subclasses of', O]$
Goal: $attribute(A, O, T, \_)$
Subgoals: $SubGoalList$
Clauses: $[(attribute(A, O, T, N1) :-$
                      $setof(X, constituent\_object(O, X), Set),$
                      $for\_each(X1, Set, attribute(A, X1, T, N2), N2, Attvals),$
                      $sum\_elements(Attvals, N1)),$
                  $(constituent\_object(Type, Obj) :-$
                      $subobj(Type, Obj)),$
                  $(constituent\_object(Type, Obj) :-$
                      $subt(Type, ST),$
                      $constituent\_object(ST, Obj)) \mid DescendantRels]$
Actions: $[]$
Precondition: $((valid\_object\_for\_type(size, A); valid\_object\_for\_type(energy, A)),$
                      $find\_all\_descendant\_objects(O, DescObjs, DescendantRels),$
                      $make\_attributes(DescObjs, A, \_, SubGoalList))$

As in Schema 4, the new subgoals generated by schema 6 are determined by the problem description. The *est_ax* goal in the precondition statement denotes the requirement that the model be spatially represented. The variable *Attributes* is instantiated to the set of all potential queries for attribute A which can be found from the problem description. This is, perhaps, rather excessive because all attributes may not be required - perhaps only a subset.

Schema 6 $[calculate, A, of, O, from, A,' of nearby objects']$
Goal: $attribute(A, O, T, \_)$
Subgoals: $[initial\_time(T),$
                  $previous\_time(T, \_),$
                  $initial\_value(A, O, \_),$
                  $in\_proximity(O, \_, T) \mid Attributes]$

Clauses: $[(attribute(A, O, T, N1) :-$
                    $\mathbf{not}\ initial\_time(T),$
                    $previous\_time(T, T1),$
                    $attribute(A, O, T1, N2),$
                    $setof\_or\_empty(O1, in\_proximity(O, O1, T), PSet),$
                    $for\_each(O2, PSet, attribute(A, O2, T1, N3), N3, Attvals),$
                    $sum\_elements(Attvals, N4),$
                    $length(Attvals, L),$
                    $((N4 = 0, N1 = N2); N1\ is\ N2$
                $(attribute(A, O, T, N5) :-$
                    $initial\_time(T),$
                    $initial\_value(A, O, N5))]$

Actions: $[]$
Precondition: $(est\_ax(\_, spatial\_representation(\_)),$
                    $find\_all\_potential\_attribute\_queries(A, Attributes))$

7.2.4   Relational Structures

Schema 7 demonstrates the use of schema actions which construct parts of the
program without user intervention. The *Clauses* list in the tail of the program is
partly made up of adjacency relations defining a grid square location representation. These relations are constructed automatically by referring to the number of
grid rows ($NRows$) and columns ($NCols$) which are obtained from the problem
description.

Schema 7 $['define\ proximity\ in\ terms\ of\ grid\ squares']$
Goal: $in\_proximity(\_, \_, \_)$
Subgoals: $[located\_at(\_, \_, \_)]$
Clauses: $[(in\_proximity(A, B, T) :-$
                    $located\_at(A, L1, T),$
                    $adjoining(L1, L2),$
                    $located\_at(B, L2, T)),$
                 $(in\_proximity(A, B, T1) :-$
                    $located\_at(A, L1, T1),$
                    $located\_at(B, L1, T1),$
                    $\mathbf{not}\ A == B)\ |\ Clauses]$
Actions: $[make\_grid\_square\_representation(NRows, NCols, Grid),$
                    $prompt\_for\_locations(Objs, NRows, NCols, Grid, Locations),$
                    $append(Grid, Locations, Clauses)]$

Precondition: $(est\_ax(\_, number\_of\_grid\_rows(NRows)),$
$\qquad\qquad\quad est\_ax(\_, number\_of\_grid\_columns(NCols)),$
$\qquad\qquad\quad get\_all\_objects(Objs))$

7.3   The Core EL System

A complete EL session is divided into four distinct phases. We first introduce these informally and then provide a formal description, which links to our detailed descriptions of each phase in subsequent sections.

- EL is initialised with a predefined sort hierarchy; a collection of ecological rules; and a store of input templates (see Section 7.3.1). These are used to help the user make an initial description of his/her problem by adding new sorts and objects to the sort hierarchy and/or adding sorted logic axioms to the problem description by editing input templates.

- The user can then indicate that he/she has said enough about the problem, at which point EL checks the sort hierarchy (augmenting it if necessary) in preparation for the next phase.

- EL then takes control of the dialogue in order to fill in remaining details of the problem description. These extra details tend to be more technical in nature – involving the use of modelling rules.

- When all refinements to the problem description are completed, EL moves to a final stage, in which schemata are applied to construct a program which is compatible with the problem description and rule base.

Algorithm 21 We write $construct\_program(\Theta, \Delta, \Psi, \Gamma_e, \Gamma_m, \Upsilon) = \pi$ to denote that π is a set of Prolog clauses constructed by EL on the basis of : an initial universe of discourse Θ ; a problem description Δ (initially empty) ; a set of program schemata Ψ ; ecological and modelling rule bases Γ_e and Γ_m ; and set of input templates Υ if :

- $describe\_ecological\_system(\Theta, \Delta, \Gamma_e, \Upsilon) = (\Theta', \Delta')$ (Algorithm 22) **AND**
- $tidy\_universe\_of\_discourse(\Theta', \Delta') = \Theta''$ (Algorithm 26) **AND**
- $refine\_problem\_description(\Theta'', \Delta', \Gamma_m) = \Delta''$ (Algorithm 27) **AND**
- $apply\_schemata(\Theta'', \Delta'', \Psi, \Gamma_e \cup \Gamma_m) = \pi$ (Algorithm 29).

In Sections 7.3.1 to 7.3.4 we provide detailed descriptions of the mechanisms used in EL's four phases of model construction. This sequence is repeated in Sections 7.4.1 to 7.4.4, which are used to step the reader through an example of the system in operation.

7.3.1 Phase 1 – Describing the Ecological System

EL needs to obtain information from the user about his/her ecological problem in order to provide appropriate guidance when constructing the simulation model. This task is non–trivial because:

- Users aren't accustomed to describing their problems in a formal notation so the system must be able to shield them from some of the formal detail without losing the precision of the notation.

- Users are often unsure about how to begin to describe a problem because they don't know how to phrase their description in terms which the program construction system will recognise.

We must rely on the user to decide exactly what information is relevant to his/her particular problem, since EL could never have a comprehensive knowledge of every user's view of any ecological system. What the system must do is to support the user in supplying initial components of the problem description and provide help in subsequently fleshing these out to provide detail sufficient to help control program generation. Our early attempts at providing this support relied on the user typing sentences in "pseudo–English", with the system parsing each sentence and converting it into the formal notation of the problem description ([Uschold *et al* 86]). This approach to extracting formal details of model structure from their descriptions in English text has also been attempted by others, including [Koshnevis & Austin 87]. Unfortunately, it doesn't seem possible to rely on a straightforward parsing system in the ecological domain because of the problems already mentioned above. Because the system is operating in an imperfectly understood domain it isn't able to represent everything which the user might say about his/her problem. This means that users are restricted to the subset of English which the system can parse, which in turn means that users must possess prior knowledge of the vocabulary known to the system. This learning requirement may be tolerable for simple models where the vocabulary is small but becomes intolerable as the range of concepts becomes large.

We describe a solution to this problem, based on a simple idea. EL provides a pool of input templates, represented as sorted logic formulae. These are statements which can be selected and edited by the user as a means of supplying problem description information to the system. These formulae are supplied with the widest permissible sort substitutions, in the expectation that a user will restrict the range of substitutions to suit his/her particular ecological problem. For instance, we provide the template:

$input\_form([A \text{ in } object, C \text{ exist } attribute\_name], has\_attribute(C, A)).$

which states that all objects of some subtype of *object* have some attribute. A user could select this template and edit it in order to say (for example) that wolves have an attribute of biomass.

A browser subsystem permits the user to locate a template which interests him and pass it into an editor, where he/she may restrict the sorts referred to in its substitution set and then add it to the problem description. By repeating this browsing and editing process, the user can construct a problem description which contains what seems to him/her to be the important features of his/her problem.

Algorithm 22 We write $describe\_ecological\_system(\Theta, \Delta, \Gamma, \Upsilon) = (\Theta'', \Delta''')$ to denote that the ecological problem description Δ''' and adapted universe of discourse Θ'' has been constructed from the initial universe of discourse Θ, problem description Δ, rule base Γ and set of input templates Υ when :

- **IF** the user applies the function $selected\_template(\Theta, \Upsilon) = \mathcal{F}$, where $\mathcal{F}$ is some selected formula in the sorted logic (Algorithm 23), **THEN** :

  - **IF** the formula selection switch is set to "display" **THEN** :
    * Generate an English statement corresponding to $\mathcal{F}$ by applying a Definite Clause Grammar **AND**
    * $describe\_ecological\_system(\Theta, \Delta, \Gamma, \Upsilon) = (\Theta'', \Delta''')$.

  - **IF** the formula selection switch is set to "describe" **THEN** :
    * Generate a more complex description of the meaning of $\mathcal{F}$, using a special purpose procedure if available **AND**
    * $describe\_ecological\_system(\Theta, \Delta, \Gamma, \Upsilon) = (\Theta'', \Delta''')$.

  - **IF** the formula selection switch is set to "edit" **THEN** :
    * $edit\_formula(\mathcal{F}) = \mathcal{F}'$ (Algorithm 24) **AND**
    * Add $\mathcal{F}'$ to Δ to form Δ' **AND**
    * $exhaustive\_deduction(\Theta, \Delta', \Gamma) = \Delta''$ (Algorithm 17) **AND**

       * $describe\_ecological\_system(\Theta, \Delta'', \Gamma, \Upsilon) = (\Theta'', \Delta''')$.

    – IF the formula selection switch is set to "remove" THEN :

       * Remove $\mathcal{F}$ from Δ to form Δ' AND

       * $describe\_ecological\_system(\Theta, \Delta', \Gamma, \Upsilon) = (\Theta'', \Delta''')$.

- OTHERWISE IF the user presses the "suggest" button (see Figure 7.3), THEN :

    – Find the set Ω of formulae $\mathcal{F}$ such that $valid\_abduction(\mathcal{F}, \Delta, \Gamma)$ (Algorithm 19) AND

    – Prompt the user to select a formula $\mathcal{F}'$ from Ω AND

    – $edit\_formula(\mathcal{F}') = \mathcal{F}''$ AND

    – Add $\mathcal{F}''$ to Δ, creating the new problem description Δ' AND

    – $exhaustive\_deduction(\Theta, \Delta', \Gamma) = \Delta''$ AND

    – $describe\_ecological\_system(\Theta, \Delta'', \Gamma, \Upsilon) = (\Theta'', \Delta''')$.

- OTHERWISE IF the user applies the function $edit\_universe\_of\_discourse(\Theta) = \Theta'$ (Algorithm 25) THEN :

    – $describe\_ecological\_system(\Theta', \Delta, \Gamma, \Upsilon) = (\Theta'', \Delta''')$.

- OTHERWISE IF the user terminates the ecological description phase THEN :

    – $\Theta'' = \Theta$ AND $\Delta''' = \Delta$.

The user interface mechanism developed for this system can be divided into several parts, corresponding to the different tasks which it must perform. We have chosen a window based architecture with a single frame holding a collection of panels, one for each task. The details of this structure are best explained by referring to the example display in Figure 7.3.

Browser We describe the browser subsystem with reference to Figure 7.3. The top panel in the display houses a pop–up walking menu depicting a section of the sort hierarchy. The left hand menu shows a path of ancestor sorts from the most general *universal* sort to the current sort (*animal*). The right hand menu shows the immediate subsorts of the current sort. Users can navigate downwards through the sort tree by selecting subsort menu options (in which case the subsort becomes the current sort and the walking menu is updated accordingly) or can go upwards by selecting options from the path to the most general ancestor. The "select" button allows users to add a current sort to the list of sorts which they consider to be of interest. These appear opposite the "SELECTIONS" prompt in the fourth panel.

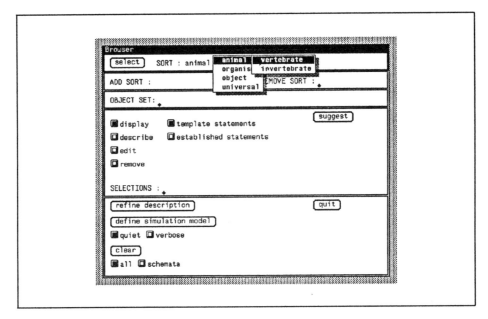

Figure 7.3
Browsing Through the Sort Hierarchy

In this fourth panel users are allowed to select from the pool of input forms those which apply to the list of sorts in which they are interested (this list having been obtained using the browser). The applicable forms are selected by finding the set of all new input forms for which there is a valid restriction to all the interesting sorts. A sort restriction is valid between two sorts if the sort to be restricted is an ancestor of or identical to the restricting sort. For example, if the object, *biomass* is of sort, *attribute_name*, then the form:

$input\_form([A$ in $object, A1$ in $attribute\_name, A2$ in $attribute\_name],$
$\qquad varies\_with(A1, A, A2, A)).$

matched to the sort list $[biomass, object]$ produces two new forms:

$input\_form([A$ in $object, A1$ in $attribute\_name],$
$\qquad varies\_with(A1, A, biomass, A)).$

$input\_form([A$ in $object, A2$ in $attribute\_name],$
$\qquad varies\_with(biomass, A, A2, A)).$

It is worth noting that this selection mechanism performs a similar role to that of the ECO browsing program ([Robertson *et al* 85]) but performs this task in a completely different way. In the ECO browser the "formulae" being located were records of specific instances of research data and the selection mechanism extracted all records which referred to sub–objects of the selected sort. For example, one record (call it record 1) might contain the information that the biomass of some observed wolf was 100 kilos; another record (record 2) might contain an equation for calculating the biomass of a mammal from various parameters. If a user were to select, using the old selection mechanism, all records referring to mammal, he/she would obtain records 1 and 2 because wolf is a subsort of mammal. If he/she selected all records referring to wolf, only record 1 would be obtained because mammal is not a subsort of wolf. Using the new selection mechanism, the results are reversed: selecting by mammal returns only record 1 since it is not possible to restrict the substitution on record 2 from wolf to mammal; selecting by wolf returns records 1 and 2 because these can both apply to wolf.

Algorithm 23 We write $selected\_template(\Theta, \Upsilon) = \mathcal{F}''$ to denote that the sorted logic formula $\mathcal{F}$ has been selected from the set of input templates Υ, given universe of discourse Θ **IF** :

- The user has supplied a non–empty set of sorts and/or objects ω which are present in Θ **AND**
- Ω is the set of all $\mathcal{F}'$, such that $selected(\Upsilon, \omega, \mathcal{F}')$ **AND**
- The user selects a formula $\mathcal{F}''$ from Ω.

$selected(\Upsilon, \omega, (Term, Substs2))$ is true **IF** :

- An input formula consisting of term $Term$ under substitution set $Substs1$ is a member of Υ **AND**
- $restrict\_substitutions(\omega, Substs1, Substs2)$.

$restrict\_substitutions(\omega, Substs1, Substs3)$ is true when :

- **IF** ω is non–empty, **THEN** :
    - $\mathcal{E}$ is the first element of ω, leaving the remaining elements ω' **AND**
    - **IF** $\mathcal{E}$ is a sort name **THEN** :
        * Find an element of $Substs1$ of the form Var **in** $Sort$ or Var **exist** $Sort$, such that $\mathcal{E} \subseteq Sort$ **AND**
        * Replace $Sort$ with $\mathcal{E}$ in $Substs1$ to form $Substs2$.
    - **OTHERWISE IF** $\mathcal{E}$ is an object name **THEN** :
        * Remove an element of $Substs1$ of the form Var **in** $Sort$ or Var **exist** $Sort$, such that $\mathcal{E} \overset{s}{\in} Sort$, returning the remaining substitutions $Substs2$ **AND**
        * Instantiate Var to $\mathcal{E}$.
    - **AND** $restrict\_substitutions(\omega', Substs2, Substs3)$.
- **OTHERWISE IF** ω is empty, $Substs3$ is empty.

When a list of selected input templates has been obtained, they are displayed as a set of options in a pop–up menu in the fourth panel (see Figure 7.4). A formula can be selected from this menu and various operations performed on it. The most important of these is editing of input templates, which is performed in a separate window (see section 7.3.1).

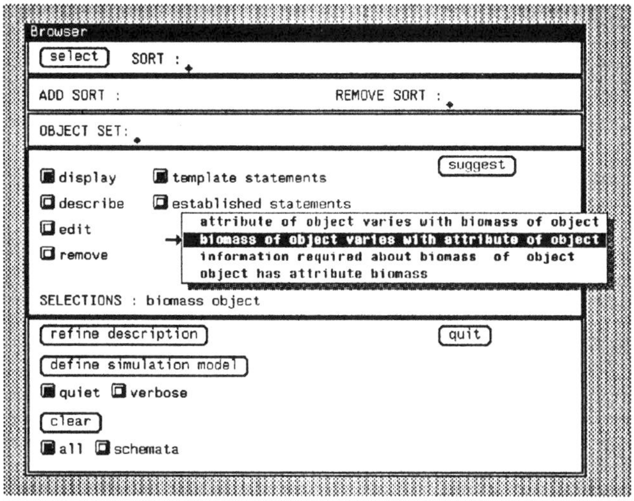

Figure 7.4
Selecting a Formula

Editor   To show how editing works we use an example which follows on from our previous discussion. Suppose that the user has selected the input template shown as the selected item in the pop–up menu of Figure 7.4. This corresponds to the sorted logic formula:

$input\_form([A$ **in** $object, A2$ **exist** $attribute],$
$\qquad varies\_with(biomass, A, A2, A)).$

The user is shown the following display:

```
            1 - For all object
            2 - There is some attribute
            biomass of object varies in response to attribute of object
```

This shows a numbered menu of substitution sorts and a rendering into pseudo–English of the term to which they apply. The text generation is done using a standard Definite Clause Grammar techniques, which are thoroughly described in most Prolog textbooks (*e.g.* [Sterling & Shapiro 85]). The user can then either restrict the sort of universal substitutions (item 1 in the menu above) or instantiate an object for existential substitutions (item 2). Suppose that substitution 1 is restricted to *wolf*, while 2 is instantiated to *c_age* (an object representing the current age of *wolf*). The resulting formula is:

$input\_form([A$ **in** $wolf],$
$\qquad varies\_with(biomass, A, c\_age, A)).$

and is displayed to the user as:

```
            1 - For all wolf

            biomass of wolf varies in response to c_age of wolf
```

The user can then add this restricted input template to his/her description of the ecological system.

Algorithm 24 We write $edit\_formula(\mathcal{F}) = \mathcal{F}'$ to denote that a sorted logic formula $\mathcal{F}$ has been converted into an adapted formula $\mathcal{F}'$ by a sequence of editing operations like those described above.

Editing the Universe of Discourse The second panel from the top of the display in Figure 7.3 allows users to attach or detach new sorts in the sort hierarchy. This is necessary because a user may want to talk about some set of objects which we had not thought of when designing the sort hierarchy. For example, the system's sort hierarchy contains the sort *vertebrate*. A user may want to attach the new sort *wolf* as a subsort of *vertebrate*. Addition of a new sort is performed by moving to the proposed parent sort, using the browser, and then typing the name of the new sort at the "add sort" prompt. Removal of sorts is done in a similar way, except that the typing is done at the "remove sort" prompt.

Addition of objects is performed in the third panel. Only sorts on the leaves of the sort hierarchy are permitted to refer to a set of objects. Once the appropriate parent sort is located, using the browser, the set of objects to which it refers can be defined in one of two ways. Either the set of objects is supplied explicitly (*e.g.* *wolf* refers to $[w1, w2, w3]$) or a user supplies a special label to indicate that he/she does not want to specify distinguishable objects for a given sort (perhaps because there are too many of them to be individually identified). Inference under these conditions is described in Chapter 6.

Algorithm 25 We write $edit\_universe\_of\_discourse(\Theta) = \Theta'$ to denote that an editing operation of the kind discussed above has been performed on universe of discourse Θ, to form the updated universe of discourse Θ'.

7.3.2 Phase 2 – Checking the Sort Hierarchy

At some point in the session it is necessary to ensure that the sorts and objects referred to in the problem description are specified in sufficient detail to support subsequent construction of a program. A good time to make this check is when a user indicates (by pressing the "refine description" button in the browser window) that he/she has volunteered enough information and wants EL automatically to extract further details. The sort hierarchy is checked in two stages : first a check is made for sorts which are referred to in the problem description but which have no defined object sets ; then any sorts which have been labelled as "undefined" by a user are supplied with objects and/or subsorts.

Algorithm 26 We write $tidy\_universe\_of\_discourse(\Theta, \Delta) = \Theta'$ to indicate that the, possibly incomplete, universe of discourse Θ has been successfully augmented with respect to the problem description Δ to form a universe of discourse Θ' sufficient to support further dialogue.

This second stage is best explained using an example. Suppose that the sort *wolf* has been labelled as "undefined" and that the user has said that the biomass of *wolf* varies with its current age (c_age) and location (c_loc). In other words, the problem description contains the statements :

$established([A \text{ in } wolf], varies\_with(biomass, A, c\_age, A)).$
$established([A \text{ in } wolf], varies\_with(biomass, A, c\_loc, A)).$

EL uses this information to distinguish c_age and c_loc as classes for subdivision of *wolf*. The reason behind this is that if there are no explicitly defined objects for a sort but we know that some of its attributes influence others then either the sort refers to a single aggregated object to which these attributes apply or the attachment of attributes to the sort should be represented by its subdivision into classes for each attribute. Suppose that the user decides to first subdivide according to c_age, supplying the subclasses *young* and *old*. These are added to the sort hierarchy as new sorts and the user is then prompted for subclasses of *young* and *old* corresponding to c_loc classes. Assume that he/she supplies the names *young_pop1*, *young_pop2* and *young_pop3* as subclasses of *young* and *oldpop* as a single subclass of *old*. This gives us the new relations:

young is a subsort of *wolf*.
old is a subsort of *wolf*.
young refers to the objects *young_pop1*, *young_pop2* and *young_pop3*
old refers to the object *oldpop*.

This technique is not altogether satisfactory, since it relies on detecting predefined relations in the problem description. In its defence, we can say that the relations involved (*varies_with* and *attribute_of*) are quite general and are not specific to ecology. For an example of this mechanism in action, see section 7.4.

7.3.3   Phase 3 – Filling in Characteristics of the Solution

At this stage the user has volunteered what information he/she feels is appropriate and EL now has the task of prompting for any extra information which might help reduce the range of candidate program structures during the final simulation construction phase. For example, it will prompt for the number of grid rows and columns in a model with a grid square spatial representation (see Section 6.1). EL generates a set of possible new formulae by applying abduction to the current problem description. These suggestions are presented to the user, who may select one of them. The selected formula is passed to the editor (see section 7.3.1) for optional adjustment by the user before being added to the problem description. Each time a new formula is added to the problem description the exhaustive deduction mechanism is fired (see section 6.5). The process stops when no further information can be generated by abduction. A more formal description of this algorithm is given below :

Algorithm 27 We write $refine\_problem\_description(\Theta, \Delta, \Gamma) = \Delta'''$ to denote that given a universe of discourse Θ, an initial problem description Δ and a set of modelling rules Γ, a final problem description, Δ''', is obtained by the following procedure:

- Find the set Ω of formulae $\mathcal{F}$ such that $valid\_abduction(\mathcal{F}, \Delta, \Gamma)$ (Algorithm 19).

  - IF Ω is non–empty THEN :

    * Prompt the user to select a formula $\mathcal{F}'$ from Ω AND
    * $edit\_formula(\mathcal{F}) = \mathcal{F}'$ (Algorithm 24) AND
    * Add the edited version of $\mathcal{F}'$ to Δ, creating the new problem description Δ' AND
    * $exhaustive\_deduction(\Delta', \Gamma) = \Delta''$ (Algorithm 17) AND
    * $refine\_problem\_description(\Theta, \Delta'', \Gamma) = \Delta'''$.

  - OTHERWISE $\Delta''' = \Delta$.

7.3.4 Phase 4 – Defining the Simulation Program

In the preceding three phases, EL has extracted from the user a description of the ecological problem which the simulation program must represent. In this final stage, the problem description will be used to restrict the range of schemata offered to the user as alternative methods to construct his/her simulation program. Recall from section 7.2 that each schema is guaranteed to provide a runnable program to solve a given Prolog query if that query matches the goal for which the schema solves and all the schema's subgoals can be established by applying schemata. Constructing a program from a problem description can therefore be divided into two stages.

First, EL decides which queries are required of the final simulation program. This is done by finding in the problem description the set of all occurrences of the formula $required\_information(A, B)$ under some substitution set ; finding all substitution instances for each of these formulae under its substitution set ; and finally rewriting each of these instances of $required\_information(A, B)$ as the Prolog query $attribute(A, B, T, N)$, where T is the time argument and N is the value for attribute A of B at T. For example, if the problem description contained the single formula $established([B$ in $wolf], required\_information(biomass, B))$ and the complete set of objects referred to by $wolf$ is $[w1, w2]$, then the extracted Prolog queries are :

$attribute(biomass, w1, T, N)$.
$attribute(biomass, w2, T, N)$.

This is a rather weak method for setting up simulation queries because it relies on detecting stipulated formulae in the problem description. Recent work described in [Uschold 90] focuses more closely on this stage of model development and presents some solutions. Description of this work is outwith the scope of this book and we shall limit our description to the simpler, though less general, solution which we have described above.

Algorithm 28 We write $\underline{extract\_queries(\Theta, \Delta) = Goals}$ to indicate that $Goals$ is a non–empty set of Prolog queries extracted from Δ, given universe of discourse Θ.

Finally, EL interactively constructs a program, by the recursive application of schemata, that can enable the extracted queries to be satisfied. The method chosen to achieve this task is similar to the Marples algorithm – a goal directed algorithm for equation extraction developed from a study by David Marples of student engineers [Marples 74]. This algorithm has also been used in the problem solving component of the MECHO system [Bundy *et al* 79] which was used automatically to generate sets of equations solving a range of mathematical problems in mechanics. Our mechanism works by taking the first goal from a list of schemata goals (initially set to the list of extracted queries). If this goal cannot be established from the set of simulation program clauses already constructed during schemata application, then the set of all schemata which are a valid means of satisfying the goal (given the user's problem description) is found. A schema is considered a valid means of solving for a given goal if it solves for that goal and its precondition statement executes successfully. The set of valid schemata are displayed to the user, who must select one of them[1]. The actions of the selected schema are then

---

[1]Note that it would be possible to provide extra help at this stage in selecting a particular schema from the short–list of options. This facility is missing from the current version of the system.

fired and its contribution to the simulation program added to the current set of program clauses. The mechanism is then applied to the subgoals of the selected schema and to the remaining members of the original schemata goal list. The recursion terminates when the schema goal list is empty. Note that this results in a depth–first application of schemata. As we shall see in Section 7.4, this variety of search doesn't always provide a natural flow of dialogue with the user.

Algorithm 29 We write $apply\_schemata(\Theta, \Delta, \Psi, \Gamma) = Clauses5$ to denote that the set of Prolog clauses $Clauses5$ constitute a runnable program constructed by the schema application mechanism, given a universe of discourse Θ, problem description Δ, database of schemata Ψ, rule base Γ and partially complete program $Clauses1$ (initially an empty set) **IF** :

- $extract\_queries(\Theta, \Delta) = Goals1$, where $Goals1$ is the set of Prolog queries which $Clauses5$ must satisfy **AND**

- $derive(\Theta, \Delta, \Psi, \Gamma, Goals1, Clauses1) = Clauses5$.

$derive(\Theta, \Delta, \Psi, \Gamma, Goals1, Clauses1) = Clauses5$ holds when :

- **IF** $Goals1$ is non–empty **THEN** :

  - Select an element $Goal1$ from $Goals1$, leaving the remaining elements $Goals2$.

    * **IF** $Goal1$ can already be satisfied from $Clauses1$, **THEN** :
      · $derive(\Theta, \Delta, \Psi, \Gamma, Goals2) = Clauses5$.

    * **OTHERWISE** :
      · Find the set Ψ' of schemata definitions of form:
      $schema(Name1, Goal2, Goals3, Clauses2, Actions1, Procedure1)$,
      such that : $Goal1 = Goal2$ **AND** $Procedure1$ executes successfully, given Θ, Δ and Γ **AND**
      · Select an element of Ψ' of the form:
      $schema(Name2, Goal3, Goals4, Clauses3, Actions2, Procedure2)$
      AND
      · Execute each Prolog procedure in $Actions2$, given Θ, Δ and Γ
      AND
      · $derive(\Theta, \Delta, \Psi, \Gamma, Goals4, Clauses1 \cup Clauses3) = Clauses4$ **AND**
      · $derive(\Theta, \Delta, \Psi, \Gamma, Goals2, Clauses4) = Clauses5$.

- **IF** $Goals1$ is empty **THEN** $Clauses5$ is the empty set.

7.4   Example of EL at Work

The definitions of Section 7.3 describe the mechanisms used in EL. In this section we work through an example of how these mechanisms are used to construct a complete Prolog model. To save time, we shall assume that the user has already added to the the sort hierarchy the sort *wolf* (a subsort of vertebrates) and, as sub-objects of *attribute*, the objects *biomass*, *c_age* and *c_loc* (denoting biomass, current age and current location, respectively). We shall pick up the model construction session at the point where the user has selected a sorted logic template to edit and is in the process of adapting that template to fit into the problem description.

7.4.1   Phase 1 – Describing the Ecological System

The user has decided to talk about some attribute with which the *biomass* of objects of sort *wolf* varies. The formula currently in the editor is the same one that we used in the example of Section 7.3.1:

$$established([A \text{ in } wolf, B \text{ exist } attribute],$$
$$varies\_with(biomass, A, B, A)).$$

The user instantiates the variable, B, by giving the command: "r 2 c_age", which may be interpreted in English as "Restrict the variable referred to in option 2 of the menu to *c_age*".

```
     STATEMENT EDITOR
     ***************

     1 - For all wolf
     2 - There is some attribute

     biomass of wolf varies in response to attribute of wolf

     EDIT >>  r 2 c_age
```

The new formula:

$$established([A \text{ in } wolf],$$
$$varies\_with(biomass, A, c\_age, A)).$$

is then added to the problem description by typing the character "**a**" (short for "add").

```
            STATEMENT EDITOR
            ***************

            1 - For all wolf

            biomass of wolf varies in response to c_age of wolf


            EDIT >>   a
```

and EL deductively establishes the following formulae:

$established([A \textbf{ in } wolf], has\_attribute(biomass, A)).$
$established([A \textbf{ in } wolf], has\_attribute(c\_age, A)).$
$established([A \textbf{ in } wolf], age\_class\_structure\_model(A)).$

The user now decides to say that the biomass of objects of sort *wolf* also varies with their current location *c_loc*. This can be done by selecting and editing the same template which was used initially.

```
            STATEMENT EDITOR
            ***************

            1 - For all wolf
            2 - There is some attribute

            biomass of wolf varies in response to attribute of wolf


            EDIT >>   r 2 c_loc
```

```
STATEMENT EDITOR
***************

1 - For all wolf

biomass of wolf varies in response to c_loc of wolf


EDIT >>  a
```

Adding to the problem description the new formula:

$$established([A \textbf{ in } wolf],$$
$$varies\_with(biomass, A, c\_loc, A)).$$

and allowing the deduction of the following new formulae:

$$established([A \textbf{ in } wolf], has\_attribute(c\_loc, A)).$$
$$established([A \textbf{ in } wolf], spatial\_representation(A)).$$

As the final statement in the problem description, the user wants to say that an attribute of interest in the problem is the *biomass* of *wolf* and so adds the formula:

$$established([A \textbf{ in } wolf], required\_information(biomass, A)).$$

This will be used to form top–level goals for the schema application mechanism.

```
STATEMENT EDITOR
***************

1 - For all wolf

you require information about the biomass of wolf


EDIT >>  a
```

7.4.2 Phase 2 – Checking the Sort Hierarchy

Having decided that enough has been said about the ecological problem, the user presses the "refine description" button in the browser window (see figure 7.3) to signify that EL should now take care of any residual description required before beginning to construct the simulation model. EL first recognises that the sort *wolf* has been labelled by the user as undefined and therefore applies its object definition mechanism to *wolf*. It determines that two attributes apply – *c_age* and *c_loc* and offers these as classes upon which *wolf* may be subdivided. The user chooses *c_age* as the first subdivision class and defines the class's divisions to be *young* and *old*.

```
            wolf

            Subdivision class [c_age,c_loc] >>  c_age
            Subtypes of class c_age >>  young old
```

The user is then prompted for the divisions of the remaining class *c_loc* as a subclass of *young*. These are defined as *young_pop1*, *young_pop2* and *young_pop3*.

```
      wolf
      young

      Objects of class c_loc >>  young_pop1 young_pop2 young_pop3
```

Finally, the user is prompted for the divisions of the remaining class *c_loc* as a subclass of *old*. These are defined as the single object *old_pop*,

```
            wolf
            old

            Objects of class c_loc >>  oldpop
```

This completes the augmentation of the sort hierarchy, resulting in the additional definitions:

subsort(*wolf, young*).
subsort(*wolf, old*).
subobj(*young, young_pop*1).
subobj(*young, young_pop*2).
subobj(*young, young_pop*3).
subobj(*old, oldpop*).

In other words, the information that *wolf* has an attribute which varies with age
has been used first to establish that the population is divided into 2 age groups (*old*
and *young*). Then the information that *wolf* also has an attribute which varies
with location has been used to subdivide these new subgroups into location units
[*oldpop*] and [*young_pop*1, *young_pop*2, *young_pop*3], respectively.

7.4.3   Phase 3 – Filling in Characteristics of the Solution

Having augmented the sort hierarchy, EL applies the abduction mechanism to generate suggestions for formulae which describe the solution to the ecological problem.
From its store of modelling rules, in combination with the problem description formula :

established([*A* in *wolf*], *spatial_representation*(*A*)).

EL generates the following menu of suggestions, from which the user chooses the
fourth item. Note that it would be useful at this point to offer the user suggestions
about the most likely of the options from the menu, rather than leaving him/her
with a completely free choice. This facility has yet to be implemented in the current
system.

```
1 - For all wolf :
 define point locations for wolf without proximity relations
2 - For all wolf :
 define locations with areas for wolf
3 - For all wolf :
 define point locations for wolf with proximity relations
4 - For all wolf :
 define a grid square representation for wolf
5 - For all wolf :
 define zone locations for wolf

Choose a formula to edit :  4
```

The formula associated with this menu item is passed to the editor before inclusion into the problem description at the user's request.

```
              STATEMENT EDITOR
              ***************

              1 - For all wolf

              define a grid square representation for wolf


              EDIT >>   a
```

The new formula is:

$$established([A \text{ in } wolf], grid\_squares(A)).$$

This addition allows EL to deduce the following formulae, without communicating with the user. These formulae all exclude particular forms of spatial representation and will therefore prevent the system from suggesting implausible spatial representations to the user.

$$established([A \text{ in } wolf], not(points\_not\_in\_proximity(A))).$$
$$established([A \text{ in } wolf], not(areas\_not\_in\_proximity(A))).$$
$$established([A \text{ in } wolf], not(points\_in\_proximity(A))).$$
$$established([A \text{ in } wolf], not(irregular\_zones(A))).$$

In addition to the formulae which can be automatically established by EL from the problem description, there are two new formulae which contain uninstantiated existentials. These formulae are presented to the user for editing before insertion into the problem description. This allows the user to specify the number of rows in the spatial grid to be 4 and the number of columns to be 3.

```
          GIVE INSTANCES OF VARIABLES
          ***************************

          1 - There is some integer

          the number of rows in your spatial grid is integer

          EDIT >>  r 1 4
```

```
          GIVE INSTANCES OF VARIABLES
          ***************************

          1 - There is some integer

          the number of columns in your spatial grid is integer

          EDIT >>  r 1 3
```

The following new formulae are added to the problem description:

$established([], number\_of\_grid\_rows(4)).$
$established([], number\_of\_grid\_columns(3)).$

No further abductions or deductions can be made using the modelling rules, so EL tells the user that this phase of description is complete.

7.4.4   Phase 4 – Defining the Simulation Program

Having completed the problem description, the user presses the "define simulation model" button in the browser window (see figure 7.3). EL then finds all instances of attribute queries which the simulation model must satisfy. These are the masses of all objects of the sort $wolf$:

$attribute(biomass, oldpop, T, N).$
$attribute(biomass, young\_pop1, T, N).$
$attribute(biomass, young\_pop2, T, N).$
$attribute(biomass, young\_pop3, T, N).$

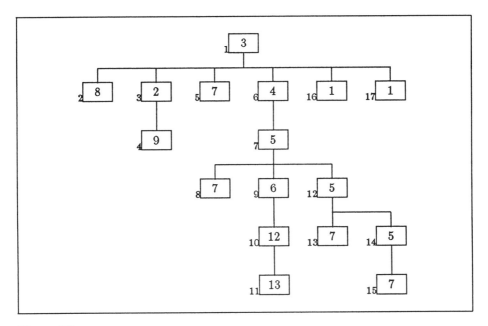

Figure 7.5
Tree of schema application

EL fires its schema application mechanism, using an initial goal list containing these
four goals. The dialogue which follows is in "verbose" mode, showing the choice
of schemata even when only a single choice is available. If "quiet" mode had been
selected these single choices would have been taken automatically by the system. To
aid the reader in relating the sequence of displays to the underlying tree of schema
application we provide, in Figure 7.5, a preview of the completed tree of application
which is obtained at the end of the program generation phase. In this diagram,
the reference number of each schema is shown within a box. An arc connecting
one schema to a schema below it signifies that the schema below was introduced to
satisfy some subgoal of the schema above. The number at the bottom left corner
of each box indicates the point in the sequence of schema displays at which that
particular schema is applied. Thus, the first schema is schema 3, at the top of
the diagram, which is applied in the first display of interaction in the discussion
below. Note that the sequence of schema application is depth–first and left to right
in the diagram. The rest of this section demonstrates how this sequence of schema
applications is performed.

EL first finds applicable schemata for the goal $attribute(biomass, oldpop, T, N)$. There are four candidate schemata (those which solve for the goal and for which the preconditions are satisfied in the problem description). These are displayed as items in a menu, from which the user selects option 3. This option refers to schema 4 from Section 7.2. Its actions are fired, prompting the user for the name of something which competes with *oldpop*. The user specifies the competitor to be *young*. Recall that this is a population which contains three sub–populations (*young_pop*1, *young_pop*2 and *young_pop*3).

```
**************************************************************
Model goal : there is some value for the biomass of oldpop
**************************************************************

1 - biomass of oldpop grows logistically
2 - biomass of oldpop is determined by a simple predator-prey equation
3 - biomass of oldpop is determined by a simple competition equation
4 - calculate biomass of oldpop from biomass of interacting objects

Choose schema >>  3
Name of object which competes with oldpop >>  young
```

EL explores the first subgoal generated when applying schema 4 – $initial\_time(T)$. Only schema 9 (see Appendix C.2) can satisfy this goal. The user chooses it (note that in "quiet" mode the system would make this choice automatically) and its actions are fired – prompting the user for a value for the initial time.

```
        there is some value for the biomass of oldpop
        **************************************************************
        Model goal : there is some initial time in the simulation
        **************************************************************

        1 - assign a value for the time at which simulation begins

        Choose schema >>  1
        Initial time >>  1
```

EL now tries to establish the second subgoal generated when applying schema 4 – $previous\_time(T, T1)$. Again, only one schema (schema 3 from Section 7.2) applies. This has no associated actions but generates a new subgoal.

```
        there is some value for the biomass of oldpop
        **********************************************************
        Model goal : we can find the previous time point from any given time
        **********************************************************

        1 - decide how to calculate a previous time in the simulation

        Choose schema >>  1
```

This subgoal can be solved only by schema 10 (see Appendix C.2), which prompts the user for a value for the time step. It would be useful to include information about units of measurement of key variables (such as time) along with their initial values but this facility does not exist in the current system.

```
        there is some value for the biomass of oldpop
            we can find the previous time point from any given time
        **********************************************************
        Model goal : there is some value for the time step in the simulation
        **********************************************************

        1 - assign a value for the time step in the simulation

        Choose schema >>  1
        Length of time step >>  1
```

EL now tries to establish the third subgoal generated when applying schema 4 – $initial\_value(biomass, oldpop, N)$. A single schema (schema 8 from Appendix C.2) is applicable, which prompts the user for the initial value.

```
        there is some value for the biomass of oldpop
        **********************************************************
        Model goal : there is some initial value for the biomass of oldpop
        **********************************************************

        1 - assign an initial value for biomass of oldpop

        Choose schema >>  1
        Initial value for biomass of oldpop >>  20
```

Since schema 8 generates no new subgoals, EL now tries to establish the fourth subgoal generated when applying schema 4 – $attribute(biomass, young, T, N)$. The user chooses to solve this goal using schema 5 (from Section 7.2).

```
        there is some value for the biomass of oldpop
        ***************************************************************
        Model goal : there is some value for the biomass of young
        ***************************************************************

        1 - biomass of young grows logistically
        2 - biomass of young is determined by a simple predator-prey equation
        3 - biomass of young is determined by a simple competition equation
        4 - biomass of young is the sum of biomass for subclasses of young
        5 - calculate biomass of young from biomass of interacting objects

        Choose schema >>  4
```

This schema generates a batch of new subgoals to find the mass of all subclass objects of $young$. These new goals are:

$attribute(biomass, young\_pop1, T, N).$
$attribute(biomass, young\_pop2, T, N).$
$attribute(biomass, young\_pop3, T, N).$

EL takes the first of the subgoals generated by schema 5 $(attribute(biomass, young\_pop1, T, N))$ and presents four candidate schemata to the user. Schema 6 (from Section 7.2) is chosen. It will turn out that this same schema will be used to determine the biomass of $young\_pop2$ and $young\_pop3$ as well. This introduces some redundancy into the program finally produced by the schema application mechanism because similar clauses are generated for each of the three objects. By using a sorted logic, such as that described in Chapter 8, we can reduce this problem.

```
        there is some value for the biomass of oldpop
            there is some value for the biomass of young
        ************************************************************
        Model goal : there is some value for the biomass of young_pop1
        ************************************************************

        1 - biomass of young_pop1 grows logistically
        2 - biomass of young_pop1 is determined by a simple predator-prey equation
        3 - biomass of young_pop1 is determined by a simple competition equation
        4 - calculate biomass of young_pop1 from biomass of interacting objects

        Choose schema >>  4
```

The first subgoal of schema 6 which isn't already establishable from the current program is $initial\_value(young\_pop1, T, N)$. This can only be established using schema 8 (see Appendix C.2).

```
        there is some value for the biomass of oldpop
            there is some value for the biomass of young
                there is some value for the biomass of young_pop1
        ************************************************************
        Model goal : there is some initial value for the biomass of young_pop1
        ************************************************************

        1 - assign an initial value for biomass of young_pop1

        Choose schema >>  1
        Initial value for biomass of young_pop1 >>  5
```

EL now continues to establish the proximity subgoal of schema 6 – $in\_proximity(young\_pop1, X, T)$. The user chooses to make this definition in terms of a grid square spatial representation (schema 7 from Section 7.2). The actions associated with this schema construct a grid with 4 rows and 3 columns, as specified in the problem description, and prompt the user for the location of each object on the grid.

```
        there is some value for the biomass of oldpop
           there is some value for the biomass of young
              there is some value for the biomass of young_pop1
        ***********************************************************
        Model goal : young_pop1 is in proximity to some object at some time
        ***********************************************************

        1 - define proximity in terms of grid squares
        2 - define proximity in terms of coordinates

        Choose schema >>  1
        Your grid square spatial representation has 4 rows and 3 columns.
        Location for young_pop1 >>  1 1
        Location for young_pop2 >>  1 2
        Location for young_pop3 >>  2 1
        Location for oldpop >>  3 3
```

EL now prompts for a means of establishing the location of any object at any
time ($located\_at(Object, Location, T)$). Only schema 13 (see Appendix C.2) is applicable.

```
        there is some value for the biomass of oldpop
           there is some value for the biomass of young
              there is some value for the biomass of young_pop1
                 young_pop1 is in proximity to some object at some time
        ***********************************************************
        Model goal : some object is located at some location at some time
        ***********************************************************

        1 - define location in terms of grid squares

        Choose schema >>  1
```

Schema 13 generates a single subgoal to establish which square an object moves
to at any time. Two alternative schemata are available for establishing this goal.
The user chooses schema 14 (see Appendix C.2).

```
        there is some value for the biomass of oldpop
           there is some value for the biomass of young
              there is some value for the biomass of young_pop1
                 young_pop1 is in proximity to some object at some time
                    some object is located at some location at some time
        **********************************************************
        Model goal : objects move between grid squares
        **********************************************************

        1 - define means of movement between grid squares by simple transition
        2 - define movement to randomly selected adjoining grid square

        Choose schema >>  2
```

All subgoals of schemata 13 and 7 have been processed so EL pops back to
consider the remaining subgoals of schema 6. The first of these is
$attribute(biomass, young\_pop2, T, N)$, for which the user chooses menu option 4 to
apply schema 6 (from Section 7.2) once more. This sudden jump back up the tree
of schema application may be disconcerting to the user and is a consequence of the
use of depth–first search. In Section 7.7 we describe a program which attempts to
remedy this problem.

```
        there is some value for the biomass of oldpop
           there is some value for the biomass of young
              there is some value for the biomass of young_pop1
        **********************************************************
        Model goal : there is some value for the biomass of young_pop2
        **********************************************************

        1 - biomass of young_pop2 grows logistically
        2 - biomass of young_pop2 is determined by a simple predator-prey equation
        3 - biomass of young_pop2 is determined by a simple competition equation
        4 - calculate biomass of young_pop2 from biomass of interacting objects

        Choose schema >>  4
```

As before, EL obtains a value for the initial biomass of $young\_pop2$ by applying
schema 8 (see Appendix C.2).

```
        there is some value for the biomass of oldpop
            there is some value for the biomass of young
                there is some value for the biomass of young_pop1
                    there is some value for the biomass of young_pop2
        *************************************************************
        Model goal : there is some initial value for the biomass of young_pop2
        *************************************************************

        1 - assign an initial value for biomass of young_pop2

        Choose schema >>  1
        Initial value for biomass of young_pop2 >>  7
```

The biomass of *young_pop3* is determined in a similar way.

```
        there is some value for the biomass of oldpop
            there is some value for the biomass of young
                there is some value for the biomass of young_pop1
                    there is some value for the biomass of young_pop2
        *************************************************************
        Model goal : there is some value for the biomass of young_pop3
        *************************************************************

        1 - biomass of young_pop3 grows logistically
        2 - biomass of young_pop3 is determined by a simple predator-prey equation
        3 - biomass of young_pop3 is determined by a simple competition equation
        4 - calculate biomass of young_pop3 from biomass of interacting objects

        Choose schema >>  4
```

```
        there is some value for the biomass of oldpop
           there is some value for the biomass of young
              there is some value for the biomass of young_pop1
                 there is some value for the biomass of young_pop2
                    there is some value for the biomass of young_pop3
        ***********************************************************
        Model goal : there is some initial value for the biomass of young_pop3
        ***********************************************************

        1 - assign an initial value for biomass of young_pop3

        Choose schema >>  1
        Initial value for biomass of young_pop3 >>  8
```

EL now pops back to the remaining subgoals of the first applied schema (4).
These are $parameter(self\_inhibition\_coefficient, oldpop, N)$. and
$parameter(competition\_coefficient, young, N)$. The former parameter is a standard ecological term used to approximate the dampening effect of increased population size on growth, while the latter is used to regulate the severity of competition
from the competing population. Both of these parameters can be obtained by applying schema 1 (see Section 7.2).

```
        there is some value for the biomass of oldpop
        ***********************************************************
        Model goal : there is some value for the self_inhibition_coefficient
                     of oldpop
        ***********************************************************

        1 - assign a value to parameter self_inhibition_coefficient of oldpop

        Choose schema >>  1
        Value for self_inhibition_coefficient of oldpop >>  0.2
```

```
        there is some value for the biomass of oldpop
        ************************************************************
        Model goal : there is some value for the competition_coefficient
                    of young
        ************************************************************

        1 - assign a value to parameter competition_coefficient of young

        Choose schema >> 1
        Value for competition_coefficient of young >> 0.3
```

No unprocessed goals remain, so the model is completed. EL prompts for a file name for the output model. The user decides just to call it 'model'.

```
            Your simulation program has been constructed.
            File name for output >> model
```

The actual program (as produced by the schemata application mechanism) is written to the file model.plist. A record of ancillary information obtained during the description of the problem and construction of the program is written to model.just. These two files are used by the program description system (section 7.5) to reconstruct the decisions made when building a given output program. A pretty–printed version of the code, which can be more easily read by humans, is written to model.prog and it is this file which is used to run the simulation . The contents of this file for our example model are shown in appendix C.5. To run the model, we simply load the file and give the appropriate query. For example we might want to know the value for the *young* population at time 4. To obtain this information we give the query:

| ?— $attribute(biomass, young, 4, N)$.

which succeeds, instantiating N to the value 47.7593.

7.5 Describing a Pre–built Simulation Model

At the end of Section 7.4.4 we mentioned that EL produces three files at the end of a program construction session:

- The list of Prolog clauses produced as raw output from EL (the `model.plist` file in our previous example).

- A pretty–printed version of this list (the `model.prog` file in our previous example). This is used for running the simulation program (see Chapter 5 for details).

- A record of ancillary information obtained during the description of the problem and construction of the program (the `model.prog` file in our previous example).

Over time, users are likely to produce a number of sets of files containing different simulation programs constructed using different implementation decisions and problem descriptions. It is important for a user to be able to reconstruct the decisions which were made when he/she or or another user built a given program. This reconstruction is extremely difficult to perform by simply looking at the appropriate files of code because they give no indication of the order in which schemata were applied or when particular strategic decisions were made. To overcome this problem, we provide a tool for automatically reconstructing a session with EL and then allowing a user to browse through this reconstruction. We first consider the mechanism by which an EL session is reconstructed and then describe the user interface.

7.5.1 Reconstructing an EL session

Recall, from section 7.3.4, that all programs generated by EL are constructed by finding an initial set of queries which the model is designed to satisfy and recursively applying schemata to satisfy those queries, plus any subgoals generated during the application of schemata. This was formally represented as a function from the universe of discourse Θ, problem description Δ, database of schemata Ψ and rule base Γ to a set of clauses *Clauses*1 constituting a program. The reconstruction system can remake Θ, Δ, Ψ and Γ from the ancillary information file which it produces at the end of the session in question. The only remaining unknowns are the instantiations of preconditions which held when schemata were applied and actions which were fired after a user selected each schema. These were also recorded by EL in an ancillary information file. Given that all this information is available, we can reconstruct the schema application session by applying a similar algorithm to that used for program construction (section 7.3.4) but using ancillary information instead of interacting with the user, and recording how each schema is applied.

Algorithm 18 The output of the reconstruction program is a list κ of Prolog terms of the form:

$j(Goal, s(Name, Goal, Subgoals, Clauses, Actions, Procedure), \kappa')$
Where : $Name$ is a list which provides a name for a schema.
     $Goal$ is the simulation goal for which the schema solves.
     $Subgoals$ is a list of new goals which the schema generates.
     $Clauses$ is a list of Prolog clauses introduced into the program by
       the schema.
     $Actions$ is a list of procedure calls which must be satisfied
       before the schema, once selected by the user, can be applied.
     $Procedure$ is a procedure call which must be satisfied before
       a schema can be used in a given context.
     κ' is a list of terms in the same form as κ.

Algorithm 30 We write $\underline{reconstruct(\Lambda, \Phi, \Psi, Goals1, Clauses1) = \kappa}$ to denote that κ is a reconstruction of schemata applications from Ψ which solve for the queries in $Goals1$ using the program $Clauses1$, given the set of schema precondition instantiations Φ and action instantiations Λ when:

- $replay(\Lambda, \Phi, \Psi, Goals1, Clauses2, \kappa, Clauses5)$, where $Clauses2$ is a partially complete reconstruction of the program (initially an empty set) and $Clauses5$ is a complete reconstructed program.
- $Clauses1 = Clauses5$.

$replay(\Lambda, \Phi, \Psi, Goals1, Clauses2, \kappa, Clauses5)$ is true when:

- If $Goals1$ is non–empty then:
  - Select the first Prolog goal $G1$ from $Goals1$, leaving the remaining elements $Goals2$.
    * If $G1$ can already be satisfied from $Clauses2$, then:
      · $replay(\Lambda, \Phi, \Psi, Goals2, Clauses2, \kappa, Clauses5)$
    * Otherwise:
      · Find a schema in Ψ of the form:
        $schema(Name, G2, Goals3, Clauses3, Actions, Procedure1)$ such that: $G1 = G2$; there is some $Procedure2$ in Φ such that $Procedure1$ instantiates to $Procedure2$; and for each schema action $\mathcal{A}$ in $Actions$, there is a corresponding action $\mathcal{A}'$ in Λ such that $\mathcal{A}$ instantiates to $\mathcal{A}'$.

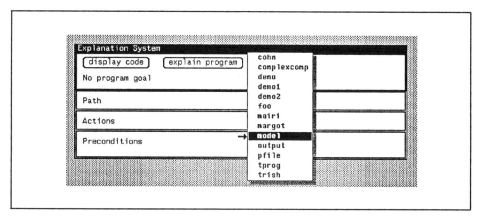

Figure 7.6
Loading a file

> $\cdot\ replay(\Lambda, \Phi, \Psi, Goals3, Clauses2 \cup Clauses3, \kappa', Clauses4).$
>
> $\cdot\ replay(\Lambda, \Phi, \Psi, Goals2, Clauses4, \kappa'', Clauses5).$
>
> $\cdot\ \kappa = \kappa'' \cup$
>
> $\{j(G1, s(Name, G2, Goals3, Clauses3, Actions, Procedure1), \kappa')\}.$

- Otherwise, if $Goals1$ is empty then κ and $Clauses5$ are also empty.

7.5.2 Interface

The user interface mechanism developed for this system is similar to that developed for the core EL system, in that most of the user interaction takes place within a single frame holding a collection of panels for performing various tasks. A separate window is used for text output from the main system. The details of this system are best explained by looking at the sequence of example displays in Figures 7.6 to 7.9.

The display in Figure 7.6 shows the main window of the system at the start of a session. The upper panel provides a pop–up menu of file names, from which the user can choose. In this example, the user has chosen the name "model", which refers to the program we constructed as an example in section 7.4. Selecting this option causes the system to read in the appropriate program and ancillary files and fire the reconstruction mechanism (see section 7.5.1), generating a nested term which represents a replay of the original model construction process.

Having made this reconstruction, the user can then browse downwards through

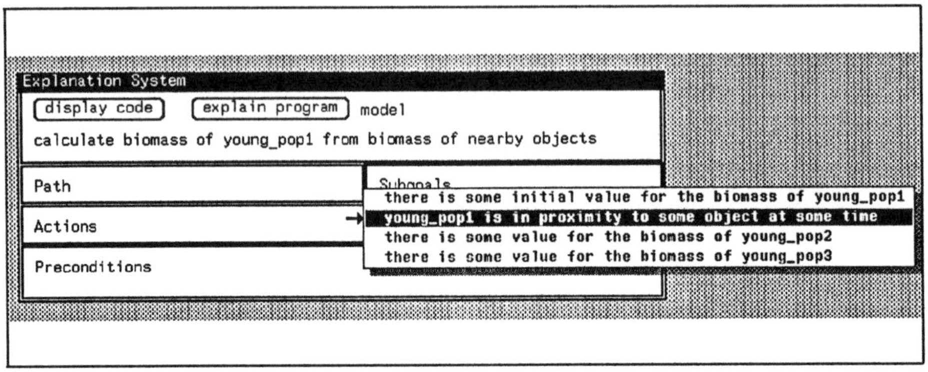

Figure 7.7
Descending to a subgoal

the nested schema applications by selecting options from the "Subgoals" panel as shown in Figure 7.7. This snapshot is taken at some depth in the nested term, at the point where schema 6 is used to solve for $attribute(biomass, young\_pop1, T, N)$. The name of this schema is printed at the top of the upper panel. The user is in the process of moving to one of the subgoals of this schema by selecting an option from the pop-up menu in the "Subgoals" panel.

The set of actions and preconditions can be displayed for any schema in the reconstruction term. For example, in Figure 7.8 the user is still positioned at the schema he was at in Figure 7.7 and has obtained a pop up menu of its preconditions. Selecting any of these menu options will provide a short description of the corresponding precondition, which is displayed in the text output window. The displays produced the two preconditions in Figure 7.8 are:

```
It has been established from the problem description that :
For all wolf :
    wolf is represented spatially in the model
```

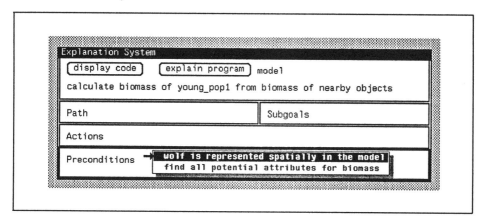

Figure 7.8
Obtaining a description of a precondition

```
          I found all potential attributes for biomass.
          These were :
           there is some value for the biomass of oldpop
           there is some value for the biomass of young_pop1
           there is some value for the biomass of young_pop2
           there is some value for the biomass of young_pop3
```

It is also possible to display the code which a particular schema contributes to the completed program by pressing the "display code" button in the upper panel. Pressing this button in Figure 7.8 produces the display:

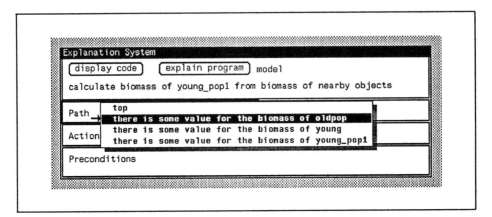

Figure 7.9
Moving back up the subgoal tree

```
attribute(biomass,young_pop1,A,B) :-
        \+ initial_time(A),
        previous_time(A,C),
        attribute(biomass,young_pop1,C,D),
        setof_or_empty(E,in_proximity(young_pop1,E,A),F),
        for_each(G,F,attribute(biomass,G,C,H),H,I),
        sum_elements(I,J),
        length(I,K),
        (J=0,B=D ; B is D+J/K/2).
attribute(biomass,young_pop1,A,B) :-
        initial_time(A),
        initial_value(biomass,young_pop1,B).
```

Finally, users may retrace their steps to higher levels in the nested schema application term by selecting an option from the pop–up menu in the "Path" panel. This gives a sequence of ancestor goals upwards from the current schema goal to a notional "top" level in the schema application. In Figure 7.9 the user is about to move to one of the top level goals.

7.6   Altering a Pre–built Simulation Model

We envisage that EL will be used not only to build one–off simulation programs but also to adapt and experiment with programs previously built using the system.

This facility is provided in the core EL system by allowing users to restore the problem description and schemata application information from the appropriate ".just" file (see last paragraph of section 7.4) by selecting the file name from a pop-up menu which appears in the lower panel of the browser window (see figure 7.3). A user can then add or remove problem description formulae or change the universe of discourse in the ways described in section 7.3 and then use the schemata application mechanism to generate a program based on this new information.

The ability to reconstruct the problem description is also important in allowing alternative simulation models to be generated from a common problem description. When constructing our example model in Section 7.4.4, a number of schemata were presented to the user as alternative methods for satisfying particular goals during the construction of the tree of schema application. Having experimented with the completed model by running it, the user might be unhappy with its behaviour and wish to apply different schemata for some components of the model. This can be done rapidly by restoring the original problem description and then re-generating the model, applying different schemata at appropriate points.

7.7 Extensions of EL: the NIPPIE System

We have described a working prototype of a system (EL) which allows users who possess no prior knowledge of Prolog programming to construct complex simulation programs in Prolog. This is made possible by the provision of a database of program schemata which are applied to ensure that the queries required of the final program can be satisfied. The task of schema application is simplified by using information from a previously elicited problem description to reduce the range of schemata which apply at any point in program construction. The resulting program is amenable to novel forms of description, thanks to its modular structure and the explicit representation of problem description information.

The chief attraction of EL is the comparatively simple mechanisms which it uses to guide dialogue during problem description and program construction. These are mostly in the form of short algorithms (we have supplied these in previous sections) which are independent of the ecology domain. There are, unfortunately, two exceptions to this rule. First, and most important, the procedure for aggregating object classes in the universe of discourse (see section 7.3.2) is *ad hoc*, relying on the detection of particular formulae in the problem description. We would like to think of better ways of performing this task. Second the way in which the initial program queries are set up (see section 7.3.4) is similarly *ad hoc* and needs to be defined more rigorously. In addition to these specific problems there are several general areas of deficiency which require attention:

- Although the formulae appearing in the problem description are sufficient to control the generation of a wide range of ecological models this is only a small proportion of the vast range of models which could, potentially, be constructed. We would like to extend this range as far as possible but this will take a large amount of effort in collecting more model structures and determining the problem description formulae necessary to control their application.

- One way to provide this extra representational capacity without suffering a massive increase in the number of schemata would be to provide more general definitions of model structure. For example, we could provide general functional relationships which apply across a wide range of problems rather than particular equations specific to a particular context. To do this requires a deeper analysis of the ecological domain in order to extract general principles from many specific modelling examples. It is also likely to place a heavier burden of responsibility on the problem description to control the application of these more general structures.

- The current EL system assumes that the problem description is complete when it begins to generate the simulation model by schema application. If the problem description is short of some crucial piece of information no means is provided for obtaining this information during the model generation phase. The onus is put on the user to supply sufficient problem description information to allow program generation to be successful but, despite the fact that we provide mechanisms for prompting the user for problem description information, there is no guarantee that the user will always get this right.

In this section we describe two systems which were built as ways of overcoming the problems listed above. They both utilise the core schema application mechanism from EL but differ in the way this algorithm is used to drive the user interface. The first such experiment was the construction of HIPPIE [Haggith 90], which overcame the problem of incomplete problem descriptions. An enhanced system, NIPPIE, was then gradually developed as the result of tackling the following issues:

- How to use more generalised model structures.

- Generating population dynamics models.

- Enhancing the user interface.

- Allowing ecologists to use more ecological terminology when supplying information.

7.7.1 HIPPIE

Because EL's problem description phase is kept distinct from model construction, there is no way of adding information if the problem description is found to be incomplete once model generation is underway. In particular, when testing schema preconditions to determine if a particular schema is applicable, a precondition may be unsatisfiable on the basis of the problem description, because the ecologist forgot to include some piece of information. For example, a grazing schema may have as a precondition that the animal in question is a herbivore. If EL is trying to find a schema to calculate the biomass of a rabbit, but the ecologist has omitted "the rabbit is a herbivore" from the problem description, the grazing schema will not have all of its preconditions satisfied. The worst case of this problem is that the ecologist may have been unable to use EL's browser and was hence unable to supply any problem description information at all. In this case, model construction cannot even get started.

It would be desirable for the system, once it has failed to satisfy a precondition on the basis of the problem description, to be able to ask the ecologist directly whether that condition is the case. In the example above, if the system could ask *"Is the rabbit a herbivore?"*, which the ecologist would affirm, then the grazing schema could become applicable. Given that the ecologist could supply further necessary information, such as what plant is grazed, and parameters such as the grazing rate, then the appropriate grazing equation could be included in the model.

This solution is implemented in HIPPIE in the following way. For a particular model goal, the set of schemata which solve for that goal are selected. Any schemata with all preconditions satisfied are offered to the ecologist in the manner of EL. If there are no such schemata, or if the ecologist does not wish to select any of those offered, then a dialogue begins. HIPPIE selects an unsatisfied precondition and converts it into a question which is then presented to the ecologist. Most of the preconditions are fairly simple statements and hence convert easily to questions with a yes or no answer, or which require a simple input like the name of an organism or a number. The herbivore example above gives a question with a yes or no answer. A schema for a competition equation will have as a precondition that a competitor is known. This will convert easily to the question *" What does the organism compete with?"* which requires the name of another organism. The schema setting up the

start time in the model has as precondition that this is known, which converts to
"What is the initial time point?" requiring a number to be given.

A number of such questions will be asked until a new schema has all preconditions
satisfied, at which point it will be suggested to the ecologist, who can either choose
it or not. If it is not chosen, the dialogue continues until a schema is chosen or all
unsatisfied preconditions are exhausted, at which point the ecologist must select
one of the applicable schemata. When a schema is selected, subgoals are generated
in the same way as in EL, and the process repeats for each of the subgoals.

The algorithms for this process are given below. The schemata application mechanism remains much the same as in EL, so it is omitted here. The major change is
to the schema choice mechanism.

First a new set of procedures, the questions, Ξ is defined. There is one element
of Ξ for each precondition and it asks the user whether the precondition is satisfied.

The questions are used to improve the schema choice mechanism, as follows:

Algorithm 31 We write $choose\_schema(\Psi, \Delta, \Xi) = (\sigma, \Delta'')$ to denote – given the
database of schemata Ψ; a problem description Δ; and the set of questions Ξ –
that σ is chosen as the schema to apply for the current goal and Δ'' is the updated
problem description. This is true when:

- *develop_context*$(\Psi, \Delta, \Xi) = \Delta'$, which means that some precondition questions for schemata in Ψ have been asked and the results used to update the
  problem description to Δ', (see next algorithm).

- and those schemata in Ψ whose preconditions are verifiable directly from the
  new problem description Δ' form the set Ψ',

- then:
  - If any of Ψ' are "new", (ie: they haven't yet been offered to the user),
    offer Ψ' to the user and
    * If the user wants to choose one of them, the chosen schema is σ, and
      $\Delta' = \Delta''$
    * If the user wants to reject any of them:
      · Let Ψ''' be the rejected schemata.
      · Let Ψ'' be the result of removing Ψ''' from the original set Ψ.
      · $choose\_schema(\Psi'', \Delta', \Xi) = (\sigma, \Delta'')$.
    * If the user doesn't want to reject any schemata then:
      $choose\_schema(\Psi, \Delta', \Xi) = (\sigma, \Delta'')$

— If there are no 'new' schemata to offer then repeat the process, *i.e.*:
$choose\_schema(\Psi, \Delta', \Xi) = (\sigma, \Delta'')$

The algorithm for developing the context is as follows:

Algorithm 32 We write $develop\_context(\Psi, \Delta, \Xi) = \Delta'$ to denote that from a given set of schemata, Ψ, a set of questions, Ξ and a problem description, Δ, a new problem description Δ' is obtained by testing some of the preconditions of the schemata in Ψ and updating Δ with the resulting information. This holds when:

- Φ is the set of all preconditions of schemata in Ψ, which are neither explicitly asserted nor explicitly denied in the problem description Δ,

- $choose\_preconditions(\Phi, \Delta) = \Phi'$ where Φ' is a subset of Φ which will be tested to see if its members are satisfied

- $test\_preconditions(\Phi', \Delta, \Xi) = \Delta'$ where Δ' is the new problem description resulting from asking the user whether the preconditions in Φ' are satisfied and adding this information to the problem description, *i.e.*: for each ϕ in Φ', with corresponding question ξ in Ξ, the user is asked ξ and

  - if ξ is answered satisfactorily, then π is asserted in Δ

  - otherwise π is denied in Δ.

Even if no problem description is given initially, HIPPIE can still acquire all necessary information via these questions. Therefore HIPPIE was implemented with no initial problem description phase, model construction beginning immediately with the initial model goal. The resulting dialogue consists of sets of questions ordered according to the depth-first search through schemata of EL's program generation algorithm. The order is hence dependent on the order of schemata in the knowledge base and of preconditions within the schemata. This can cause the following sorts of problems:

- It may begin by asking specific questions about the ecological problem like *"Does the rabbit compete with another organism?"* and *"Is the rabbit preyed upon by another animal?"* and then ask a question about a general modelling issue, like *"Do you want to use a spatial representation model?"*. It would be better to ask general questions before specific ones.

- HIPPIE does not follow up answers to questions, as a human modeller would. It may ask about the nature of a spatial representation model by saying *"Do you want to use a coordinate representation?"* and receive the reply "No".

A human modeller would probably follow up by immediately asking about alternative representations, like grid squares, but unless the schemata have been specially ordered in the knowledge base, HIPPIE is just as likely to ask next *"Is the rabbit a mammal?"* and may ask several other questions, before suggesting a grid representation. The user would probably be fairly bewildered by this stage.

- If HIPPIE had a schema for a predation relationship with two preconditions - one giving the prey, and one saying that the predator is a carnivore - in that order, then HIPPIE would ask *"What does the rabbit prey on?"* and then *"Is the rabbit a carnivore?"*. This causes what is known in linguistics as 'presupposition failure' because the first question presupposes an affirmative reply to the second.

HIPPIE should be able to cope with these situations and not be dependent on something as implicit as the ordering of schemata in the knowledge base, and of preconditions within schemata.

These problems are solved by giving HIPPIE meta-level information about preconditions, such as subject matter or specificity, which is used when selecting which question to ask the ecologist next (ie: in the *choose_preconditions* stage of the algorithm for *develop_context* given above. The selection is done on the basis of heuristics to group related questions, to order them from general to specific, and to avoid asking questions which are dependent on the answers of other questions which have not yet been asked. For details of this see [Haggith 90].

To conclude:

- HIPPIE is a solution to the problem of how to build simulation models from an incomplete or even empty problem description, by allowing it to be completed as model construction goes on. This allows for the common experience of ecological modellers that precisely what information will be required for the construction of a model does not become apparent until the model is partially built.

- HIPPIE acquires model information by asking questions which determine whether or not schemata preconditions are satisfied. The resulting dialogue, being totally in the hands of the system, is said to be "system initiative".

- Improvements to the structure of the dialogue are made by the use of meta-level information about preconditions and heuristics which use this information to order questions.

- The generative power of EL is retained as the underlying model generation algorithm is the same.

7.7.2 NIPPIE

HIPPIE was used as the basis of some further experiments with improved model generation techniques, leading to the enhanced system, NIPPIE. The major additional features implemented in NIPPIE are described in the remainder of this section.

In Section 2.3 a brief description was given of how a population is often modelled by aggregating it together and treating it as a unit with properties such as number, rather than modelling so many separate entities. It was further described how refinement of such models may involve disaggregating the population according to dimensions such as spatial location, age, sex or species. The growth of a population may, for example, be modelled by taking into account the different fecundity rates of different age-classes in the population. The grazing rates of members of the same population may perhaps vary according to location (food availability may vary from place to place), but not according to age. A mechanism is hence required to allow a population to be disaggregated across different (orthogonal) dimensions in one model. This mechanism is present in the EL system but is applied only in a restricted form at the point where the problem description is refined, prior to the generation of the simulation model, (see Sections 7.3.2 and 7.4.2). It is necessary to provide the user with some control over disaggregation during model generation, rather than forcing the decision to be made entirely as part of the problem description phase.

To provide this facility, schemata were included in NIPPIE which would allow ecologists to select appropriate disaggregation and aggregation mechanisms in their models. For example, the total biomass of a population may be found by summing the biomasses of subpopulations, say those in each of three locations. The fecundity rate of a population as a whole may be the average fecundity rate of each age-class in the population, weighted by the proportion of females in each class. Schemata were hence included to represent the aggregation methods: sum, maximum, minimum, mean and weighted average.

A means was also required whereby an ecologist could supply the dimensions by which a population should be disaggregated (age, sex etc) and the values these dimensions should take (the age-class ranges, location names etc). The ecologist would also need to show in which parts of the model the disaggregation is relevant, for example, which parameters take different values according to the value of some dimension. Using our previous example, the ecologist must be also to state that the rabbit's grazing rate depends on location, but not sex or age; that fecundity varies according to age, but not location and so on.

This problem has two main aspects. The first is the question of how to represent such information in NIPPIE's schemata in a manner in which it can be used unambiguously and accurately both in the generation of appropriate subgoals when building the model, and in actual model calculations when the simulation is run. It is hence the problem of finding a suitable notation.

The second aspect is how to acquire the appropriate information from the user, given that NIPPIE inherits HIPPIE's "system–initiative" approach to knowledge acquisition. Put more simply, what are the right questions to ask about disaggregation? So far we have found only *ad hoc* solutions to these problems, though they are sufficient to allow simple models incorporating these ideas to be constructed automatically. A brief description of our approach to this problem is given below.

A population is represented by the term:

$$pop([name : Name, Dim_1 : Val_1, Dim_2 : Val_2, \cdots Dim_N : Val_N])$$

where *Name* is a name by which the population can be referred to, the Dim_I are the dimensions by which the population will be disaggregated and the Val_I are dimension values or a variable indicating any value. For example a population of 2-year old bucks (male rabbits) spread over several warrens may be represented as:

$$pop([name : rabbit, age : 2, location : L, sex : male]) :- member(L, [a, b, c])$$

Where $[a, b, c]$ is a set of possible locations. A parameter or other model variable may also have dimensions, so in our rabbit example, as fecundity varies according to age and sex, the fecundity of female, adult rabbits (does) would be represented as follows:

$$parameter(fecundity, [rabbit\_sex\_class : female, rabbit\_age\_class : adult], Value)$$

This notation allows variable dimension values to be instantiated by Prolog unification and hence "passed down" the goal-tree in model construction and the running of the final simulation program.

This is a notational variant of the formalism used in [Bundy & Uschold 89]. However, its use in acquiring disaggregation information from an ecologist is rather clumsy and counter–intuitive, and further research is required to determine whether it can be made to work more effectively.

NIPPIE also differs from HIPPIE with respect to its user interface. As anticipated users of the system are ecologists with little experience with using a computer system, it is important that such a system is easy to use. Hence, a window-based interface was developed which allows users to answer questions by clicking a mouse on clearly labelled buttons, choosing from suggestions on menus or typing simple answers in a clearly marked place. In addition, as the problem description is built up, it is displayed in windows, as are decisions about chosen schemata. This allows the ecologist to see what happens as a result of answering NIPPIE's questions, and to help keep track of the information given to the system so far. It is interesting to note that the interfaces for NIPPIE and EL (although both window based) are differently organised. This is because EL places heavy responsibility on the user to decide on the sequence of dialogue during model construction and therefore has to provide a battery of pop-up menus, toggles and other display tools to support this flexibility. By contrast, users of NIPPIE assume a more passive role – simply responding to the dialogue generated by the system. This allows the complexity of the interface (from the user's perspective) to be reduced.

7.8   Conclusion

In this chapter we have described some software tools for helping users to supply descriptions of problems in a restricted domain and for using this information to control the generation of simulation models. This draws together our work on the use of Prolog for model representation (see Chapter 3) and our use of a sorted logic for problem description (see Chapter 6). The modularity of logic programming languages permits us to define self–contained model schemata, which may be thought of as plans for constructing standard components of the model. This supports a view of model construction as a search through a large space of possible plans. Even with a small number of schemata, this space can be vary large and ecologists can't be expected to navigate through it without help in deciding which schemata are appropriate to their ecological problems. This raises two problems: how to extract a formal problem description from the user and how to employ this problem description to reduce the size of the space of schemata appropriate to a given problem. We have tackled the first of these problems by introducing the idea of template ecological statements which may be selected and edited, using a simple interface, to describe key aspects of the ecological problem. Deduction and abduction mechanisms are used to establish ancillary problem description information and to provide suggestions for further statements which the user might want to add. The task of linking the problem description to schemata is performed by supplying each schema with a set of preconditions which must be established in the problem description in order for that schema to be considered appropriate for the user's ecological problem.

Within the general framework of schema application it is possible to have two contrasting forms of dialogue. The first requires the user initially to describe the ecological problem and subsequently uses this description to control the generation of the model by schema application. The second approach drives all dialogue from the schema application mechanism, with requests to establish schema preconditions from the problem description being used to prompt users for ecological information. This second approach has the advantage of constraining dialogue to topics which are relevant to the construction of the simulation model but it has the disadvantage of tending to enforce a rigid ordering on the sequence of dialogue.

As well as improving model comprehension during program construction (by subdividing the task of programming into manageable "chunks" which are presented in the context of the ecological problem) the use of schemata aids model comprehension by allowing users to reconstruct the sequence of schema applications used to build a completed program. This facility is important because it allows users who had no part in constructing a program to analyse how it was produced and to examine which parts of the problem description were prerequisites for the components of the model. This, in turn, makes it easy to experiment with alterations to the problem description and/or choice of schemata and to study their effect on the completed program.

In the next chapter we shall consider a contrasting approach to program construction, which moves away from the use of model schemata and relies, instead, on enhancements to the sorted logic meta–interpreter from Chapter 4.

8 Model Construction in the Sorted Logic

We have shown, in Chapter 7, that it is possible to utilise the modularity of Prolog to provide users with a library of standard simulation model structures (schemata) and that domain–specific information (expressed in the sorted logic) can be used partially to automate the process of model construction. There were, however, some drawbacks with this approach – in particular:

1. Complex Prolog procedures in the actions and preconditions of schemata are used to connect the Prolog simulation program to the sorted logic problem description and this makes it quite difficult to link together the two languages during model construction. Note that we cannot make the link between Prolog and the sorted logic simply by translating the Prolog into sorted logic because we have no general purpose algorithm for making this conversion. The translation algorithm of Section 5.3 is from the sorted logic to Prolog, which is the reverse of what is required here.

2. Since the final simulation program is constructed by repeated application of schemata, it is essential that each schema introduces a complete, runnable section of Prolog code and that each section of code is compatible with the others. The modularity of Prolog code reduces this problem but EL is reliant on the schema actions and preconditions (and through them the problem description) to ensure that the code contributed by each schema to the simulation program is correct. Given the complexity problems which we noted above, this means that we cannot provide a *guarantee* that any program constructed using EL, HIPPIE or NIPPIE will be runnable. This is because our schemata are like plans of programs which are pieced together without testing that the program they produce actually runs.

The obvious solution to problem 1 is to rewrite program schemata using the sorted logic, thus maintaining a uniform language for both model and problem description. Unfortunately, this doesn't solve problem 2 because, although we could perhaps provide more of an assurance that our completed programs would run, this assurance could not be absolute. In this chapter we describe a more radical solution – that of constructing a program *as part of the process of running it*. The basic idea is that instead of assuming that the sorted–logic interpreter will always operate on a static set of axioms in order to answer some query about the model we allow the user to add further axioms whenever a solution cannot be found using the existing axioms. In this way new axioms are accumulated until there are sufficient to solve the initial goal, at which point the model is complete. Since the search strategies used to construct and run the model are the same, we can guarantee that the final program will run. Casting one's mind back to the run times which we gave in Chapter 5, it may seem that this idea is a non–starter because it takes such a long time to run logic–based simulations. However, recall that run–time tends to increase exponentially with the number of time points over which the simulation is run. Many simulation models have the same computational structure during the course of a simulation and, for these, the axioms required to run them over the initial few time points may be all that are required, regardless of how many other time points one wanted to consider later on. Provided that the length of this stable time period is known, it is then possible to construct quickly a model which runs over this small range of time points and only later extend the range of time points, thus alleviating the exponential run–time problem during model construction.

In the rest of this chapter we shall describe a program, named SL, which constructs a simulation program in the sorted logic, using the approach sketched above. After the style of our description of EL in Chapter 7, we first describe the algorithms used in program construction (Section 8.1) and then provide a detailed example of SL at work (Section 8.2).

8.1   Program Construction Algorithms

In SL, the process of program construction is divided into three chronologically distinct phases:

Development of the sort hierarchy (Section 8.1.1) in which the user describes the sorts and objects which are present in the simulation model.

Specification of modelling goals (Section 8.1.2) which involves the selection and refinement of a top–level goal in the sorted logic, for which the completed simulation model must provide a solution.

Selecting axioms for the working model (Section 8.1.3) which uses an augmented version of the sorted logic interpreter from Section 4.4 to drive the interactive selection of axioms for inclusion in the simulation model.

We now consider each of these in turn.

8.1.1   Developing the Sort Hierarchy

The purpose of this part of the program construction algorithm is to prompt the user for any extensions of the sort hierarchy which he/she requires. We could have used a browsing system for this purpose, perhaps similar to the one described in Section 7.4.1 but, instead, we have chosen a more directed method of extracting sort information from the user. The reason for giving less freedom to users to determine which parts of the sort hierarchy they want to visit is that we want to make sure that all portions of the sort hierarchy are brought to the users' attention, unless they specifically say otherwise. To this end, the algorithm is basically an interactive, exhaustive search. Starting at the most general element of the sort hierarchy (see Figure 4.1 for an example hierarchy), the system checks which of the immediate subsorts of this node the user is interested in looking at. For any sort in which the user expresses an interest, the system may prompt the user to introduce objects belonging to this sort. A library of default sorts is provided as indications of typical objects which might be included. The system may also attempt to introduce structured sort terms by finding any **sort schemata** which apply to the given sort. These sort schemata are similar in structure to the *sort_term* declarations of Section 4.1.4 and represent possible complex objects which may appear in a particular simulation model but do not always appear in all simulation models. For example, a user might want to represent objects in a population using terms ranging over some user defined index (denoted using the reserved name *"index"* for which the user may substitute any list of objects) and age class. This corresponds to the sort schema declaration:

sort_schema(population, population(P, A), [P in index, A in age_class]).

which, with the *index* sort instantiated to an appropriate index set might be asserted as a sort term:

sort_term(population, population(P, A), [P in [1, 2, 3], A in age_class]).

The user might go on to define age classes as being terms ranging over some other index (say *young* and *old*) and sex classes, using the sort schema:

sort_schema(age_class, age_class(G, S), [G in index, S in sex_class]).

which might be asserted, with *index* instantiated appropriately, as the sort term:

sort_term(age_class, age_class(G, S), [G in [young, old], S in sex_class]).

If the user now allocated the objects *male* and *female* to the sort *sex_class* (using the *subobj* declaration from Definition 2) then this would define the set of all objects included within the *population* sort to be:

$[population(1, age\_class(young, male)), population(1, age\_class(young, female)),$
$\quad population(1, age\_class(old, male)), population(1, age\_class(old, female)),$
$\quad population(2, age\_class(young, male)), population(2, age\_class(young, female)),$
$\quad \ldots population(3, age\_class(old, female))]$

Once a user has specified a given sort to his/her satisfaction, the system finds any subsorts of this sort and applies the same algorithm to them. Alternatively, the user may state that they don't want to talk about the current sort at all – in which case it is tagged as being of no interest and none of its subsorts are explored. This process continues until all the sorts have either been specified or blocked off as being of no interest.

Algorithm 33 We write $\underline{develop\_sort(Sort)}$ to denote that $Sort$ has been described to the user's satisfaction when :

- **IF** $Sort$ has already been visited **THEN STOP** .

- **OTHERWISE IF** $Sort = (Sort1 \text{ and } Sort2)$ **OR** $Sort = (Sort1 \text{ or } Sort2)$ **THEN** :
    - $develop\_sort(Sort1)$ **AND**
    - $develop\_sort(Sort2)$.

- **OTHERWISE IF** $sort\_test(Sort, \_, \_)$ (Definition 6) **THEN STOP** .

- **OTHERWISE IF** $sort\_term(Sort, \_, Sortlist)$ (Definition 4 **THEN** :
    - For each element of $Sortlist$ of the form X in $Sort1$: $develop\_sort(Sort1)$.

- **OTHERWISE EITHER** :
    - Introduce a sort schema as follows :
        * Find the set of sort $Schemata$ which could be added without introducing any infinite sort paths into the sort hierarchy **AND**
        * Prompt the user to choose a schema, consisting of a sort term $Term$ under substitution set $Substs$, from $Schemata$ **AND**
        * Add the term $sort\_term(Sort, Term, Substs)$ to the set of sort terms currently active in the system **AND**
        * $develop\_sort\_schema(Sort, Term, Substs)$.
    - **OR** continue development of the sort hierarchy as follows:
        * Find the set, $Defobjs$, of all default objects associated with $Sort$ **AND**

* Find the set, *Subsorts*, of all subsorts of *Sort* **AND**
* *continue_develop_sort(Sort, Defobjs, Subsorts)*.

Algorithm 34 We write *develop_sort_schema(S, T, C)* to denote that a sort schema, *S*, consisting of a term, *T*, under a set of sort constraints, *C*, has been incorporated into the sort hierarchy, when:

- The user restricts the initial set of sort substitutions to form a new set of substitutions, *C*1 appropriate for his/her problem **AND** .

- The new sort term: *sort_term(S, T, C1)* is added to the sort hierarchy **AND**

- For each element of *C*1 of the form *X* in *S*1 : *develop_sort(S1)* (Algorithm 33) **AND**

- Prompt the user for another restriction of the original sort schema:

  - **IF** another restriction is required **THEN** *develop_sort_schema(S, T, C)*.

  - **OTHERWISE STOP** .

8.1.2 Specifying Modelling Goals

Having fully defined the sets of objects over which the sorted logic axioms will range, the user is then taken through the specification of a top–level goal for which the simulation model must solve (*i.e.* the output of the simulation model).

Algorithm 35 We write *provide_goal = Goal* to denote that the user has specified a *Goal*, in the sorted logic when:

- *choose_initial_goal = Goal1* (Algorithm 36) **AND**
- *develop_goal(Goal1) = Goal2* (Algorithm 37) **AND**
- *expand_goal(Goal2) = Goal* (Algorithm 38).

To do this, the user first chooses a preliminary description of the goal, from a menu of options. For example, this might be the goal:

([*A* in *attribute_name*, *X* in *object*], [])#
          fplot(([*T* in *time*], [])#*attribute*(*A, X, T*), ([*T* in *time*], [])#*T*)

which denotes a plot of some attribute of some object against time.

Algorithm 36 We write *choose_initial_goal = Goal* when the user has selected an initial, partially specified goal from a menu of options presented by the system.

Given this preliminary goal, the next step is to restrict, if necessary, any of the variables appearing in it. In the example above, the variables of interest are A and X – restricted to *attribute_name* and *object*, respectively. A variable can be restricted in three ways:

- Its sort restriction may be made more specific (*e.g.* *object* could be restricted to *animal*.

- The variable could be instantiated to a particular object (*e.g.* X could be instantiated to *deer_pop*).

- A new function could be substituted for the variable, which would return a result consistent with the variable's original sort restriction. For example, the function $x\_values/1$ takes a list of coordinate pairs and returns their x coordinate values. In our function definition notation introduced in Definition 11 this is written as:

$$def(x\_values(L),\ fun([L\ \text{in}\ coordinate\_list],[],number\_list)).$$

Now if we had a preliminary goal which was to find the maximum of some list of values, expressed as the term:

$$([X\ \text{in}\ number\_list],[])\#maximum(X).$$

then we could restrict the variable X by inserting the x_values function, giving the new goal:

$$([L\ \text{in}\ coordinate\_list],[])\#maximum(x\_values(L)).$$

Note that we have removed the sort restriction applying to X from the substitution set and added the sort restrictions applying to the x_values function.

Algorithm 37 We write $develop\_goal((I,O)\#Term) = (FinalI, FinalO)\#Term$ to denote that a goal in the sorted logic, consisting of a $Term$ restricted over some initial set of input sort substitutions (I) and output sort substitutions (O), has been edited to form a more restricted formula, with new sort substitutions $FinalI$ and $FinalO$, when:

- **IF** the set I is non–empty **THEN** :

  - Take the first element, Var in $Sort$, of I, leaving the remaining elements R **AND**

  - Find the possibly empty set, D, of function definitions, Def, such that $function\_source(Sort, Def)$ **AND**

  - Present the user with the choice of **EITHER** :

    * Choosing a definition statement, of form $(I1, O1)\#Term$, from D – in which case:
      - $Var = Term$ **AND**
      - $develop\_goal(I1 \cup R, O1 \cup O)\#Term = (FinalI, FinalO)\#Term$.

    * **OR** supplying an object, Obj, such that Obj in $Sort$ – in which case:
      - $Var = Obj$ **AND**
      - $develop\_goal(R, O)\#Term = (FinalI, FinalO)\#Term$.

    * **OR** supplying a sort, $Sort1$, such that $Sort1 \subseteq Sort$ – in which case:
      - $develop\_goal(R, O)\#Term = (I3, FinalO)\#Term$ **AND**
      - $FinalI = [Var \text{ in } Sort1] \cup I3$.

    * **OR** leave the existing sort restriction, $Sort$, unchanged – in which case:
      - $develop\_goal(R, O)\#Term = (I3, FinalO)\#Term$ **AND**
      - $FinalI = [Var \text{ in } Sort] \cup I3$.

Once a user has restricted the variables in his/her current goal, the system considers the possibility of elaboration of the goal statement. This applies only to functions and consists of finding any defined functions for which the current goal could be an argument (similar to the refinement step described above but applied "in reverse"). For example, suppose that the current goal is to plot the mass of $deer\_pop$ against time – written formally as:

$$fplot(([T \text{ in } time], [])\#attribute(mass, deer\_pop, T), ([T \text{ in } time], [])\#T)$$

The function $fplot/2$ is defined as returning a list of coordinate pairs. There exists in the system a function, $optimum/1$, which takes as its argument a list of coordinate points and returns a number which is the optimum value of that list of points[1]. It is defined as:

$$def(optimum(C), \ fun([C \ \textbf{in} \ coordinate\_list], [], number)).$$

Using this function definition, we could elaborate our *fplot* goal by inserting it as an argument of *optimum*, thus:

$$optimum(fplot(([T \ \textbf{in} \ time], [])\#attribute(mass, deer\_pop, T), \ ([T \ \textbf{in} \ time], [])\#T))$$

which represents the optimum of a plot of mass of *deer_pop* against time.

Algorithm 38 We write $expand\_goal(Goal) = ExpandedGoal$ to denote that a sorted logic *Goal* has been elaborated to form a new, more complex goal, *ExpandedGoal*, when:

- **IF** $def(Goal, fun(\_, \_, \_ \ \textbf{in} \ ESort)$ (Definition 10) **THEN** :
  - Find the set, *ESet*, of elements E such that $goal\_expansion(Goal, ESort, E)$ **AND**
  - Prompt the user to choose a member, *Goal1*, of *ESet* **AND**
  - $develop\_goal(Goal1) = Goal2$ (Algorithm 37) **AND**
  - $expand\_goal(Goal2) = ExpandedGoal$
- **OTHERWISE** $ExpandedGoal = Goal.$

$goal\_expansion((Ins, Outs)\#Term, \ ESort, \ (NewIns, NewOuts)\#NewTerm)$ is true when:

- $def(NewTerm, fun(Ins1, Outs1, \_))$ **AND**
  1. An element of the form Var in $Sort1$ can be removed from $Ins1$ leaving the remaining elements, R, such that $Sort1 \subseteq Sort$ **AND** $Var = Term$ **AND** $NewIns = R \cup Ins$ **AND** $NewOuts = Outs1 \cup Outs$.
  2. **OR** There is some subterm, T, of $NewTerm$ of the form: $(Ins2, Outs2)\#SubTerm$ for which $Term$ is a valid instantiation of a variable in $Ins2$ according to the procedure given in part 1 (above) giving the new subterm, $T1$, **AND** T is replaced by $T1$ in $NewTerm$ **AND** $NewIns = Ins$ **AND** $NewOuts = Outs$.

---

[1]There are various ways of calculating the optimum value and the user would choose one of these during subsequent model construction.

At this point in the model construction process we have completed our definition of the sets of objects present in the model (Section 8.1.1) and have provided a top–level goal. The final phase of model construction requires the selection of sorted logic axioms capable of solving for this top–level goal. In other words, we have described the output which we want from the model, which in the example above was:

$$optimum(fplot(([T \text{ in } time], [])\#attribute(mass, deer\_pop, T), \ ([T \text{ in } time], [])\#T))$$

and we must now provide clauses which will allow us to obtain this output. In our example, this would require us to obtain axioms for calculating *optimum* and *attribute* (*fplot* being a system function). Normally, there is a choice of which axiom to apply. For example, the optimum of a list of coordinates may be calculated in a number of different ways, one being to take the maximum of the "y" coordinates in the list – formally:

$$([C \text{ in } coordinate\_list], [])\#optimum(C) \Leftarrow maximum(y\_values(C))$$

The task performed in the next phase of model construction is to present these axioms to the user who can then select those appropriate to his/her model.

8.1.3 Constructing a Working Model

Since we want to guarantee that the programs which we construct are runnable, the basic algorithm for constructing the model is identical in most respects to the sorted logic interpreter described in Section 4.4. The idea is that we first try to use the standard interpreter mechanism to satisfy a given goal from the set of sorted logic axioms which define the current model. If no solution can be found using the standard, non–interactive, interpretation mechanism then it is necessary to prompt the user to decide if he/she wants to add further axioms which would enable the goal to be satisfied – thus extending the model. Our first requirement is for a replicate of the standard sorted logic interpreter described in Algorithm 9 of Section 4.4. We shall then add to this basic framework the facility for obtaining extra axioms while running the model.

Algorithm 39 We write $g\_solve(Term, Result)$ to denote that the sorted logic *Term* is interactively solved to obtain its *Result* when :

- $term\_class(primitive, Term)$ THEN $Result = Term$.

- **OTHERWISE IF** $Term = (Obj$ in $Sort)$ **THEN** :
  - **IF** Obj in $Sort$ **THEN** $Obj = Result$.
- **OTHERWISE IF** $Term = (A$ and $B)$ **THEN** :
  - $g\_solve(A, RA)$ **AND**
  - $g\_solve(B, RB)$ **AND**
  - $Result = RA$ $andRB$.
- **OTHERWISE IF** $Term = (A$ or $B)$ **THEN** :
  - $g\_solve(A, RA)$ **AND** $Result = RA$ **OR**
  - $g\_solve(B, RB)$ **AND** $Result = RB$
- **OTHERWISE IF** $Term = [H|T]$ **THEN** :
  - $g\_solve(H, R)$ **AND**
  - $g\_solve(T, Rest)$ **AND**
  - $Result = [R|Rest]$.
- **OTHERWISE IF** $Term = ((Ins, Outs)\#Tm)$ **THEN** :
  - $satisfiable\_constraints(Ins)$ (Algorithm 4) **AND**
  - $g\_solve(Tm, Result)$ **AND**
  - $satisfiable\_constraints(Outs)$.
- **OTHERWISE IF** $g\_meta\_fun(Term, Result, Call)$ **THEN** :
  - $execute\ Call$.
- **OTHERWISE IF** $g\_meta\_pred(Term, Call)$ **THEN** :
  - $execute\ Call$ **AND**
  - $Term = Result$.
- **OTHERWISE IF** $nonvar(Term)$ **THEN** :
  - $standardise\_term(Term, ETerm)$ (Algorithm 10) **AND** :
    * **IF** $term\_class(function, ETerm)$ **THEN** $g\_eval(ETerm, Result)$ (Algorithm 11).
    * **OTHERWISE IF** $term\_class(predicate, ETerm)$ **THEN** $g\_establish(ETerm, Result)$ (Algorithm 12).

The procedure for standardising terms, prior to attempting to satisfy them from the database of axioms, is also similar to the corresponding procedure in the sorted logic interpreter (Algorithm 10).

Algorithm 40 We write $g\_standardise\_term(Term, ETerm)$ to denote that a $Term$ in the sorted logic has been interactively standardised to form the term, $Eterm$, with all its arguments fully evaluated, when:

- $Term$ has functor F and ordered set of arguments $Args$ **AND**

- For each A in $Args$ $g\_solve(A, R)$ (Algorithm 39) and return the values for R in the ordered set $RArgs$.

- $ETerm$ has functor F and set of arguments $RArgs$.

The difference between the model construction and model execution algorithms lies in the procedures used to evaluate functions (Algorithm 41) and establish predicates (Algorithm 42). The strategy used by both these algorithms is similar so we shall give a description of the evaluation procedure in the knowledge that the same general principles are used to establish predicates:

- First try to evaluate the current goal using the non–interactive evaluation algorithm (Algorithm 11). This means that the user will not be prompted for new axioms if the current goal can be already solved from the existing axioms.

- If that fails, then look for any existing sorted logic axiom which would allow the evaluation of the current goal and try to evaluate interactively the body of that axiom. The reason for doing this is that there may exist axioms which would provide a solution to the current goal but these may refer to goals which are not yet solvable. In this case it is preferable to attempt to solve those subgoals before considering adding any new axioms for the current goal.

- If all else fails (*i.e.* there is no way of non–interactively solving for the current goal) then the only recourse is to add a new axiom which solves for this goal. To do this the system looks up a library of sorted logic schemata – axioms which define standard model structures, rather like the Prolog schemata of Section 7.2. These schemata are necessary to represent choices between different implementations of model structure. Consider, for example, a definition of the parameter $carrying\_capacity$. This could be defined simply as a constant value, using the axiom schema:

$$a\_schema(([X \text{ in } population, N \text{ in } number], []) \#$$
$$parameter(carrying\_capacity, X) \Leftarrow N).$$

Alternatively, it might be defined using a more complex function, involving other model variables. For instance, it could be defined as the maximum value of the "x" coordinates at "y" coordinate values of 0 of the plot of reproduction rate against numbers. This would be expressed using the schema:

$$a\_schema(([X \text{ in } population, T \text{ in } time], [])\#$$
$$parameter(carrying\_capacity, X) \Leftarrow$$
$$maximum(x\_values\_at\_y(0,$$
$$fplot(attribute(reproduction\_rate, X, T),$$
$$attribute(numbers, X, T)))))).$$

The system selects one of these schemata which is capable of solving for the current goal and presents it to the user as a statement which he/she might want to make about the model. The user can restrict the range of objects over which this suggested axiom ranges, provided that the sort restrictions are not restricted to a point where they exclude the objects referred to in the current goal (this check ensures that the edited axiom is capable of solving for that goal). The new axiom is then added to the set of axioms describing the model and the body of the new axiom is interactively evaluated by recursively applying the algorithm.

Algorithm 41 We write $g\_eval(Term, Result)$ to denote that a sorted logic function, $Term$, evaluates to produce the value, $Result$, when:

- $eval(Term, Result)$ (Algorithm 11).

- **OTHERWISE :**
    - $(Ins, Outs)\#Term1 \Leftarrow Body$ **AND**
    - $standardise\_term(Term1, Term2)$ (Algorithm 10) **AND**
    - $Term = Term2$ **AND**
    - $satisfiable\_constraints(Ins)$ (Algorithm 4) **AND**
    - $g\_solve(Body, Result)$ (Algorithm 39) **AND**
    - $satisfiable\_constraints(Outs)$.

- **OTHERWISE :**
    - $a\_schema((Ins, Outs)\#Term1 \Leftarrow Body)$ **AND**

 – Make a copy of the term $(Ins, Outs)\#Term1 \Leftarrow Body$, standardising all variables apart, to obtain a copy, $GeneralTerm$ **AND**

 – $g\_standardise\_term(Term1, Term3)$ (Algorithm 40) **AND**

 – $Term = Term3$ **AND**

 – $satisfiable\_constraints(Ins)$ **AND**

 – $edit\_axiom(GeneralTerm, Term1, Term4)$ **AND**

 – Add $Term4$ to the set of sorted logic axioms representing the program.

 – $GeneralTerm = (Ins, Outs)\#Term1 \Leftarrow Body$ **AND**

 – $g\_solve(Body, Result)$ **AND**

 – $satisfiable\_constraints(Outs)$.

Algorithm 42 We write $g\_establish(Term, Result)$ to denote that a sorted logic predicate, $Term$, is interactively established to produce a ground instance, $Result$, when:

- $establish(Term, Result)$ (Algorithm 12).

- **OR** :

 – $(Ins, Outs)\#Term1 \leftarrow Body$ **AND**

 – $standardise\_term(Term1, Term2)$ **AND**

 – $Term = Term2$ **AND**

 – $satisfiable\_constraints(Ins)$ **AND**

 – $g\_solve(Body, \_)$ (Algorithm 39) **AND**

 – $satisfiable\_constraints(Outs)$ **AND**

 – $Result = Term4$.

- **OR** :

 – $a\_schema((Ins, Outs)\#Term1)$ **AND**

 – Make a copy of the term $(Ins, Outs)\#Term1$, standardising all variables apart, to obtain a copy, $GeneralTerm$ **AND**

 – $g\_standardise\_term(Term1, Term3)$ (Algorithm 40) **AND**

 – $Term = Term3$ **AND**

 – $satisfiable\_constraints(Ins)$ **AND**

 – $edit\_axiom(GeneralTerm, Term1, Term4)$ **AND**

- Add *Term4* to the set of sorted logic axioms representing the program.
- $GeneralTerm = (Ins, Outs)\#Term1$ **AND**
- $satisfiable\_constraints(Outs)$ **AND**
- $Result = Term4$.

- **OR :**

  - $a\_schema((Ins, Outs)\#Term1 \leftarrow Body)$ **AND**
  - Make a copy of the term $(Ins, Outs)\#Term1 \leftarrow Body)$, standardising all variables apart, to obtain a copy, *GeneralTerm* **AND**
  - $g\_standardise\_term(Term1, Term3)$ **AND**
  - $Term = Term3$ **AND**
  - $satisfiable\_constraints(Ins)$ **AND**
  - $edit\_axiom(GeneralTerm, Term1, Term4)$ **AND**
  - Add *Term4* to the set of sorted logic axioms representing the program.
  - $GeneralTerm = (Ins, Outs)\#Term1 \Leftarrow Body$ **AND**
  - $g\_solve(Body, \_)$ (Algorithm 39) **AND**
  - $satisfiable\_constraints(Outs)$ **AND**
  - $Result = Term4$.

This completes our definition of the sorted logic model construction phases. To complete the algorithm we simply string these together in sequence.

Algorithm 43 We write $makemodel(Goal, Result)$ to denote that a model has been constructed which solves for a given *Goal* and in the process returns the *Result* of solving the *Goal*, when:

- $develop\_sort(entity)$ (Algorithm 33) **AND**
- $provide\_goal = Goal$ (Algorithm 35) **AND**
- $g\_solve(Goal, Result)$ (Algorithm 39).

8.2 Example of SL at work

Having provided (in Section 8.1) descriptions of the algorithms used to construct the
sorted logic simulation models, we now step through an example of the construction
of a simulation model using these algorithms. To save space, portions of the dialogue
which do not contribute to our explanation of the algorithm have been pruned out.
The model which is finally constructed is the one which we used as an example in
Section 4.5, where we first demonstrated the use of the sorted logic to represent
a complete simulation model. The sorted logic axioms for the model are shown
in Figure 4.3, while the sort hierarchy for the model appears in Figure 4.2. The
example below will show how this model can be constructed using SL.

SL is started via the top–level goal:

$$| \ ?- \ makemodel(G, R).$$

If this goal succeeds, it will bind G to the modelling goal supplied by the user
and R to the output of the model resulting from the evaluation of the goal G,
having introduced into the Prolog database the axioms necessary to perform this
evaluation.

8.2.1 Developing the Sort Hierarchy

The session begins with the development of the sort hierarchy. The system first
introduces the sort which is currently being considered (*entity*) and tells the user
about its immediate subsorts (*attribute_name*, *external_variable_name*, *etc*). It
then asks the user if he/she is interested in talking about *entity* and the user types
"y" to indicate that he/she does. The system then prompts the user to add any
objects to the sort *entity* but the user presses the carriage return key to indicate
that no objects need be added directly to this sort. The system then prompts the
user to indicate which of the displayed subsorts of *entity* he/she wants to explore.
The user types "y" to accept the default set of subsorts (all of them).

```
            Let's talk about things in the sort : entity
            I know about these subsorts of entity
                 attribute_name
                 external_variable_name
                 list
                 location_point
                 number
                 object
                 parameter_name
                 rate_name
                 spatial_area
                 time
            ------------------------------------------------------------
            Are you interested in this kind of thing ?
                 y = yes
                 <cr> = not interested
            INPUT >> y
            Do you want to give some objects in sort : entity ?
                 list of names = objects in this sort
                 <cr> = not interested
            INPUT >> (cr)
            Which subsorts of entity are you interested in ?
                 list of names = subsorts of this sort
                 y = accept default subsorts
                 <cr> = not interested
            INPUT >> y
```

The system then takes the first of the subsorts of *entity*: *attribute_name*. This sort contains no subsorts but has a set of default objects. The reason for supplying these default objects is to give users an indication of the kinds of objects which normally appear at a given point in the sort hierarchy. It also gives users who just want to try out the system an opportunity to avoid having to make up their own object names. The user is asked if he/she wants to assign any of these default objects (or an object of his/her own devising) to the set of attribute names. The user assigns mass to this set.

```
      Let's talk about things in the sort : attribute_name
      The default objects which you might assign to this set are :
          energy
          intrinsic_growth_rate
          length
          mass
          reproduction_rate
          volume
      -------------------------------------------------------------
      Are you interested in this kind of thing ?
          y = yes
          <cr> = not interested
      INPUT >>  y
      Do you want to give some objects in sort : attribute_name ?
          list of names = objects in this sort
          y = accept default objects
          <cr> = not interested
      INPUT >>  mass
```

The system now moves on to another subsort of *entity* – *external_variable_name* – which the user doesn't want to consider (*i.e.* there are no external variable names in the model) so that branch of the sort hierarchy is not explored.

```
      Let's talk about things in the sort : external_variable_name
      The default objects which you might assign to this set are :
          temperature
      -------------------------------------------------------------
      Are you interested in this kind of thing ?
          y = yes
          <cr> = not interested
      INPUT >> ⟨cr⟩
```

The system now moves on to the sort *population*, to which the user assigns 3 objects: *deer_pop*, *young_deer* and *old_deer*.

```
            Let's talk about things in the sort : population
            The default objects which you might assign to this set are :
                wolf_population
                deer_population
            ------------------------------------------------------------
            Are you interested in this kind of thing ?
                y = yes
                <cr> = not interested
            INPUT >>  y
            Do you want to give some objects in sort : population ?
                list of names = objects in this sort
                y = accept default objects
                <cr> = not interested
            INPUT >>  deer_pop young_deer old_deer
```

To the sort *rate_name* the user assigns the objects *growth_rate* and *mortality_rate*.

```
            Let's talk about things in the sort : rate_name
            The default objects which you might assign to this set are :
                growth_rate
                mortality_rate
                birth_rate
            ------------------------------------------------------------
            Are you interested in this kind of thing ?
                y = yes
                <cr> = not interested
            INPUT >>  y
            Do you want to give some objects in sort : rate_name ?
                list of names = objects in this sort
                y = accept default objects
                <cr> = not interested
            INPUT >>  growth_rate mortality_rate
```

The set of valid time points is taken to be the default of the integers from 0 to 5. This means that the set of times over which the simulation may be run will be constrained to these time points. It would be easy for the user to specify a longer time span but this would slow down program construction because (as we discussed at the start of this chapter) the model is being run during the construction session. The assumption is that the structure of the model (*i.e.* the set of sorted logic axioms) which are obtained for times 0 to 5 will be sufficient to run the program over longer time spans.

```
        Let's talk about things in the sort : time
        The default objects which you might assign to this set are :
            0
            1
            2
            3
            4
            5
        You could also decide to talk about these subsorts of time
            initial_time
        ----------------------------------------------------------------
        Are you interested in this kind of thing ?
            y = yes
            <cr> = not interested
        INPUT >> y
        Do you want to give some objects in sort : time ?
            list of names = objects in this sort
            y = accept default objects
            <cr> = not interested
        INPUT >> y
        Which subsorts of time are you interested in ?
            list of names = subsorts of this sort
            y = accept default objects
            <cr> = not interested
        INPUT >> y
```

The initial time is given the default value of 0 because this is the lowest value in the set of times from 0 to 5, which were defined earlier.

```
        Let's talk about things in the sort : initial_time
        The default objects which you might assign to this set are :
            0
        --------------------------------------------------------------
        Are you interested in this kind of thing ?
            y = yes
            <cr> = not interested
        INPUT >> y
        Do you want to give some objects in sort : initial_time ?
            list of names = objects in this sort
            y = accept default objects
            <cr> = not interested
        INPUT >> y
```

The system now prompts the user to supply any subpopulation relations (see

Section 4.5). The user states that the objects *young_deer* and *old_deer* are subpopulations of the object *deer_pop*. This adds to the sort hierarchy the sort relation:

sort_relation(*subpopulation*(*A, deer_pop*), [*A* in [*young_deer, old_deer*]]).

```
          Define any relations of the form :
          for A in population
          for B in population
          A is a subpopulation of B
          ----------------------------------------------------------------
          Restrict A from population to something else ?
               subsort name = new name for this sort
               y = keep existing sort
               <cr> = not interested
          INPUT >>  young_deer old_deer
          ----------------------------------------------------------------
          Restrict B from population to something else ?
               subsort name = new name for this sort
               y = keep existing sort
               <cr> = not interested
          INPUT >>  deer_pop
          Do you want to give another definition ?
               y = yes
               <cr> = not interested
          INPUT >>  <cr>
```

The description of the sort hierarchy is now complete and the system moves on to the specification of a top–level modelling goal.

8.2.2 Specifying Modelling Goals

The phase of specification of a modelling goal commences with the user being shown a menu of possible initial goals. These range from finding the optimum of a list of coordinate pairs to simply finding the value of some attribute in the model. Suppose that the user chooses a plot of an attribute against time. This is formally represented (inside the system) by the sorted logic expression:

$$([A \text{ in } attribute\_name, X \text{ in } object], []) \#$$
$$fplot((([T \text{ in } time], []) \# attribute(A, X, T), ([T \text{ in } time], []) \# T)$$

The system then selects the first sort restricted variable in the input sort list of this expression and prompts the user to restrict the sort of this variable from

attribute_name to something more specific. The user decides to instantiate it to
mass.

```
            The current goal is :
            the plot of : for A in time
                          the B of C at A
                          against A

            Consider the collection of objects : attribute_name
            which is represented by : B
                r = restrict to some smaller sort of objects
                <cr> = leave it as it is
            INPUT >> r
            Restrict attribute_name to :   mass
```

The system then prompts for restriction of the second variable from *object* to
something more specific. The user chooses to instantiate this variable to *deer_pop*.
The current goal expression is now as shown below:

$$fplot((([T \text{ in } time], []) \#attribute(mass, deer\_pop, T), \ ([T \text{ in } time], []) \#T)$$

```
            The current goal is :
            the plot of : for A in time
                          the mass of B at A
                          against A

            Consider the collection of objects : object
            which is represented by : B
                r = restrict to some smaller sort of objects
                <cr> = leave it as it is
            INPUT >> r
            Restrict object to :   deer_pop
```

The system now finds possible elaborations of the current goal by finding all the
defined functions into which it could be substituted as an argument. These are
displayed to the user as a menu of possible goal expansion statements. For example
the function for taking the optimum of a list of coordinate pairs is defined as:

$$def(optimum(C), \ fun([C \text{ in } coordinate\_list], [], number)).$$

Now *fplot*/2 (the current goal function) returns as its result a list of coordinate pairs so a valid elaboration can be obtained by inserting it as an argument to *optimum*/1, thus:

$$optimum(fplot(([T \text{ in } time], [\,])\#attribute(mass, deer\_pop, T),\ ([T \text{ in } time], [\,])\#T))$$

Which means that the user wants to find the optimum value of a plot of mass of *deer_pop* against time. This appears as option 1 in the menu. However, the user refuses to provide further elaboration of his/her goal so the current *fplot* goal remains unchanged. In other words, the user just wants a straightforward plot of results, without the need to obtain the optimum (or similar) from the plot of values.

```
        1 the optimum value of the plot of : for A in time
                    the mass of deer_pop at A
                    against A
        ------------------------------------------------------------
        2 the "x" coordinate values for the plot of : for A in time
                    the mass of deer_pop at A
                    against A
        ------------------------------------------------------------
        3 the "y" coordinate values for the plot of : for A in time
                    the mass of deer_pop at A
                    against A
        ------------------------------------------------------------
        4 for A in number
        the "y" coordinate values for the plot of : for B in time
                    the mass of deer_pop at B
                    against B at "x" value A
        ------------------------------------------------------------
        5 for A in number
        the "x" coordinate values for the plot of : for B in time
                    the mass of deer_pop at B
                    against B at "y" value A

        Choose an expansion or press <return> to continue.
        INPUT >> ⟨cr⟩
```

This completes the goal extraction phase. All that remains is to select the axioms necessary to solve the top–level goal, given the objects and sort hierarchy defined in Section 8.2.1.

8.2.3 Constructing a Working Model

Recall that the top–level goal provided by the user is:

$$fplot((([T \text{ in } time], []) \# attribute(mass, deer\_pop, T),\ ([T \text{ in } time], []) \# T)$$

The function $fplot/2$ is system defined so no axioms are required for it. The system therefore begins with an attempt to find an axiom which will solve for the goal:

$attribute(mass, deer\_pop, 0)$

having instantiated the time argument to 0 as part of its function standardisation algorithm. It first selects an axiom which allows the mass of *deer_pop* to be set to a constant value at this initial time but the user is not satisfied with this definition and rejects it by typing "n".

```
            for A in attribute_name
            for B in object
            for C in initial_time
            for D in number
            the A of B at C
                 is derived from D

            1 D can be anything of sort : number
            2 A can be anything of sort : attribute_name but must include mass
            3 B can be anything of sort : object but must include deer_pop
            4 C can be anything of sort : initial_time but must include 0
            Edit >>  n
```

The system then selects another possible definition which states that the mass of *deer_pop* is derived from the sum of the masses of all subpopulations of *deer_pop*. The user is interested in this definition and begins to edit the axiom by instantiating the *attribute_name* variable to *mass*. This is done by giving the command "r 1" which tells the system to restrict the sort of the variable in menu option 1 to the most specific sort possible, which in this case is the object *mass*.

```
for A in attribute_name
for B in population
for C in time
the A of B at C
    is derived from the sum of the collection of things such that :
        for D such that : D is a subpopulation of B
        the A of D at C can be found

1 A can be anything of sort : attribute_name but must include mass
2 B can be anything of sort : population but must include deer_pop
3 C can be anything of sort : time but must include 0
4 D can be anything of sort : srelation(subpopulation(D,B))
Edit >> r 1
```

The user now restricts the *population* sort to *deer_pop*.

```
for A in population
for B in time
the mass of A at B
    is derived from the sum of the collection of things such that :
        for C such that : C is a subpopulation of A
        the mass of C at B can be found

1 A can be anything of sort : population but must include deer_pop
2 B can be anything of sort : time but must include 0
3 C can be anything of sort : srelation(subpopulation(C,A))
Edit >> r 1
```

At this point, the user is satisfied with the current axiom and doesn't want to impose any further restrictions to the sorts over which it applies. The command "y" is used to confirm that this axiom can be added to the database. The formula added is:

$$([T \text{ in } time], [])\#attribute(mass, deer\_pop, T) \Leftarrow$$
$$sum(bagof((([Y \text{ in } srelation(subpopulation(Y, deer\_pop))], [])\#$$
$$attribute(mass, Y, T))).$$

```
for A in time
the mass of deer_pop at A
    is derived from the sum of the collection of things such that :
        for B such that : B is a subpopulation of deer_pop
        the mass of B at A can be found

1 A can be anything of sort : time but must include 0
2 B can be anything of sort : srelation(subpopulation(B,deer_pop))
Edit >> y
```

The system now attempts to evaluate the body of the axiom which the user introduced and, as part of this process, needs to find the mass of *young_deer* (which is a subpopulation of *deer_pop*). It again suggests that this should be set to some constant value at the initial time and this time the user is interested in the axiom, instantiating the *attribute_name* variable to *mass*.

```
for A in attribute_name
for B in object
for C in initial_time
for D in number
the A of B at C
    is derived from D

1 D can be anything of sort : number
2 A can be anything of sort : attribute_name but must include mass
3 B can be anything of sort : object but must include young_deer
4 C can be anything of sort : initial_time but must include 0
Edit >> r 2
```

After further editing the current axiom is added to the database. Its final form is:

$$([T \text{ in } initial\_time], [])\#attribute(mass, young\_deer, T) \Leftarrow 10.$$

```
        for A in initial_time
        the mass of young_deer at A
              is equal to 10

        1 A can be anything of sort : initial_time but must include 0
        Edit >>  y
```

The system now suggests that the same axiom schema that was used to calculate the initial mass of *young_deer* should be used to calculate the initial mass of
old_deer. The user edits this in a similar manner and adds to the database the
resulting formula :

$$([T \textbf{ in } initial\_time], []) \# attribute(mass, old\_deer, T) \Leftarrow 20.$$

```
        for A in initial_time
        the mass of old_deer at A
              is equal to 20

        1 A can be anything of sort : initial_time but must include 0
        Edit >>  y
```

The system now suggests an axiom which would solve for the mass of *young_deer*
at times other than the initial time. The user is interested in this axiom but not
just for *young_deer* so it is edited to apply to both young and old deer.

```
for A in attribute_name
for B in object
for C in time and not initial_time
the A of B at C
     is derived from
          the A of B at the time previous to C
            plus the sum of the set of things such that : for D in rate_name
                 the D of B at the time previous to C

1 A can be anything of sort : attribute_name but must include mass
2 B can be anything of sort : object but must include young_deer
3 C can be anything of sort : time and inv(initial_time) but must include 1
4 D can be anything of sort : rate_name
Edit >>  r 2 young_deer old_deer
```

After further editing the axiom is in shape and is duly added to the database. The finished version is:

$$([X \text{ in } [young\_deer, old\_deer], T \text{ in } time \text{ and } inv(initial\_time)], [])\#$$
$$attribute(mass, X, T) \Leftarrow$$
$$\qquad attribute(mass, X, previous\_time(T))$$
$$\qquad + sum(bagof(([R \text{ in } rate\_name], [])\#$$
$$\qquad\qquad\qquad rate\_of\_change(R, X, previous\_time(T)))).$$

```
for A in young_deer old_deer
for B in time and not initial_time
the mass of A at B
     is derived from
          the mass of A at the time previous to B
          plus the sum of the set of things such that : for C in rate_name
                 the C of A at the time previous to B

1 A can be anything of sort : [young_deer, old_deer]
     but must include young_deer
2 B can be anything of sort : time and inv(initial_time) but must include 1
3 C can be anything of sort : rate_name
Edit >>  y
```

The next axiom required by the system is one for calculating the previous time point. The user sets the time decrement value of the axiom suggested by the system to 1.

```
            for A in time
            for B in number
            the time previous to A
                 is derived from A minus B

            1 B can be anything of sort : number
            2 A can be anything of sort : time but must include 1
            Edit >>  r 1 1
```

The user then adds this axiom to the database – the final version being:

$$([T \text{ in } time], []) \#previous\_time(T) \Leftarrow T - 1.$$

```
            for A in time
            the time previous to A
                 is derived from A minus 1

            1 A can be anything of sort : time but must include 1
            Edit >>  y
```

The system now suggests an axiom for calculating the rate of growth of *young_deer* as a function of some attribute of it. The user decides to use this axiom for old as well as young deer.

```
            for A in rate_name
            for B in object
            for C in time
            for D in attribute_name
            for E in number
            the A of B at C
                 is derived from E times the D of B at C

            1 E can be anything of sort : number
            2 A can be anything of sort : rate_name but must include growth_rate
            3 B can be anything of sort : object but must include young_deer
            4 C can be anything of sort : time but must include 0
            5 D can be anything of sort : attribute_name but must include mass
            Edit >>  r 3 young_deer old_deer
```

After further editing (for example, editing the value of E to 0.3) the user is satisfied with the current axiom which will calculate the growth rates of old or young deer at any time. The finished axiom is:

$$([X \textbf{ in } [young\_deer, old\_deer], T \textbf{ in } time], [])\#$$
$$rate\_of\_change(growth\_rate, X, T) \Leftarrow$$
$$0.3 * attribute(mass, X, T).$$

```
    for A in young_deer old_deer
    for B in time
    the growth_rate of A at B
        is derived from 0.3 times the mass of A at B

    1 A can be anything of sort : [young_deer, old_deer] but must include young_deer
    2 B can be anything of sort : time but must include 0
    Edit >>  y
```

A similar editing process, using the same schema, is used to define an axiom for determining the mortality rate of old and young deer as a function of their respective masses. The completed axiom is:

$$([X \textbf{ in } [young\_deer, old\_deer], T \textbf{ in } time], [])\#$$
$$rate\_of\_change(mortality\_rate, X, T) \Leftarrow$$
$$-0.2 * attribute(mass, X, T).$$

```
        for A in young_deer old_deer
        for B in time
        the mortality_rate of A at B
            is derived from -0.2 times the mass of A at B

        1 A can be anything of sort : [young_deer and old_deer]
            but must include young_deer
        2 B can be anything of sort : time but must include 0
        Edit >>  y
```

The top–level goal:

| ?− $makemodel(G, R)$.

will now succeed, instantiating G to the user's modelling goal:

$fplot((([T \ \textbf{in} \ time], [\,])\#attribute(mass, deer\_pop, T), ([T \ \textbf{in} \ time], [\,])\#T)$

and instantiating R to the result of evaluating that goal – the list of coordinate pairs in a plot of *mass* of *deer_pop* against time:

$[(0, 30), (1, 32.9999), (2, 36.2999), (3, 39.9299), (4, 43.9229), (5, 48.3151)]$

The final phase of model construction is to produce an automatic translation of the sorted logic program into standard Prolog code, using the Algorithm 13, and to output the two equivalent versions of the simulation model to appropriate files. In this case, the sorted logic program could also have been translated into our imperative language, using Algorithm 15.

8.3 Conclusion

The SL program described in this chapter is an experiment in using the search strategy of the sorted logic interpreter to control dialogue during model construction. This has the advantage of being a straightforward extension to the meta–interpreter which we described in Chapter 4, rather than involving the introduction of complex Prolog schemata (as we did in Chapter 7). We also make use of the representation of nested functions in the sorted logic to provide a mechanism for specification and refinement of modelling goals. However, like the NIPPIE system of Section 7.7, SL's dialogue is constrained by the demands of the meta–interpreter and so does not provide for a high level of initiative on the part of the user. Further work is required to integrate the tightly controlled dialogue used in the SL and NIPPIE systems with the more flexible style of dialogue adopted by the EL system. We shall consider these and other general issues arising from our research in the next (and final) chapter.

9 Conclusions

Throughout most of this book we have concentrated on the technical aspects of using logic–based approaches to the construction of ecological models. In this final chapter we shall take the opportunity to return to the topic of model comprehension and discuss what we consider to be our main contributions in this field (see Section 9.1). It is in the nature of scientific research that progress in one area makes one aware of several new areas which would merit exploration (if only there were enough time). In Section 9.2 we look at some of the directions in which the ideas presented within this book could be developed.

9.1   Contributions of the Eco–Logic Project

The Eco–Logic project is (to our knowledge) the first attempt to explore extensively the use of logic as a tool for improving users' comprehension of simulation models. Our experience in using logic for this purpose has largely been positive and we have been able to represent a wide variety of models using standard techniques, borrowed from the Artificial Intelligence and Logic Programming communities. Indeed, the discipline imposed by the use of logic in our experiments has helped to provide direction to our research among an otherwise confusing variety of modelling systems. A key contribution of our work has been in demonstrating the value of applying techniques from logic to the domain of modelling. However, we have found that in order to apply logic–based techniques to this domain it was necessary to address more fundamental problems associated with model comprehension. The rest of this section summarises what these problems are and how we have tackled them.

9.1.1   Model Description

In Chapter 3 we demonstrate the use of Prolog for representing a variety of simulation models. Its utility as a model representation language is derived from its modularity (which allows us to provide a clear separation between the components of the model) and its declarative interpretation (which allows us to represent the structure of the model without considering how it is to be run). While it is true that Prolog programs can be inefficient to run for some models, this deficiency is compensated by the ease with which it can be used to represent models which would be difficult to describe in conventional imperative languages (see Sections 3.1.2 and 3.1.3 for examples). Furthermore, it is possible to produce augmented forms of the standard Prolog interpreter which reduce the computational overhead for a class of the most inefficient models (see Chapter 5).

Prolog is adequate for our purposes in terms of its generality of notation and its computational efficiency but, in Chapter 4, we identify two areas in which it can be enhanced to fit more closely to the requirements of the ecological modelling domain. These enhancements were a means of representing functions explicitly, rather than treating them as relations, and the ability to restrict the scope of variables over objects defined in a hierarchy of sorts, thus clearly separating the definition of objects in the model from the axioms ranging over these sets of objects. These extensions do not increase the representational capacity of Prolog but are intended to make the notation for describing models more concise and easier to use. By finely tuning the notation to the domain in this way we make it easier to tackle the problem of model comprehension. Note, however, that the enhanced notation does not, in itself, provide a solution to this problem because the potential users of ecological models aren't any more familiar with the new notation than they are with Prolog. This leads us to the requirement for a problem description, which we discuss below.

9.1.2 Problem Description

Even with enhanced notation, such as that described in Chapter 4, there remains a fundamental problem in model comprehension. The structure of the simulation model is normally mathematical, with various equations controlling its dynamic behaviour. By contrast, the concepts familiar to ecologists who might use ecological models are often non–mathematical and/or qualitative. It is therefore unrealistic to expect users to comprehend the model purely at the mathematical level. It is necessary also to provide a formal representation of the problem, viewed from the users' perspective, and to link this to the solution of the problem, expressed as a simulation model.

The task of representing problem descriptions is more difficult than that of representing simulation models because the information used to describe problems is often vague and/or poorly defined. To counter this problem we show (in Chapter 7) how users can be provided with a library of template statements, expressed in a sorted logic, and may edit these to describe a limited range of ecological problems. This provides users with the advantage of being able to state formally key aspects of their problem without having to descend immediately to the details of model structure. The price paid for this advantage is that the domain in which users can describe their problems is limited to that for which template statements are provided.

The practical benefit obtained by using formal problem descriptions is that they can be used to guide the synthesis of simulation models. To provide this guidance it is necessary to provide a formal link between components of the model and statements in the problem description. In the EL and NIPPIE systems (see Chapter 7) this was done by providing a library of standard model structures (schemata) and attaching to each schema a set of preconditions which must hold in the problem description in order for that schema to be applicable to the user's problem. In this way the information supplied by the user about the problem can be used to reduce the search space of possible model structures, making it easier to choose a plausible structure for the model.

9.1.3 Multi-Level Cooperative Dialogue

Much of our work has been in defining appropriate notations in which to represent models and the problems which they are intended to solve. As far as users are concerned, this notation is of no consequence unless it can be used to control a dialogue which they can readily understand. This dialogue must be conducted both at the "high" level of the problem description and at the "low" level of the simulation model. It must also be cooperative, in the sense that neither system nor user should assume full control over the dialogue and the system should be responsive to the requirements of the user. All of the systems described in Chapters 7 to 8 are involved in some form of cooperative dialogue but each employs a different strategy. A major contribution of our research has been in demonstrating how these strategies can be implemented in the domain of simulation modelling. We summarise our results below and refer the reader to [Robertson 90] for a more detailed account.

Perhaps the most obvious way of tackling the problem of integrating high and low level dialogue is to separate the interaction with the user into two distinct phases: the first phase covering the high level dialogue and the second phase taking care of the residual low level details. In this scheme, the information obtained in the high level phase provides a way of constraining the scope of the dialogue in the low level phase, thus making it possible for users to cope with the (otherwise overwhelming) low level details. This is the architecture used in the EL system (see Chapter 7). A clear separation between high and low level dialogue can be convenient because it allows different forms of inference mechanism to be employed in each phase without fear of conflict between the mechanisms. However, it also poses problems because users often want to interpose sections of low level information within a high level dialogue. Furthermore, it provides no route by which low level information may influence the collection of high level information, since all high level information is assumed to have been provided before the low level dialogue begins. This can result in the high level dialogue providing insufficient information on which to base the low level dialogue required for model generation. We experimented with two methods of countering this problem.

The first method involved retaining the existing EL architecture and representing some of the modelling information within the problem description. This allowed users to describe general properties of their models (such as whether spatial representation was to be implemented using grid squares or coordinate points, *etc*) prior to the phase of low level dialogue. In EL, this could only be a partial solution to the general problem because some of the low level information remained within the schemata which were used to generate the final simulation program.

Our second, more radical approach, was to drive all dialogue (including high level dialogue) from the requirements of the schema application mechanism. This approach is used in the HIPPIE and NIPPIE systems (Chapter 7.7) and a related technique is employed in the SL system (Chapter 8). The NIPPIE program uses the basic low level schema application mechanism from EL to control dialogue at both high and low levels. This basic mechanism does not, itself, require much alteration. The key difference between EL's schema application mechanism and NIPPIE's version is that in EL the information needed to apply each schema is assumed to have already been supplied from earlier high level dialogue. In NIPPIE this assumption is relaxed and techniques are provided for establishing information needed at the low level by resuming dialogue at the high level. Therefore, in NIPPIE high level dialogue is constrained by the requirements of the application and so the problem of mismatch between high and low level dialogue is solved. However, this new approach brings it own problems. In particular, it has been necessary to add extra facilities for ensuring that the low level requirements of the schema application mechanism are translated into a coherent high level dialogue.

9.1.4 Providing Explanations

Explanations in the domain of simulation modelling can be important, both during model construction (to help users understand how the model is being constructed) and afterwards (to allow the sequence of model development to be reconstructed). It is important that explanations of model structure should be linked not only to the structure of the model itself but also to the features of a user's problem which indicated that a particular model structure should be used.

Our contribution in this area has centred around the EL system. EL's schema application mechanism provides a good foundation for providing explanations of model structure because the nested application of schemata gives a way of decomposing the completed program into a number of subcomponents. The schema which was applied in order to introduce each subcomponent will also have referenced information in the problem description. This provides a link between each subcomponent and the aspects of the problem description which were instrumental in including it in the model. In Section 7.5 we describe a mechanism which allows the tree of schema applications to be reconstructed for any program constructed using EL. This tree provides a structure through which users may browse, examining at any point the code contributed by the appropriate schema and/or the conditions in the problem description which led that schema to be used.

9.1.5 Idealisation

Whenever ecological modellers construct simulation programs they must examine complex real–world problems; extract from them the key principles on which they seem to operate; and represent these in a computationally tractable form in their simulation models. We refer to this process as idealisation. Consider, for example, the problem of representing an animal population, which we shall call '*pop*'. The discussions of previous chapters have shown several possible ways of idealising this population and we recap on a few of these below:

- The most straightforward way is simply to state that '*pop*' is a subsort of '*population*' and then enumerate the objects which it contains (as described in Sections 4.1.2 and 4.1.3). Formally, we could write:

  $pop \subseteq population \ \& \ a_1 \in pop \ \& \cdots \& \ a_N \in pop$

  where a_1 to a_N are the names of individual animals in '*pop*'.

- Complications arise when '*pop*' is considered to have substructure. This may be incorporated into the model in several ways, two of which are described below:

  - If '*pop*' divides into subgroups then it is possible to represent these as subsorts. For instance, we might have '*old*', '*mature*' and '*young*' as subgroups:

    $old \subseteq pop \ \& \ mature \subseteq pop \ \& \ young \subseteq pop$

    This type of representation is discussed in Section 4.1.3 and used in Section 7.4.

  - Membership of objects in some subsorts of '*pop*' may be contingent on the existence of objects within other sorts. For example, we might have a sort named '*new_born*' which contains an object, $n\_b(X)$, for each object, X, existing in the sort, '*mature*'. Formally, we express this as:

$$pop \supseteq \{n\_b(X) \mid X \in mature\}$$

This method of allocating objects to sorts is described in Section 4.1.4 and used in Section 8.2.

- Sometimes '*pop*' may, for all practical purposes, be considered to act as if it were a single entity. In these circumstances it may be appropriate to represent it in the model as a single object of sort '*population*':

$$pop \in population$$

The decision to simplify a population by representing it as a single object is illustrated in Sections 7.4 and 8.2.

The examples given above illustrate the wide range of formal representations which may be obtained when idealising a single component of an ecological problem (in this case a population). The representations which we have described are not always alternatives but may sometimes be combined to produce complex descriptions (for example, the use of subsort relations and complex objects is combined in Section 8.2). This variety of choices, coupled with the dearth of explicit knowledge about how modellers perform the task of idealisation, makes it hard to provide guidance to users as they apply their knowledge of how an ecological system works to obtain a simulation model. We have experimented with some partial solutions to this problem:

- We have attempted to make the statements describing the model match as closely as possible to the form in which users might be expected to state the information. This is the primary motivation for using the sorted logic, which is designed to provide a "natural" way of representing common types of ecological statement. Of course, there is a tension between the demands on the notation to be easily understood by users, versus the requirement for representational power and computational efficiency. For this reason, it is unrealistic to expect the notation to be used directly by users – hence the need for interface packages, such as those described in Chapters 7 and 8.

- Within these interface packages it is insufficient simply to provide a passive interface to a standard notation and leave the user to get on with the task of model construction. Users need advice about how to use the notation in appropriate ways. Taking the EL system (Chapter 7) as an example, this advice is available at several stages:

— During the the initial problem description phase, an abduction mechanism is employed to provide users with suggestions of new statements which they might wish to make (Sections 7.3.1 and 7.4.1).

— Between the phase of problem description and model construction, EL checks that the sort hierarchy is specified in sufficient detail to support subsequent construction of the model. Where necessary, it prompts users for further subsorts and objects (Sections 7.3.2 and 7.4.2).

— Information from the problem description is used to reduce the range of schemata which are presented to the user as alternatives for incorporating components into the completed model (Sections 7.3.4 and 7.4.4).

Although they provide a considerable amount of guidance during model construction, our experimental systems do not provide all the guidance which is necessary. As a general rule, users should be able to obtain advice on which choice to make whenever they are presented with a set of alternatives by the program construction system. All of our systems provide such advice only in limited form. For example, the schema application mechanism in EL presents a choice of schemata to the user but offers no advice about which of the schemata might be the most appropriate to choose; nor does it supply advice about appropriate values or units of measurement for variables. Research continues into providing enhancements to the guidance provided by our systems while maintaining the logic–based approach to model construction.

9.2 Future Directions of Research

Our ultimate goal is to make the arguments embodied in simulation models accessible to people who must use the models to make decisions. To achieve this goal, it is necessary to solve some challenging problems which occur in a number of different (but related) areas of research. The areas which seem, to us, to be most relevant are summarised in Figure 9.1.

There is a natural tendency to hone the language which is being used to represent a model – customising it to the requirements of the task for which it is to be used. This is represented by our first entry in Figure 9.1, depicting the transition from standard logic programming languages to special purpose logic programming languages for simulation. A key problem in providing these enhanced languages is that of providing interfaces which allow them to be understood readily by users. Along with the interest in "designer logics" for simulation comes the desire to

Current technology		Required technology
Standard L.P. languages	$\Longrightarrow$	Special purpose L.P. languages
Standard L.P. interpreters	$\Longrightarrow$	Efficient L.P. simulation interpreters
Partially represented domain	$\Longrightarrow$	Comprehensive domain representation
Weak links problem to model	$\Longrightarrow$	Deep representation of idealisation
Restrictive interfaces	$\Longrightarrow$	Flexible, user–friendly interfaces

Figure 9.1
Major avenues of research

develop more efficient forms of inference which take advantage of special features of the new notation. Standard logic programming techniques remain inefficient for some modelling tasks and improvements in run times may be produced either by improved interpreters or through translation to more efficient implementation languages.

The third avenue of research concerns the completeness of problem descriptions – a topic which is discussed in Section 6.8. The problem descriptions which we provided for the EL and NIPPIE systems (Chapter 7) are designed to support the use of the limited range of program schemata which are available to each system. If we were to extend the range of schemata then it is likely that the range of elements of the problem description would also have to increase. The problem is then how to ensure the ecological validity of the problem description – to detect which concepts are key to the operation of the domain and which are peripheral. Such decisions rely on a depth of formal analysis of the domain which, for ecology, is lacking. Progress in this direction depends primarily on efforts from within the domain and, in ecology, the beginnings of such work are starting to emerge.

Assuming that formal notations can be found for simulation models and problem descriptions, this takes us to the fourth topic in Figure 9.1 – being able to link a simulation model to the problem description. In the EL and NIPPIE systems this link is made through preconditions attached to program schemata. Clearly, this is an incomplete model of how users' perceptions of real world problems are refined and simplified to produce a simulation model. We refer to this process as idealisation and must acknowledge that our systems provide no deep insight into how it takes place. The process of refinement of the problem description, culminating in selection of model schemata through preconditions, provides only a superficial description of idealisation. New insights are required into the deeper mechanisms which allow human modelling experts to take idealisation decisions.

Our final direction for research is the requirement for user interfaces which are capable of supporting the manipulation of expressive model and problem specification languages. This aspect of system construction is often overlooked but is an essential requirement. As new techniques and interface paradigms become available, these may provide better ways of representing model specifications. For example, the availability of window management systems with associated graphics facilities, provided us with opportunities to develop more flexible dialogue mechanisms in the EL and NIPPIE systems. More fundamentally, there is a need to explore more fully the use of general strategies for conducting coherent, cooperative dialogue during the construction and analysis of models. The systems described in this book have made some progress in this respect but much work remains to be done in developing a theoretical basis for conducting cooperative dialogue.

9.3   Concluding Remarks

This book presents the results of experiments in the application of logic–based techniques to the problem of improving users' comprehension of ecological models. This is a task fraught with difficulty because the problem of model comprehension encompasses numerous sub-problems which cut across many different areas of research. We believe that further progress in improving model comprehension will be best achieved by promoting collaboration between researchers in simulation, software engineering, logic programming and artificial intelligence, and that this research must be motivated by the demands of a non–trivial domain of application. We have described what seem to us to be the most important and interesting areas of research and have demonstrated the progress which we have made in these areas. In doing this, we hope to have kindled in the reader an interest in pursuing the topic further.

The thread which we have used to weave together our research has been the use of techniques from logic: to provide notations in which to represent models; to describe the contextual information which supports model construction; and to supply general purpose inference mechanisms which can be used to aid model comprehension. It seems to us that the use of a well understood, soundly based knowledge representation scheme is particularly important as a means of ensuring that our model comprehension systems are, themselves, comprehensible to others.

Our motivation for this research is the concern that simulation models, if they are not open to inspection by their users, may be used incorrectly or, worse, employed to justify false claims and erroneous courses of action. This is properly the concern not only of the user community but also of simulation modellers, who should welcome the notion of tools which would make it easier to exercise their intellectual skills and for others to appreciate the results of their work. Society is already influenced in fundamental ways by the use of simulation models and if we are to place our trust in these models we should be informed of the basis on which our reliance is founded. To do this, we must understand in more detail how models and modellers work.

Bibliography

[Abel 90]   D.E. Abel. Application of a formal specification language to animal ecology.
                            1. environment. *Ecological Modelling*, 50:205–212, 1990.

[Aytac & Oren 86]   Z.K. Aytac and T.I. Oren. Magest: a model-based advisor and certifier for
                            gest programs. In M. Elzas, T. Oren, and B. Zeigler, editors, *Modelling and
                            Simulation Methodology in the Artificial Intelligence Era*, pages 299–307, Elsevier
                            Science Publishers, 1986.

[Barstow 88]   D. Barstow. Artificial intelligence and software engineering. In H. E.
                            Shrobe, editor, *Exploring Artificial Intelligence: Survey Talks from the National
                            Conferences on Artificial Intelligence*, pages 641–671, 1988.

[Bundy & Uschold 89] A. Bundy and M.. Uschold. *The Use of Typed Lambda Calculus for Requirements
                            Capture in the Domain of Ecological Modelling*. Research Paper 446, Dept. of
                            Artificial Intelligence, Edinburgh, 1989. To appear in journal of Logic and
                            Computation.

[Bundy 84]   A. Bundy. Intelligent front ends. In J. Fox, editor, *State of the Art Report on
                            Expert Systems*, pages 15–24, Pergamon Infotech, 1984. also in proceedings
                            of British Computer Society Specialist Group on Expert Systems 1984 and
                            available from Edinburgh as DAI Research Paper 227.

[Bundy 87]   A. Bundy. How to improve the reliability of expert systems. In S. Moralee,
                            editor, *Research and Development in Expert Systems IV*, pages 3–17, British
                            Computer Society Specialist Group on Expert Systems, Cambridge Uni-
                            versity Press, 1987. Also available from Edinburgh as Research Paper No.
                            336.

[Bundy *et al* 79]   A. Bundy, L. Byrd, G. Luger, C. Mellish, R. Milne, and M. Palmer. Solving
                            mechanics problems using meta-level inference. In B.G. Buchanan, editor,
                            Proceedings of IJCAI-79, pages 1017–1027, International Joint Conference on
                            Artificial Intelligence, 1979. Reprinted in 'Expert Systems in the microelec-
                            tronic age' ed. Michie, D., Edinburgh University Press, 1979. Also available
                            from Edinburgh as DAI Research Paper No. 112.

[Cleary 89]   J.G. Cleary. *Colliding Pucks Solved Using a Temporal Logic*. Research Re-
                            port 89/358/20, Department of Computer Science, University of Calgary,
                            1989.

[Clocksin & Mellish 84] W.F. Clocksin and C.S. Mellish. *Programming in Prolog*. Springer-Verlag,
                            1984.

[Cohn 89]   A.G. Cohn. Taxonomic reasoning with many-sorted logics. *Artificial Intelli-
                            gence Review*, 3(2):89–129, 1989.

[Cox & Pietrzykowski 86] P.T. Cox and T. Pietrzykowski. Causes for events: their computa-
                            tion and applications. In J. Siekmann, editor, *Lecture Notes in Computer
                            Science: Proceedings of the 8th International Conference on Automated Deduction*,
                            pages 608–621, Springer-Verlag, 1986.

[Forrester 61]   J. W. Forrester. *Industrial Dynamics*. MIT Press, 1961.

[Futo & Gergely 86]   I. Futo and T. Gergely. Problems and advantages of simulation in pro-
                       log. In M. Elzas, T. Oren, and B. Zeigler, editors, *Modelling and Simulation
                       Methodology in the Artificial Intelligence Era*, pages 385–397, Elsevier Science
                       Publishers, 1986.

[Haggith 90]   M. Haggith. Interactive program construction. In S.L.H. Clarke, editor,
                       Proceedings of UK IT 90, pages 227–33, Brighton, England, 1990.

[Jackson 86]   P. Jackson. *Introduction to Expert Systems*. Addison-Wesley, 1986.

[Koshnevis & Austin 87] B. Koshnevis and W.M. Austin. An intelligent interface for system
                       dynamics modelling. In P.A. Luker and G. Birtwistle, editors, *Proceedings
                       of the Conference on AI and Simulation*, pages 81–86, Society for Computer
                       Simulation, San Diego, California, January 1987.

[Krebs 78]   C.J. Krebs. *Ecology: the Experimental Analysis of Distribution and Abundance*.
                       Harper and Row, 1978.

[Lewis 86]   J. Lewis. Stella: a model of its kind. *Practical Computing*, 66–67, September
                       1986.

[Marples 74]   D. Marples. *Argument and technique in the solution of problems in Mechanics and
                       Electricity*. CUED/C-Educ/TRI, Dept. of Engineering, Cambridge, Eng-
                       land, 1974.

[Mostow & Cohen 85]   J. Mostow and D. Cohen. Automating program speedup by deciding what
                       to cache. In *Proceedings of the ninth IJCAI*, pages 165–172, International Joint
                       Conference on Artificial Intelligence, Los Angeles, California, 1985.

[Muetzelfeldt *et al* 88] R. Muetzelfeldt, D. Robertson, A. Bundy, and M. Uschold. The use of
                       prolog for improving the rigour and accessability of ecological modelling.
                       Ecological Modelling, 1988.

[Niven 82]   B.S. Niven. Formalisation of the basic concepts of animal ecology. *Erktennis*,
                       17:307–320, 1982.

[Owen 87]   S. Owen. *The Development of Explicit Interpreters and Transformers to Control
                       Reasoning about Protein Topology*. Technical Report HPL-ISC-TM-88-015,
                       Hewlett Packard Laboratories, 1987.

[Pave & Rechenmann 85] A. Pave and F. Rechenmann. Computer-aided modelling in biology:
                       an artificial intelligence approach. In E.J.H. Kerchoffs, G.C. Vansteenkiste,
                       and B. Zeigler, editors, *Working Conference on Artificial Intelligence in Simula-
                       tion*, pages 52–66, Society for Computer Simulation, University of Ghent,
                       Belgium, February 1985.

[Prieditis & Mostow 87] A.E. Prieditis and J. Mostow. Prolearn: towards a prolog interpreter
                       that learns. In *Proceedings of the Sixth National Conference on Artificial In-
                       telligence*, pages 494–498, American Association for Artificial Intelligence,
                       Seattle, Washington, 1987.

[Radiya & Sargent 87] A. Radiya and R.G. Sargent. Logic programming and discrete event simu-
                       lation. In P.A. Luker and G. Birtwistle, editors, *Proceedings of the Conference
                       on AI and Simulation*, pages 64–71, Society for Computer Simulation, San
                       Diego, California, January 1987.

[Robertson 88]   D. Robertson. *An Experiment in Increasing the Execution Speed of Prolog Simulation Programs Using Meta-Interpreters.* Technical Report 2, Department of Artificial Intelligence, University of Edinburgh, 1988.

[Robertson 90]   D. Robertson. Multi-level cooperative dialogue in intelligent front ends. *Journal of Artificial Intelligence in Engineering,* (special issue on Intelligent Front Ends), 1990. (in press).

[Robertson *et al* 85]   D. Robertson, R. Muetzelfeldt, D. Plummer, M. Uschold, and A Bundy. The eco browser. In *Expert Systems 85,* pages 143–156, British Computer Society Specialist Group on Expert Systems, Coventry, England, 1985.

[Robertson *et al* 88]   D. Robertson, M. Uschold, A. Bundy, and R. Muetzelfeldt. The eco program construction system: ways of increasing its representational power and their effects on the user interface. *International Journal of Man Machine Studies,* 31:1–26, 1988.

[Sterling & Shapiro 85] L. Sterling and E. Shapiro. *The Art of Prolog.* MIT Press, 1985.

[Ulgen & Thomasma 89] O.M. Ulgen and T. Thomasma. Computer simulation modelling in the hands of decision-makers. In W. Webster, editor, *Proceedings of Society for Computer Simulation Western Multiconference,* pages 89–95, Society for Computer Simulation, San Diego, California, January 1989.

[Uschold 90]   M. Uschold. *The Use of Types Lambda Calculus for Comprehension and Construction of Simulation Models in the Domain of Ecology.* Unpublished PhD thesis, Department of Artificial Intelligence, University of Edinburgh, submitted 1990.

[Uschold *et al* 86]   M. Uschold, N. Harding, R. Muetzelfeldt, and A. Bundy. An intelligent front end for ecological modelling. In T. O'Shea, editor, *Advances in Artificial Intelligence,* Elsevier Science Publishers, 1986. Also in Proceedings of ECAI-84, and available from Edinburgh University as Research Paper 223.

[Walther 85]   C. Walther. *A Classification of Many-Sorted Unification Problems.* Technical Report, Institut fur Informatik, Karlsruhe University, W. Germany, 1985.

[Zajicek 86]   W.A. Zajicek. Transforming a discrete-event system into a logic programming formalism. In M. Elzas, T. Oren, and B. Zeigler, editors, *Modelling and Simulation Methodology in the Artificial Intelligence Era,* pages 181–192, Elsevier Science Publishers, 1986.

[Zeigler 84]   B.P. Zeigler. *Multifaceted Modelling and Discrete Event Simulation.* Acedemic Press, 1984.

A Glossary of Terms

Throughout the book it has been necessary to introduce terminology which readers may find unfamiliar. A glossary of some of the more esoteric terms appears below:

Abduction : A non–standard rule of inference which, given a statement that "A implies B" and the knowledge that B is true, allows the suggestion that A has caused B and therefore A might also be true. Note that this form of inference isn't logically sound because the fact that B is true and that A implies B doesn't require A always to be true – B could be true for some other reason.

Antecedent : The term represented by A in a statement of the form "A implies B".

Argument : The terms used in Prolog always have a functor which applies to zero or more arguments. For example, the term $father(fred)$ has the functor, $father$, and the argument, $fred$.

Atom : Atoms are primitive constants within a Prolog program. They are normally represented by lower case words or by a sequence of symbols within single quotes. Thus, $fred$ is an atom and '$Joe\ Bloggs$' is also an atom. However, Joe is not an atom and neither is $father(fred)$ (see definitions of variable and ground term below).

Axiom : A logical formula assumed to be true without proof.

Branching rate : In a search tree, a measure of the number of subnodes which are connected as immediate descendants of parent nodes in the tree. Thus, if the search tree in question has 2 subnodes appearing from each parent node the branching rate is 2. In trees where there are varying numbers of subnodes from different parents it is common to express an average branching rate, which gives a guide to the "bushiness" of the tree.

Browser : A piece of software which is used to allow users to scan through a database of information, looking for the information which interests them. Many browsers rely on the provision of some tree or network through which users can "move" with the assistance of the browser package.

Clause : The basic building block of Prolog programs. The set of clauses which comprise a program are used by the Prolog interpreter to answer queries supplied by the user.

Conjunction : A statement that two or more propositions are both true. For example, one might write $big(X)$ & $bad(X)$ to denote the conjunction of the statements $big(X)$ and $bad(X)$. In English this would be interpreted as "X is big and bad." A variety of operators are used to represent conjunctions between statements. The symbol '&' is common in logic texts. In Prolog, a comma is used to separate the elements of a conjunction in the body of a clause. We have also used the word 'and' to stand for conjunction in the rule definitions of later chapters.

Consequent :The term represented by B in a statement of the form "A implies B".

Cut : A special symbol (normally written as an exclamation mark) which is used in Prolog programs to tell the interpreter when it should commit to a particular clause as a means of satisfying some goal. Cuts are a procedural device which exist to control the execution of the program and are therefore unpopular with "pure" logic programmers who wish to retain the declarative interpretation of their programs. Nevertheless, they appear frequently within Prolog applications.

Deduction : The process of establishing, from some set of assumptions, logically sound conclusions. The application of the rule of *modus ponens*, which allows us to conclude B given the information that A is true and that A implies B, is an example of deductive inference. Abduction is an example of non–deductive inference (see above).

Declarative : A program is called "declarative" if it has a meaning independent of how it behaves when executed. In particular, a logic program is declarative because its clauses can be interpreted as assertions in a logical theory.

Depth–first search : A search strategy which involves exploring to their furthest extent the parts of the search tree which are first encountered. In Prolog, this occurs because the interpreter (in trying to solve for some goal) will try every way to obtain a solution using the first clause for that goal before it moves on to consider other clauses.

Disjunction : A statement that one of a number of different propositions may be true. For example, one might write $big(X)$ *or* $bad(X)$ to denote the disjunction of the statements $big(X)$ and $bad(X)$. In English this would be interpreted as "X is either big or bad." A variety of operators are used to represent disjunctions between statements. We use the word '*or*' to stand for disjunction in the rule definitions of later chapters. In Prolog, a semicolon is used to separate the elements of a disjunction in the body of a clause.

Existential quantification : Used when we want to say that there exists at least one object with some property. In standard first order predicate logic this is usually written using an expression such as: $\exists X\ p(X)$, which is interpreted as "There exists some X such that $p(X)$ is true". In some of the sorted logic definitions of Chapters 6 and 7 we used the notation, X **exist** S, to denote that there is some instance of an object, X, of sort, S.

Function : Generally speaking, an expression which evaluates to some value. We use the term in a more restricted sense to denote an expression which evaluates to a single value. Thus the expression $2 + 3$ is a function which evaluates to the value, 5.

Goal : A relation which the Prolog interpreter must attempt to establish from the set of clauses comprising the program. Goals can arise either as queries provided by the user to the Prolog interpreter or may be generated as subgoals for a clause during the execution of the program.

Ground term : A Prolog term in which all its arguments are either atoms or numbers. For example, $father(fred, joe)$ is a ground term but $father(fred, X)$ isn't ground because it contains a variable (X).

Imperative program : A term used to refer to programs constructed solely with the intention of executing instructions to the computer in a pre–specified sequence. This compares to the logic programming approach in which it is possible to define a program without prior consideration of precisely how it will be run. The distinction between imperative and logic programs can become blurred because of the use of non–declarative features, such as cut, in logic programming languages.

Implication : By saying "A implies B" we mean that if A is true then B must also be true. This is often written more formally as the expression, $A \rightarrow B$, or sometimes with the implication arrow pointing in the other direction to obtain $B \leftarrow A$.

Instantiation : The act of binding a variable to some other term. This takes place during unification. For example, in the term $father(fred, X)$ it is possible to instantiate the variable, X, to the term joe, thus obtaining the term $father(fred, joe)$.

Interpreter : A program used for executing other programs. In our particular case this normally refers to the mechanism used in Prolog to establish a given query from a set of clauses.

Lemma : A result obtained during an intermediate stage in a proof or, in our case, the execution of a logic program.

Meta–interpreter : A program written in Prolog which interprets Prolog programs. This makes it possible to represent in Prolog the search strategy used by the Prolog interpreter and to adapt that search strategy in various ways, which are often different from the standard interpreter.

Meta–predicate : A Prolog predicate which treats other Prolog predicates as objects. For example, the standard built–in predicate, $var(X)$, succeeds if X is a Prolog variable. It is classed as a meta–predicate because it denotes a property of an object level term.

Predicate : A relation between objects which is defined by the clauses of a Prolog program.

Query : A goal which the user supplies to the Prolog system and which is established by the Prolog interpreter from the set of clauses constituting the Prolog program. A query which cannot be established by the interpreter is said to have "failed".

Recursion : Occurs when the Prolog interpreter, in attempting to establish a given predicate, generates a subgoal involving the same predicate.

Relation : A definition of some relationship between objects. For example the term $father(X,Y)$ might be used to denote the relationship of fatherhood between X and Y.

Run time : The time taken to run a program or, in Prolog terms, to answer some query. Sometimes referred to as execution time.

Search tree : The execution of a Prolog program is often represented as the construction of a tree which records the search performed in order to solve some initial Prolog goal. Each point (node) in the tree represents a goal which the Prolog interpreter attempted to establish and branches (arcs) in the tree connect "parent" goals to subgoals which were necessary in order to achieve the appropriate parent goal. This notion is used widely as a means of describing a variety of search problems, not just those of the Prolog interpreter.

Search space : A way of referring to the amount of search which has to be performed by the Prolog interpreter (or other search algorithm) in order to achieve some task. The idea is that one can think of the search tree as occupying some imaginary space. Search is then viewed as an exploration of this space. If the tree grows large then so does the search space. The search spaces of non–terminating programs are usually considered to be infinite.

Topological sort : We use this term to refer to the process of sorting a set of equations into an ordered set with each equation preceding any other equations which rely on it for input values.

Unification : The means by which it is decided whether two terms may be instantiated to identical terms. We restrict our discussion to the use of Prolog unification, which allows us to decide whether any two terms can be matched together by binding variables in either (or both terms). For example, the term produced by unifying $father(fred,Y)$ with $father(X,joe)$ is: $father(fred,joe)$.

Universal quantification : Used when we want to say that all objects have some property. In standard first order predicate logic this is usually written using an expression such as: $\forall X\ p(X)$, which is interpreted as "For all X $p(X)$ is true". In some of the sorted logic definitions of Chapters 6 and 7 we shall use the notation, X in S, to refer to any object, X, of sort, S.

Variable : A symbol which may be bound to any other term (including another variable). This binding process is often referred to as instantiation. In this book, variables are always represented by words beginning with a capital letter. Thus, X and $Fred$ are both variables.

B Summary of Models

A variety of models are used throughout the text. The core of the book is built around a standard example of a simple deer population model but other models are used to illustrate particular points. To help the reader keep track of these models we include below a table which gives the location and summarises the purpose of each model.

Model	Location	Purpose
Height growth	Chapter 1	Simple introduction to notion of model as argument.
Rabbit population	Section 2.3	Simple example of the process of idealisation.
Rabbit–grass energy flow	Section 3.1.1	System Dynamics example
Structural growth	Figure 3.3	A simple example of simulation driven by the manipulation of data structures.
State transition	Figure 3.5	Simulation represented as state space search.
Deer population model	Figure 3.7	(1) A more complex imperative model of population growth with substructure.
	Figure 3.8	(2) A Prolog implementation of version 1. Used for meta–interpreter experiments of Chapter 5
	Section 4.5	(3) A sorted logic implementation of version 2. Used for meta–interpreter experiments of Chapter 5
	Figure 4.4	(4) A translation into Prolog of version 3. Used for meta–interpreter experiments of Chapter 5
	Figure 5.9	(5) A translation of version 3 into an imperative language.
Spatial competition	Appendix C.5	A more complex model. Used in Chapter 7 as an example of model construction using the EL program.

C Ancillary Definitions

In this appendix we provide definitions of ancillary information referred to in other parts of the book.

C.1 Utility Predicates

We provide descriptions of Prolog predicates which are used to form the definitions of the main text but which do not, in themselves, merit detailed scrutiny. For convenience, these are divided into three sub–sections: those used for general "chores" during program description ; those used in the meta–interpreter descriptions of Chapter 5 ; and those used specifically as part of the Prolog schemata definitions of Section 7.2.

C.1.1 General Utilities

This section contains short descriptions of general utility predicates used throughout the text. More detailed descriptions of most of these can be obtained from standard Prolog text books and/or programming manuals.

- $append(L1, L2, L3)$ joins list $L1$ to list $L2$ to form the concatenation of the two lists, $L3$.

- $bagof(X, Call, List)$ returns the $List$ of all instances of X such that $Call$ succeeds. Fails if there are no successful calls. $List$ may contain duplicate elements. Hard core Prolog hackers might like to note that we have assumed that $bagof$ will return the exhaustive list of instances for all free variables in $Call$. In standard implementations of $bagof$ this normally can only be achieved by using the "hat" symbol to flag the appropriate variables but we assume that all variables are "hatted" in this way (e.g. $bagof(X, foo(A, X), L)$ is identical to $bagof(X, A\hat{}foo(A, X), L)$).

- $clause(Head, Body)$ searches the Prolog program for a clause whose head and body unify with $Head$ and $Body$, respectively. If the clause is a fact (i.e. it has no preconditions in its body) then $Body$ is unified with the atom 'true'.

- $direct\_distance(X1, Y1, X2, Y2, N)$ returns as a value for N the direct distance between coordinate points $(X1, Y1)$ and $(X2, Y2)$.

- $for\_each(Item, List, Call, Result, ResultList)$ applies $Call$ to each $Item$ in $List$, storing the $Result$ of each $Call$ in $ResultList$.

- $integer(X)$ tests that X is an integer.

- $length(List, Number)$ returns the $Number$ of elements in a given $List$.

- $member(Element, List)$ succeeds if $Element$ is a member of $List$.

- $nonvar(X)$ succeeds if X is not a Prolog variable.

- $random\_float(Label, Number)$ generates a random floating point $Number$ between 0 and 1. $Label$ is used as a flag to prevent different random numbers being generated if a random value for the same term is accessed more than once during a run of the program.

- $random\_select\_member(Label, Item, List)$ selects an $Item$ at random from a $List$. The purpose of $Label$ is as given above.

- $setof(X, Call, Set)$ is similar to $bagof/3$ but finds the Set of elements, X, such that $Call$ is successful. Fails if there are no successful calls.

- $setof\_or\_empty(X, Call, Set)$ is like $setof/3$ but returns an empty Set if there are no successful calls.

- *sum_elements*(*List*, *Sum*) returns the *Sum* of a *List* of numbers.
- *var*(*X*) tests that *X* is a Prolog variable.

C.1.2   Meta–Interpreter Utilities

- *add_lemma*(*Goal*) adds the assertion *lemma*(*Goal*) to the Prolog database if it hasn't been added already.
- *blank_term*(*Term*, *Blank*) produces a term, *Blank* with the same functor and arity as *Term* but with all its arguments as variables.
- *direct_call*(*Term*) succeeds if *Term* is a Prolog predicate which is implemented using compiled procedures which can't be referenced by meta–interpretation mechanisms.

C.1.3   Schemata Preconditions and Actions

We list below several utility procedures used as part of the definitions of Prolog schemata in Section 7.2 and Appendix C.2.

- *prompted_input*(*Prompt*, *Test*, *Commands*, *Result*) prompts the user for input by displaying *Prompt*; reads in the *Result* ; fires any *Commands* appropriate to *Result*; and applies *Test* to the final outcome. If any of these fails, the user is reprompted and the sequence repeated.
- *valid_object_for_type*(*Sort*, *Obj*) succeeds if *Obj* is an object contained within the set referred to by *Sort*.
- *find_all_descendant_objects*(*Obj*, *D*, *R*) returns the set, *D*, of objects which are sub–objects of *Obj* and the sub–object relations, *R*, defining that portion of the object hierarchy.
- *make_attribute*(*Objs*, *Att*, *T*, *List*) constructs an attribute goal for each object on the list *Objs*, with attribute name *Att* and time *T* and collects the resulting terms in *List*.
- *est_ax*(*K*, *Axiom*) succeeds if sorted logic *Axiom* is established in the knowledge base *K*.
- *find_all_potential_attribute_queries*(*Att*, *Set*) obtains from the problem description the *Set* of all potential queries which the user might want to make concerning the attribute named *Att*.
- *make_grid_square_representation*(*R*, *C*, *Grid*) constructs a set of relations defining adjoining squares in a spatial *Grid* consisting of number of rows *R* and number of columns *C*.
- *prompt_for_locations*(*Objs*, *R*, *C*, *Grid*, *Locations*) prompts the user for the location of each object in the list *Objs* on a spatial *Grid* consisting of number of rows *R* and number of columns *C*.
- *get_all_objects*(*Set*) returns the *Set* of all physical objects in the universe of discourse.

C.2   Ancillary Schemata Definitions

This section contains some extra schema definitions which were not necessary when introducing the use of schemata in Section 7.2 but were required for the large program construction example of Section 7.4. These are not a complete set of schemata for the EL or NIPPIE systems, merely a representative set.

Schema 8 is a simple schema for obtaining an initial value, *N*, for the attribute, *A*, of some object, *O*. Its action prompts the user to supply this initial value.

Schema 8	$['assign\ an\ initial\ value\ for', A, of, O]$
Goal:	$initial\_value(A, O, \_)$
Subgoals:	$[]$
Clauses:	$[(initial\_value(A, O, X) :- X = N)]$
Actions:	$[prompted\_input(['Initial\ value\ for', A, of, O,' >>'], number(N), [], [N])]$
Precondition:	$true$

Schema 9 obtains the initial time, N, at which the simulation commences. Like schema 8, it prompts the user for this value.

Schema 9	$['assign\ a\ value\ for\ the\ time\ at\ which\ simulation\ begins']$
Goal:	$initial\_time(\_)$
Subgoals:	$[]$
Clauses:	$[(initial\_time(X) :- X = N)]$
Actions:	$prompted\_input('Initial\ time >>', number(N), [], [N])]$
Precondition:	$true$

Schema 10 obtains the time step, N, to be used when moving either forwards or backwards through time during the simulation. The user is prompted for this value.

Schema 10	$['assign\ a\ value\ for\ the\ time\ step\ in\ the\ simulation']$
Goal:	$time\_step(\_)$
Subgoals:	$[]$
Clauses:	$[(time\_step(X) :- X = N)]$
Actions:	$prompted\_input('Length\ of\ time\ step >>', (number(N), N > 0), [], [N])]$
Precondition:	$true$

Schema 11 obtains the value for an attribute, L, of some object, O, at times other than the initial time point in the simulation by generating a random number, Rnd, and multiplying the value of the attribute at the previous time point by this random value. At the initial time, the value of the attribute is simply its initial value (which must be obtained as one of the subgoals of this schema). A common use for this schema is in updating each of the coordinates of an object's position in space, thus producing a "random walk" effect.

Schema 11	$[determine, L,' of', O,' as\ a\ random\ function\ of\ its\ previous', L]$
Goal:	$attribute(L, O, Tm, \_)$
Subgoals:	$[initial\_time(Tm),\ previous\_time(Tm, \_),\ initial\_value(L, O, \_)]$
Clauses:	$[(attribute(L, O, T, N1) :-$

$$\textbf{not}\ initial\_time(T),$$
$$previous\_time(T, T1),$$
$$attribute(L, O, T1, N2),$$
$$random\_float(attribute(L, O, T), Rnd),$$
$$N1\ is\ Rnd * N2),$$
$$(attribute(L, O, T, N3) :-$$
$$initial\_time(T),$$
$$initial\_value(L, O, N3))]$$

Actions: []
Precondition: *true*

Schema 12 determines whether objects in the model are in proximity to each other in terms of their spatial (X and Y) coordinates. The code in this schema defines two objects to be in proximity if the direct distance between their two coordinate positions is less than some constant threshold of proximity. For this schema to be applied it is necessary to find all the objects in the problem description; construct sets of goals to obtain the X and Y coordinates for each of these objects; and add these sets of goals to the list of schema subgoals.

Schema 12 $['define\ proximity\ in\ terms\ of\ coordinates']$
Goal: $in\_proximity(O, \_, \_)$
Subgoals: $[attribute(x\_coordinate, O, \_, \_),$
                  $attribute(y\_coordinate, O, \_, \_),$
                  $constant(proximity\_distance, \_)\ |\ Attributes],$
Clauses: $[(in\_proximity(A, B, T) :-$
                  $\quad attribute(x\_coordinate, A, T, XA),$
                  $\quad attribute(y\_coordinate, A, T, YA),$
                  $\quad attribute(x\_coordinate, B, T, XB),$
                  $\quad attribute(y\_coordinate, B, T, YB),$
                  $\quad constant(proximity\_distance, PD),$
                  $\quad direct\_distance(XA, YA, XB, YB, DD),$
                  $\quad DD < PD)]$
Actions: []
Precondition: $(get\_all\_objects(Objs),$
                  $make\_attributes(Objs, x\_coordinate, \_, XCA),$
                  $make\_attributes(Objs, y\_coordinate, \_, YCA),$
                  $append(XCA, YCA, Attributes))$

Schema 13 determines the location of an object, O, in terms of a grid square spatial representation. The code contained within this schema calculates the location at times other than the initial time by finding all the grid squares adjoining the square in which the object is currently located and then selecting one of those squares as the square to visit. A subgoal is added to obtain a schema for determining the choice of square. This schema is only applicable if grid squares have been specified in the problem description as the required form of spatial representation.

Schema 13 $['define\ location\ in\ terms\ of\ grid\ squares']$
Goal: $located\_at(O, \_, \_)$
Subgoals: $[move\_to\_square(\_, O, \_, \_, \_)]$
Clauses: $[(located\_at(A, L, T) :-$
                  $\quad not\ initial\_time(T),$
                  $\quad previous\_time(T, T1),$
                  $\quad located\_at(A, L1, T1),$
                  $\quad setof(X, next\_to(L1, X), Squares),$
                  $\quad move\_to\_square(Squares, A, T1, L1, L)),$
                  $(located\_at(A, L, T) :-$

$$initial\_time(T),$$
$$initial\_location(A, L))]$$

Actions: []
Precondition: $est\_ax(\_, grid\_squares(\_))$

Schema **14** defines movement to a square in a list, $Squares$, of grid squares by randomly selecting an element of the list.

Schema 14   [$'define\ movement\ to\ randomly\ selected\ adjoining\ grid\ square'$]
Goal: $move\_to\_square(\_, \_, \_, \_, \_)$
Subgoals: []
Clauses: [$(move\_to\_square(Squares, A, T, \_, grid(XN, YN))$:−
                 $random\_select\_member(move(A, T), grid(XN, YN), Squares))]$
Actions: []
Precondition: $true$

C.3   Problem Description Rules

This section contains some examples of rules which are used in the EL system as a basis for conducting a high level dialogue about users' ecological problems. Note that this set is just a representative sample and is not the complete set.

An object, **A**, has attribute, $Att1$, if the value of $Att1$ varies with some attribute $Att2$.

$pd\_rule((([A$ **in** $object, Att1$ **in** $attribute\_name, Att2$ **in** $attribute\_name], [])\#$
       $has\_attribute(Att1, A) \leftarrow$
       $varies\_with(Att1, A, Att2, A)).$

An object, **A**, has attribute, $Att2$, if the value of $Att2$ varies with some attribute $Att1$.

$pd\_rule((([A$ **in** $object, Att1$ **in** $attribute\_name, Att2$ **in** $attribute\_name], [])\#$
       $has\_attribute(Att2, A) \leftarrow$
       $varies\_with(Att1, A, Att2, A)).$

An object, **A**, has attribute, Att, if information is required from the model about Att.

$pd\_rule((([A$ **in** $object, Att$ **in** $attribute\_name], [])\#$
       $has\_attribute(Att, A) \leftarrow$
       $required\_information(Att, A)).$

There is an age structure representation with respect to object, **A**, if an attribute, Att, of **A** varies with the age of **A**.

pd_rule((([*A* in *object*, *Att* in *attribute_name*, *Age* in *age*], []))#
       age_class_structure_model(*A*) ←
       varies_with(*Att*, *A*, *Age*, *A*)).

An organism, *A*, bears young if it has seasonal births.

pd_rule((([*A* in *organism*], []))#
       bears_young(*A*) ←
       seasonal_births(*A*)).

An organism, *A*, bears young if its natality (*i.e.* birth rate) varies with some attribute, *Att*.

pd_rule((([*A* in *organism*, *Natality* in *natality*, *Att* in *attribute_name*], []))#
       bears_young(*A*) ←
       varies_with(*Natality*, *A*, *Att*, *A*)).

An object, *A*, dies if its mortality varies with some attribute of *A*.

pd_rule((([*A* in *object*, *Mortality* in *mortality*, *Att* in *attribute_name*], []))#
       dies(*A*) ←
       varies_with(*Mortality*, *A*, *Att*, *A*)).

An organism, *A*, is eating an organism, *B*, if predation occurs between *A* and *B*.

pd_rule((([*A* in *organism*, *B* in *organism*], []))#
       eating(*A*, *B*) ←
       predation(*A*, *B*)).

An organism, *A*, is eating an organism, *B*, if grazing occurs between *A* and *B*.

pd_rule((([*A* in *organism*, *B* in *organism*], []))#
       eating(*A*, *B*) ←
       grazing(*A*, *B*)).

An organism, *A*, grows if some attribute of size of *A* increases with the age of *A*.

pd_rule((([*A* in *organism*, *S* in *size*, *X* in *age*], []))#
       grows(*A*) ←
       increases_with(*S*, *A*, *X*, *A*)).

An organism, A, grows if it grows exponentially.

$pd\_rule(([A \text{ in } organism], [])\#$
$\qquad grows(A) \leftarrow$
$\qquad exponential\_growth(A)).$

An organism, A, grows if it grows logistically.

$pd\_rule(([A \text{ in } organism], [])\#$
$\qquad grows(A) \leftarrow$
$\qquad logistic\_growth(A)).$

An object, A, is spatially represented if it moves.

$pd\_rule(([A \text{ in } object], [])\#$
$\qquad spatial\_representation(A) \leftarrow$
$\qquad moves(A)).$

An object, A, is spatially represented if an attribute of A varies with the location of A.

$pd\_rule(([A \text{ in } object, Att \text{ in } attribute\_name, Loc \text{ in } location], [])\#$
$\qquad spatial\_representation(A) \leftarrow$
$\qquad varies\_with(Att, A, Loc, A)).$

An object, A, is spatially represented if it is migratory.

$pd\_rule(([A \text{ in } object], [])\#$
$\qquad spatial\_representation(A) \leftarrow$
$\qquad migratory(A)).$

C.4   Modelling Rules

This section contains some examples of rules which are used in the EL system as a basis for conducting dialogue during the phase of extraction of high level details of model structure. As was the case for the problem description rules of Section C.3, this set is just a representative sample and is not the complete set.

An object, A, is spatially represented if its location in the model is represented by coordinate points which are not connected to each other by proximity relations.

$model\_rule((([A \text{ in } object], []) \#$
    $\quad spatial\_representation(A) \leftarrow$
    $\quad points\_not\_in\_proximity(A)).$

An object, A, is spatially represented if its location in the model is represented by spatial areas which are not connected to each other by proximity relations.

$model\_rule((([A \text{ in } object], []) \#$
    $\quad spatial\_representation(A) \leftarrow$
    $\quad areas\_not\_in\_proximity(A)).$

An object, A, is spatially represented if its location in the model is represented by coordinate points which are connected to each other by proximity relations.

$model\_rule((([A \text{ in } object], []) \#$
    $\quad spatial\_representation(A) \leftarrow$
    $\quad points\_in\_proximity(A)).$

An object, A, is spatially represented if its location in the model is represented by grid squares.

$model\_rule((([A \text{ in } object], []) \#$
    $\quad spatial\_representation(A) \leftarrow$
    $\quad grid\_squares(A)).$

An object, A, is spatially represented if its location in the model is represented by zones of irregular shape.

$model\_rule((([A \text{ in } object], []) \#$
    $\quad spatial\_representation(A) \leftarrow$
    $\quad irregular\_zones(A)).$

An object, A, has a location point if its location in the model is represented by spatial areas which are not connected to each other by proximity relations.

$model\_rule((([A \text{ in } object], []) \#$
    $\quad has\_location\_point(A) \leftarrow$
    $\quad areas\_not\_in\_proximity(A)).$

An object, A, has a location with some area if its location in the model is represented by spatial areas which are not connected to each other by proximity relations.

$model\_rule((([A \text{ in } object], [])\#$
    $has\_location\_area(A) \leftarrow$
    $areas\_not\_in\_proximity(A)).$

An object, A, has a location point if its location in the model is represented by coordinate points which are connected to each other by proximity relations.

$model\_rule((([A \text{ in } object], [])\#$
    $has\_location\_point(A) \leftarrow$
    $points\_in\_proximity(A)).$

The number of rows in the model's spatial grid is $N1$ if an object, A, has a grid square spatial representation in the model.

$model\_rule((([A \text{ in } object, N1 \text{ in } integer, N2 \text{ in } integer], [])\#$
    $number\_of\_grid\_rows(N1) \leftarrow$
    $grid\_squares(A)).$

The number of columns in the model's spatial grid is $N1$ if an object, A, has a grid square spatial representation in the model.

$model\_rule((([A \text{ in } object, N1 \text{ in } integer, N2 \text{ in } integer], [])\#$
    $number\_of\_grid\_columns(N1) \leftarrow$
    $grid\_squares(A)).$

It is not true that an object, A, has a spatial representation in terms of areas without proximity relations if it is true that A has a spatial representation in terms of coordinate points without proximity relations.

$model\_rule((([A \text{ in } object], [])\#$
    $not(areas\_not\_in\_proximity(A)) \leftarrow$
    $points\_not\_in\_proximity(A)).$

It is not true that an object, A, has a spatial representation in terms of coordinate points with proximity relations if it is true that A has a spatial representation in terms of coordinate points without proximity relations.

$model\_rule((([A \text{ in } object], [])\#$
    $not(points\_in\_proximity(A)) \leftarrow$
    $points\_not\_in\_proximity(A)).$

It is not true that an object, A, has a spatial representation in terms of grid squares if it is true that A has a spatial representation in terms of coordinate points without proximity relations.

$model\_rule((([A\ \mathbf{in}\ object], [])\#$
          $not(grid\_squares(A)) \leftarrow$
          $points\_not\_in\_proximity(A)).$

It is not true that an object, A, has a spatial representation in terms of irregularly shaped zones if it is true that A has a spatial representation in terms of coordinate points without proximity relations.

$model\_rule((([A\ \mathbf{in}\ object], [])\#$
          $not(irregular\_zones(A)) \leftarrow$
          $points\_not\_in\_proximity(A)).$

It is not true that an object, A, has a spatial representation in terms of coordinate points without proximity relations if it is true that A has a spatial representation in terms of areas without proximity relations.

$model\_rule((([A\ \mathbf{in}\ object], [])\#$
          $not(points\_not\_in\_proximity(A)) \leftarrow$
          $areas\_not\_in\_proximity(A)).$

It is not true that an object, A, has a spatial representation in terms of coordinate points with proximity relations if it is true that A has a spatial representation in terms of areas without proximity relations.

$model\_rule((([A\ \mathbf{in}\ object], [])\#$
          $not(points\_in\_proximity(A)) \leftarrow$
          $areas\_not\_in\_proximity(A)).$

It is not true that an object, A, has a spatial representation in terms of grid squares if it is true that A has a spatial representation in terms of areas without proximity relations.

$model\_rule((([A\ \mathbf{in}\ object], [])\#$
          $not(grid\_squares(A)) \leftarrow$
          $areas\_not\_in\_proximity(A)).$

It is not true that an object, A, has a spatial representation in terms of irregularly shaped zones if it is true that A has a spatial representation in terms of areas without proximity relations.

$model\_rule(([A \textbf{ in } object], [])\#$
$\qquad not(irregular\_zones(A)) \leftarrow$
$\qquad areas\_not\_in\_proximity(A)).$

It is not true that an object, A, has a spatial representation in terms of coordinate points without proximity relations if it is true that A has a spatial representation in terms of coordinate points with proximity relations.

$model\_rule(([A \textbf{ in } object], [])\#$
$\qquad not(points\_not\_in\_proximity(A)) \leftarrow$
$\qquad points\_in\_proximity(A)).$

It is not true that an object, A, has a spatial representation in terms of areas without proximity relations if it is true that A has a spatial representation in terms of coordinate points with proximity relations.

$model\_rule(([A \textbf{ in } object], [])\#$
$\qquad not(areas\_not\_in\_proximity(A)) \leftarrow$
$\qquad points\_in\_proximity(A)).$

It is not true that an object, A, has a spatial representation in terms of grid squares if it is true that A has a spatial representation in terms of coordinate points with proximity relations.

$model\_rule(([A \textbf{ in } object], [])\#$
$\qquad not(grid\_squares(A)) \leftarrow$
$\qquad points\_in\_proximity(A)).$

It is not true that an object, A, has a spatial representation in terms of irregularly shaped zones if it is true that A has a spatial representation in terms of coordinate points with proximity relations.

$model\_rule(([A \textbf{ in } object], [])\#$
$\qquad not(irregular\_zones(A)) \leftarrow$
$\qquad points\_in\_proximity(A)).$

It is not true that an object, A, has a spatial representation in terms of coordinate points without proximity relations if it is true that A has a spatial representation in terms of grid squares.

$model\_rule(([A \textbf{ in } object], [])\#$
$\qquad not(points\_not\_in\_proximity(A)) \leftarrow$
$\qquad grid\_squares(A)).$

It is not true that an object, A, has a spatial representation in terms of areas without proximity relations if it is true that A has a spatial representation in terms of grid squares.

$model\_rule(([A \text{ in } object], [])\#$
$\qquad not(areas\_not\_in\_proximity(A)) \leftarrow$
$\qquad grid\_squares(A)).$

It is not true that an object, A, has a spatial representation in terms of coordinate points with proximity relations if it is true that A has a spatial representation in terms of grid squares.

$model\_rule(([A \text{ in } object], [])\#$
$\qquad not(points\_in\_proximity(A)) \leftarrow$
$\qquad grid\_squares(A)).$

It is not true that an object, A, has a spatial representation in terms of irregularly shaped zones if it is true that A has a spatial representation in terms of grid squares.

$model\_rule(([A \text{ in } object], [])\#$
$\qquad not(irregular\_zones(A)) \leftarrow$
$\qquad grid\_squares(A)).$

It is not true that an object, A, has a spatial representation in terms of coordinate points without proximity relations if it is true that A has a spatial representation in terms of irregularly shaped zones.

$model\_rule(([A \text{ in } object], [])\#$
$\qquad not(points\_not\_in\_proximity(A)) \leftarrow$
$\qquad irregular\_zones(A)).$

It is not true that an object, A, has a spatial representation in terms of areas without proximity relations if it is true that A has a spatial representation in terms of irregularly shaped zones.

$model\_rule(([A \text{ in } object], [])\#$
$\qquad not(areas\_not\_in\_proximity(A)) \leftarrow$
$\qquad irregular\_zones(A)).$

It is not true that an object, A, has a spatial representation in terms of coordinate points without proximity relations if it is true that A has a spatial representation in terms of irregularly shaped zones.

$model\_rule((([A \text{ in } object], []) \#$
$\qquad not(points\_in\_proximity(A)) \leftarrow$
$\qquad irregular\_zones(A)).$

It is not true that an object, A, has a spatial representation in terms of grid squares if it is true that A has a spatial representation in terms of irregularly shaped zones.

$model\_rule((([A \text{ in } object], []) \#$
$\qquad not(grid\_squares(A)) \leftarrow$
$\qquad irregular\_zones(A)).$

C.5 Example Output Program

This section contains a listing of the Prolog program constructed by EL in Section 7.4. Short comments are included for each predicate.

The following two clauses give the parameter values for the competition coefficient of *young* and the self inhibition coefficient of *oldpop*.

$parameter(competition\_coefficient, young, A) :-$
$A = 0.3.$
$parameter(self\_inhibition\_coefficient, oldpop, A) :-$
$A = 0.2.$

The initial values of all the subpopulations of *young* and of *oldpop* are given by the *initial_value* definitions.

$initial\_value(biomass, young\_pop3, A) :-$
$\qquad A = 8.$
$initial\_value(biomass, young\_pop2, A) :-$
$\qquad A = 7.$
$initial\_value(biomass, young\_pop1, A) :-$
$\qquad A = 5.$
$initial\_value(biomass, oldpop, A) :-$
$\qquad A = 20.$

The next three pairs of clauses define the attribute of *biomass* for each of the subpopulations of *young*. The calculations are similar, involving the detection of those populations in proximity to the given population at the appropriate time and calculating the biomass of the stipulated object from the biomasses of the objects in proximity.

$attribute(biomass, young\_pop3, A, B) :-$
        $initial\_time(A),$
        $initial\_value(biomass, young\_pop3, B).$
$attribute(biomass, young\_pop3, A, B) :-$
        $\textbf{not } initial\_time(A),$
        $previous\_time(A, C),$
        $attribute(biomass, young\_pop3, C, D),$
        $setof\_or\_empty(E, in\_proximity(young\_pop3, E, A), F),$
        $for\_each(G, F, attribute(biomass, G, C, H), H, I),$
        $sum\_elements(I, J),$
        $length(I, K),$
        $(J = 0, B = D \; ; \; B \; is \; D + J/K/2).$

$attribute(biomass, young\_pop2, A, B) :-$
        $initial\_time(A),$
        $initial\_value(biomass, young\_pop2, B).$
$attribute(biomass, young\_pop2, A, B) :-$
        $\textbf{not } initial\_time(A),$
        $previous\_time(A, C),$
        $attribute(biomass, young\_pop2, C, D),$
        $setof\_or\_empty(E, in\_proximity(young\_pop2, E, A), F),$
        $for\_each(G, F, attribute(biomass, G, C, H), H, I),$
        $sum\_elements(I, J),$
        $length(I, K),$
        $(J = 0, B = D \; ; \; B \; is \; D + J/K/2).$

$attribute(biomass, young\_pop1, A, B) :-$
        $initial\_time(A),$
        $initial\_value(biomass, young\_pop1, B).$
$attribute(biomass, young\_pop1, A, B) :-$
        $\textbf{not } initial\_time(A),$
        $previous\_time(A, C),$
        $attribute(biomass, young\_pop1, C, D),$
        $setof\_or\_empty(E, in\_proximity(young\_pop1, E, A), F),$
        $for\_each(G, F, attribute(biomass, G, C, H), H, I),$
        $sum\_elements(I, J),$
        $length(I, K),$
        $(J = 0, B = D \; ; \; B \; is \; D + J/K/2).$

The biomass of the population, $young$, is determined by summing its constituent sub–populations ($young\_pop1$, $young\_pop2$ and $young\_pop3$).

$attribute(biomass, young, A, B) :-$
        $setof(C, constituent\_object(young, C), D),$
        $for\_each(E, D, attribute(biomass, E, A, F), F, G),$
        $sum\_elements(G, B).$

The biomass of the population, *oldpop*, is calculated from a competition equation, involving the population, *young*.

$attribute(biomass, oldpop, A, B) :-$
        $initial\_time(A),$
        $initial\_value(biomass, oldpop, B).$
$attribute(biomass, oldpop, A, B) :-$
        not $initial\_time(A),$
        $previous\_time(A, C),$
        $attribute(biomass, oldpop, C, D),$
        $attribute(biomass, young, C, E),$
        $parameter(self\_inhibition\_coefficient, oldpop, F),$
        $parameter(competition\_coefficient, young, G),$
        B *is* $D + (1 - D * F - E * G).$

Movement between grid squares is achieved by randomly selecting a square, (E, F), from the list of neighbouring squares, A.

$move\_to\_square(A, B, C, D, grid(E, F)) :-$
        $random\_select\_member(move(B, C), grid(E, F), A).$

The location of an object, A, at time, C, is B if either C is the initial time and B is the initial location of A, or The set of neighbouring squares is found and a move is chosen.

$located\_at(A, B, C) :-$
        $initial\_time(C),$
        $initial\_location(A, B).$
$located\_at(A, B, C) :-$
        not $initial\_time(C),$
        $previous\_time(C, D),$
        $located\_at(A, E, D),$
        $setof(F, next\_to(E, F), G),$
        $move\_to\_square(G, A, D, E, B).$

The following four clauses give the initial locations for the spatially represented objects in the model.

$initial\_location(oldpop, grid(3,3)).$
$initial\_location(young\_pop3, grid(2,1)).$
$initial\_location(young\_pop2, grid(1,2)).$
$initial\_location(young\_pop1, grid(1,1)).$

The predicate, $adjoining(A, B)$, denotes that a grid square, A, is next to grid square, B in the spatial grid.

$adjoining(grid(3,4), grid(2,4)).$
$adjoining(grid(3,4), grid(3,3)).$
$adjoining(grid(3,3), grid(2,3)).$
$adjoining(grid(3,3), grid(3,2)).$
$adjoining(grid(3,2), grid(2,2)).$
$adjoining(grid(3,2), grid(3,1)).$
$adjoining(grid(3,1), grid(2,1)).$
$adjoining(grid(2,4), grid(1,4)).$
$adjoining(grid(2,4), grid(2,3)).$
$adjoining(grid(2,3), grid(1,3)).$
$adjoining(grid(2,3), grid(2,2)).$
$adjoining(grid(2,2), grid(1,2)).$
$adjoining(grid(2,2), grid(2,1)).$
$adjoining(grid(2,1), grid(1,1)).$
$adjoining(grid(1,4), grid(1,3)).$
$adjoining(grid(1,3), grid(1,2)).$
$adjoining(grid(1,2), grid(1,1)).$

An object, A, is in proximity to an object, B, at time, C, if either A and B are in the same grid square at time C, or A and B are in adjoining grid squares at time C.

$in\_proximity(A, B, C)$:—
        $located\_at(A, D, C),$
        $located\_at(B, D, C),$
        $\textbf{not}\ A == B.$
$in\_proximity(A, B, C)$:—
        $located\_at(A, D, C),$
        $adjoining(D, E),$
        $located\_at(B, E, C).$

The following three facts provide the sub–objects of the population, $young$. This replicates the sort membership relation from Section 4.1.2.

$subobj(young, young\_pop3).$
$subobj(young, young\_pop2).$
$subobj(young, young\_pop1).$

The predicate, $constituent\_object(A, B)$, denotes that the object, B, belongs to the sort, A. This replicates the recursive sort membership definition of Sections 4.1.2 and 4.1.3.

$constituent\_object(A, B) :-$
$\qquad subt(A, C),$
$\qquad constituent\_object(C, B).$
$constituent\_object(A, B) :-$
$\qquad subobj(A, B).$

The time step in the simulation is 1.

$time\_step(A) :-$
$\qquad A = 1.$

The time point, B, is previous to A, if B equals A minus the time step for the simulation or if A equals B plus the time step. Both conditions must be given in Prolog because of the restrictions on the degree of instantiation of the arithmetic evaluation predicate, $is/2$.

$previous\_time(A, B) :-$
$\qquad integer(B),$
$\qquad var(A),$
$\qquad time\_step(C),$
$\qquad A \ is \ B + C.$
$previous\_time(A, B) :-$
$\qquad integer(A),$
$\qquad var(B),$
$\qquad time\_step(C),$
$\qquad B \ is \ A - C.$

The initial time point in the simulation is 1.

$initial\_time(A) :-$
$\qquad A = 1.$

Index

Index

run time, 219

S

schema, <u>123</u>
  action, 124
  complex procedure, 127
  constant, 124
  equation, 126
  precondition, 124
  relational structure, 129
search space, 38, 83, 178, 219
search tree, 219
selection mechanism, 135
SHIRKA, 123
sort constraints, 55, 100
sort schema, 179
sort, <u>49</u>–50, 73
sorted logic, <u>48</u>, 97, 111, 131, 177, 208
spatial representation, 19, <u>33</u>, 128, 148, 155,
  164, 171
Starlog, 21
state transition model, <u>30</u>
state variable, 22, 26
STELLA, 6
structural growth model, <u>29</u>
substitution, <u>111</u>
suggestion generation, 108, 148
system dynamics model, <u>22</u>

T

T-Prolog, 21
template editing, <u>131</u>, 136, 144, 183, 199
template formulae, <u>131</u>, 136, 144
topological sort, 100, 219
translation, <u>40</u>, 86
  formulae to pseudo-English, 131, 138
  sorted logic to conventional imperative, 100
  sorted logic to Prolog, 78
unification, 64, 70, <u>111</u>, 174, 219
universal quantification, 107, 219
validity of rules, 109
variable, 220
Z specification language, 117

The MIT Press, with Peter Denning as general consulting editor, publishes computer science books in the following series:

ACM Doctoral Dissertation Award and Distinguished Dissertation Series

Artificial Intelligence
Patrick Winston, Founding editor
Michael Brady, Daniel Bobrow, and Randall Davis, editors

Charles Babbage Institute Reprint Series for the History of Computing
Martin Campbell-Kelly, editor

Computer Systems
Herb Schwetman, editor

Explorations with Logo
E. Paul Goldenberg, editor

Foundations of Computing
Michael Garey and Albert Meyer, editors

History of Computing
I. Bernard Cohen and William Aspray, editors

Information Systems
Michael Lesk, editor

Logic Programming
Ehud Shapiro, editor; Fernando Pereira, Koichi Furukawa, Jean-Louis Lassez, and David H. D. Warren, Associate editors

The MIT Press Electrical Engineering and Computer Science Series

Research Monographs in Parallel and Distributed Processing
Christopher Jesshope and David Klappholz, editors

Scientific and Engineering Computation
Janusz Kowalik, editor

Technical Communication
Ed Barrett, editor